Interpersonal and Group Dynamics in Law Enforcement

SECOND EDITION

Bruce Bjorkquist

2004
EMOND MONTGOMERY PUBLICATIONS LIMITED
TORONTO, CANADA

Printed in Canada.

Edited, designed, and typeset by WordsWorth Communications, Toronto.
Cover design by Susan Darrach, Darrach Design.

We acknowledge the financial support of the Government of Canada through the
Book Publishing Industry Development Program (BPIDP) for our publishing
activities.

The events and characters depicted in this book are fictitious. Any similarity to
actual persons, living or dead, is purely coincidental.

Library and Archives Canada Cataloguing in Publication

Bjorkquist, Bruce D., 1942–
    Interpersonal and group dynamics in law enforcement / Bruce Bjorkquist. —
2nd ed.

Includes index.
ISBN 1-55239-099-3

    1. Police training.   2. Group relations training.   I. Title.

HV7936.P75B46 2004   363.2'071   C2004-904487-7

To Bob, Jean, and Maureen

Contents

Preface

More than 20 years ago I taught my first course in interpersonal and group dynamics, a new course offered within a nursing program. Nursing educators and practitioners had long recognized a need for leadership and group skills, and college nursing programs responded with a variety of offerings designed to assist students in this area. Today, virtually all college programs require group work in their curricula. The Police Foundations Program is no exception.

My first attempt at teaching group dynamics was something of a disaster, both from the students' point of view and mine. I did what many a college teacher has done. I selected a textbook, prepared and delivered lectures, planned and directed exercises, and developed and administered tests. In this rather traditional way, I tried to teach group dynamics. The students were kind but clear in their course-end evaluation. I learned two important things from their review.

The first thing I learned was that students do not develop practical group skills by reading about groups, listening to lectures about groups, talking about groups, doing exercises in groups, and writing tests about groups. In short, I learned that my initial approach to teaching group dynamics was sadly inadequate, providing students with a "head trip" but little in the way of practical skills. I remedied the methodology problem the next school year in a way that has proved most effective.

My experiential model for teaching and learning group skills is an important addition to this second edition of *Interpersonal and Group Dynamics in Law Enforcement*. The model is described in both appendix A of this text and in units 2 and 3 of the Teacher's Guide. The inclusion of the model and its attendant resources is an expression of my now longstanding commitment to skill acquisition. That commitment began with the student feedback on my first effort to teach interpersonal and group dynamics many years ago.

The second thing I learned from the student feedback on that first course was that the textbook that I had selected was also focused on theory and, for the most part, unconcerned with practice. Moreover, it was too difficult. Written by a university professor for second- or third-year university students, it was undoubtedly an excellent text for students at those levels in that setting. The text was composed almost entirely of theoretical explanations of various facets of group life. The theoretical orientation, technical terminology, and conceptual complexity, however, hindered access to the practical fundamentals of group work.

Although I was able to remedy the methodology concern almost immediately, the textbook problem took me close to 20 years to address. The first edition of *Interpersonal and Group Dynamics in Law Enforcement*, with its simple style and its focus on practical skills, remedied that longstanding problem. The second edition continues with a clear and concise presentation of the basics, while adding significant, practical strategies for skill development. It remains a practical manual for building an effective team. In addition, it remains a simple account of the essentials of interpersonal and group dynamics.

Part of the book's simplicity is to be found in its style. I have written the book in the form of a training manual rather than a traditional textbook. It employs, for example, the conversational tone of a coach. Moreover, it is light on theoretical analyses of group dynamics, and it is heavy on basic "how-to" explanations. Teachers familiar with the first edition will note that the second edition is somewhat more personal in its presentation, a feature that should make the material even more accessible to students. It is a practical guide written in a simple style that is both conversational and personal.

It is also a simple book in the sense that it attempts to present only the essential concepts associated with interpersonal and group dynamics. In educator terminology, I have included the "need to knows," consciously avoiding the "nice to knows." Without question, much more could be included. Many teachers who use this book will, no doubt, supplement these essentials with additional materials of their own choosing.

Throughout, I have also tried to keep the language simple. Where technical terms can't be avoided, I have provided clear definitions and simple examples. In order to make ideas more easily understood, many more examples have been added to the second edition. All in all, this book is a simple manual covering the essentials of group work. I believe that it can serve college students well as they prepare themselves for working in groups in the police services field. I hope, too, that it will serve police services well by equipping officers with the ability to understand and practise the essentials of effective interpersonal and group dynamics.

FEATURES OF THE SECOND EDITION

The Experiential Model

New to the second edition is appendix A. Here you will find a description of five student teams that teachers can use to teach interpersonal and group dynamics in an exciting and practical way. The model includes a Teaching Team, an Executive Team, a Lesson Review Team, an Energizer Team, and an Evaluation Team. Teachers can choose to use one or more of these teams depending on the teacher's circumstances and preferences. The more teams that the teacher uses, the more that teacher functions as a consultant, coaching the various teams as they plan and carry out their tasks. Appendix A describes the experiential model, providing detailed job descriptions for both teams and individual team members. Units 2 and 3 of the Teacher's Guide also describe the model.

The Experiential Exercises

Also new to the second edition is appendix B. It provides detailed instructions for conducting experiential exercises that are keyed to topics in each of the ten chapters of the text. In the experiential model, the Teaching Team has responsibility for teaching the lesson of the day to their classmates. Their lesson is always a two-step lesson. First, they lead the class in the assigned experiential exercise. Second, they provide an explanation of related concepts from the assigned chapter. The exercise provides the class with an experience of chapter topics before they receive an exposition of the topics.

Note that teachers who choose not to use the experiential model can still use the exercises of appendix B. They will conduct the exercises themselves rather than coaching student teams to conduct them. Note further, that unit 9 of the Teacher's Guide provides resources for use in the experiential exercises. Resources that the class needs in order to do certain exercises (role-play instructions, for example) are ready in the Teacher's Guide for duplication by the teaching team or the teacher.

Practising Your Group Skills

Another new feature of the second edition is a chapter section called "Practising Your Group Skills." In each chapter, this section provides students with specific team assignments pertinent to the chapter or, in the case of the Lesson Review Team, to the previous chapter. The Executive, Lesson Review, Energizer, and Evaluation teams get their assignment in its entirety in this section. The Teaching Team, which always has the major responsibility for a class session, gets its basic assignment in this section but is also directed to appendix B. There, as we saw above, they get further details regarding the experiential-exercise portion of their lesson assignment.

Mastering the Material

As in the first edition, each chapter of the second edition includes a section called "Mastering the Material." The items in this section are intended to assist students in learning the chapter material, checking their comprehension, and preparing for tests and exams. The items focus on recall of information, not recognition. The goal is mastery of the words and ideas that are fundamental to a basic understanding of interpersonal and group dynamics. Students who can complete the worksheets without looking up the answers will be well prepared for test situations. The Teacher's Guide includes correct responses to all items in this section.

Applying the Ideas in Policing

Each chapter of the second edition includes a section called "Applying the Ideas in Policing." This section is designed to take the student from mastery of general concepts to their application in particular settings within policing. Working with policing scenarios, students are encouraged to apply the ideas from each chapter to situations that might occur in the workplace. The scenarios include on-duty situations such as community liaison assignments and raids on biker bunkers. They also include off-duty situations such as association meetings and family dilemmas. The Teacher's Guide includes sample responses for all exercises in this section.

Presentation of Chapter Content

As with the first edition, each chapter of the second begins with a statement of chapter objectives followed by an introduction to the chapter topic. The detailed presentation of chapter content follows and the chapter concludes with a summary.

The addition of many more examples should enhance the exposition of chapter topics, assisting readers with comprehension of the material. Moreover, the conscious repetition of key concepts within and between chapters contributes to greater coherence throughout the text. This repetition should enhance learning overall. The expansion of chapter summaries in the second edition is also significant. The summaries now give readers more detailed reviews of the key ideas in each chapter. In addition, they can better serve as additional introductions to chapters for those readers who choose to use them in this way. The expanded summaries should also assist readers as they prepare for both classes and tests.

The Sequence of Chapters

The sequence in which the chapters are presented in the second edition reflects my preferred order of study. However, each chapter has been written so that it can precede or follow any other. The actual course of study, therefore, is at the discretion of the teacher.

Teachers who choose to use the experiential model in its entirety may wonder about the wisdom of leaving the assessment of team performance (chapter 10) to the end. In the model, performance evaluation (not to be confused with grading!) is a regular part of every class session. I continue to follow the sequence of chapters in the text, but I require all evaluation teams to study a portion of chapter 10 before they facilitate an evaluation session. You will see this requirement in both appendix A (the job description for the Evaluation Team) and the "Practising Your Group Skills" section (the instructions for the Evaluation Team) in each chapter.

The Teacher's Guide

A Teacher's Guide accompanies the second edition and is available to teachers who adopt the text or consider it for adoption. Unit 1 introduces the guide, providing an overview of its contents. Unit 2 gives a general description of the experiential model for teaching group skills, and unit 3 describes the model in detail. Appendix A of the text and these two units of the guide together provide a thorough description of the experiential model for teaching interpersonal and group dynamics.

Units 4 and 5 provide forms for duplication by the teacher for use in class. In particular, unit 4 offers communication forms that can be used by Leaders, Recorders, Reporters, and Participant-Analysts in the experiential model. Unit 5 also contains forms for reproduction by the teacher. These are grading forms that can be used to calculate scores for various skills taught in the course. Both types of forms will, no doubt, be of interest to teachers who use the experiential model and those who opt for a more traditional approach.

A test bank of over 300 questions with answers is found in unit 6. The correct answers to all "Mastering the Material" items of the various chapters are given in unit 7. Sample responses for all "Applying the Ideas in Policing" items occupy unit 8.

Unit 9 of the guide provides detailed instructions for conducting the 10 experiential exercises that are assigned to teaching teams in the "Practising Your Group Skills" section of the various chapters of the text. Unit 9 also includes resources necessary for conducting the exercises, including items that can be duplicated for handout or other purposes. The materials in unit 9 are most effective when used in the context of the experiential model described in units 2 and 3 of the guide and in appendix A of the text.

Acknowledgments

Over the 20-plus years that I have taught interpersonal and group dynamics at Conestoga College, I have worked with students in the fields of nursing, recreation, engineering, security, and policing. Except for one of those years, all my students have worked on their group skills using the structures of a teaching model that is now an important addition to the second edition of *Interpersonal and Group Dynamics in Law Enforcement.*

The development and successful use of this model has been one of the most rewarding aspects of my professional career. I frequently tell colleagues, with all sincerity, that the best lessons ever taught in my classroom were taught by my students. To all — dare I say it? — the thousands of students who embraced the model, worked with me, learned from me, and taught me so much about teamwork I express my sincere thanks.

In recent years, teaching interpersonal and group dynamics in the Police Foundations Program has put me in the midst of police officers and security specialists who have contributed to my understanding of policing in general and, most importantly, to the critical role that small groups play within police and security services. In this regard, I give special thanks to Al Hunter, Andy Knetsch, Harry Stavrou, Dave Stewart, and Brent Walker. You have taught me much more than you may realize.

I am also grateful for many colleagues who administer programs and coordinate activities in the best interests of our students. In particular, I thank Greg Burns, Don Douglas, Carolyn Harrison, Bill Jeffrey, Tony Martinek, Bob McIver, and Jal Wadia for their collegial approach to our common tasks at Conestoga College. Your teamwork in the offices of the College has made the teaching of teamwork in the classrooms of the College more effective.

Three colleagues deserve special mention and special thanks. At one of the busiest times in his career, Bob Bamford joined me in teaching interpersonal and group skills to Conestoga's first class of degree-level students. He mastered the experiential model in record time and brought his considerable interpersonal skills to bear on this new challenge. Thanks, Bob, for the courage to jump in and for the very valuable contributions that you made. You are an important part of this second edition.

I also wish to thank Jean LeForge for her many contributions to the development of the second edition. She has used the experiential learning model successfully with students in security and policing, and she has adapted it for use with human relations students as well. Her classroom experience is very much a part of this second edition. Thank you, Jean, for securing essential resources, for sharing your teaching strategies, for reading and rereading the manuscript, for providing valuable feedback, and for encouraging me in my work.

In addition to teaching security students and policing students, Maureen Murphy-Fricker teaches welding technicians. Maureen has successfully employed the experiential learning model with all three groups of students, adapting it to special circumstances where necessary. Her experience in the classroom has contributed in important ways to this second edition. In particular, her creativity shows up in experiential exercises that she has personally developed and kindly permitted me to use. Thank you, Maureen, for your enthusiasm, your creativity, your support, and your generosity.

Finally, I would like to express my sincere appreciation to the congenial, dedicated, and professional staff at both Emond Montgomery Publications Limited and WordsWorth Communications. For their encouragement and assistance in getting this second edition to press, I especially thank James Black, Peggy Buchan, and Karen Davidson of Emond Montgomery. I also thank Jim Lyons and the editorial staff of WordsWorth Communications for their many contributions to this project.

Bruce Bjorkquist
Waterloo, Ontario
April 2, 2004

Member Roles: Participating Effectively in Your Group

Chapter Objectives

After completing this chapter, you should be able to:

- Define the terms *culture*, *norm*, and *role*.

- Distinguish between helpful and harmful group member roles.

- Describe the difference between a task goal and a social goal.

- Identify and describe six task actions that constitute a group member's task role.

- Identify and describe six social actions that constitute a group member's social role.

- Identify and describe six harmful group member roles.

INTRODUCTION

We are all familiar with the fact that actors play roles in plays, movies, and television series. Kelsey Grammer, for example, played the role of Frasier Crane in the long-running TV series *Frasier*. When actors play roles, they portray particular characters in a story. Those of us who aren't actors also play roles, but not the kinds associated with movies or plays. We play various roles in our families and in society. In this case we don't really *play* the roles the way an actor does; rather, we *live* the roles that family and society require of us. Within our families, we live the roles of son or daughter, husband or wife, brother or sister. Beyond our families, we fulfill other roles as well. These roles are often work related. We are police officers, chefs, servers, mechanics, and pilots. Throughout society, we observe people living roles on a daily basis. People are detectives, plumbers, firefighters, nurses, and students. The variety of such roles in any society is virtually endless.

Many readers of this book are, or plan to be, police officers. Take note that the roles and rules that we describe in this chapter and later in this book are the roles and rules associated with being an effective group member in *any setting*, not just police settings. Those of you who serve as police officers will need to know both the essentials of interpersonal and group dynamics and a great deal about the legal and ethical requirements of policing. Eventually, what you have studied here with respect to being an effective group member will form part of your experience in a particular social context — the police service. You will apply your knowledge of group dynamics in the context of the legal and ethical requirements of your profession. Thus, you need to know the essentials of group dynamics, and you also need to know the requirements of the legal and the ethical standards that apply to police officers.

A final point: Everything we study about interpersonal and group dynamics will apply to your personal life as well as your professional life. You will work in many groups as a private citizen, not as a police officer. Whether in your family, a service club, your church, or another community organization, you can be an effective member of your group by knowing and practising the essentials of interpersonal and group dynamics that we are about to explore.

SOCIETAL ROLES AND SMALL-GROUP ROLES

culture
the way of life of people in a given society or group

Among other things, social scientists study **culture**, the way of life of the people in a given society or group. They remind us that a society's way of life includes many different roles. Every society requires a variety of roles to be lived or fulfilled in order for its members to survive and thrive as a people. Complex, interdependent roles within a society allow the members of that society to meet their basic needs and, in wealthier societies, to enjoy some of the luxuries of life. A **role**, in this sense of the word, is a set of expectations associated with particular responsibilities within a society. For example, police officers are expected to behave in certain ways when carrying out their responsibilities. So, too, we have expectations of what mothers, doctors, or electricians should do when fulfilling their particular roles. Because each one of us fulfills many different roles in our society, we are subject to many different sets of expectations.

role
a set of expectations associated with a particular responsibility

norm
a written or unwritten rule of a group

The expectations that society has for a particular role amount to a set of **norms** or rules for the proper fulfilling of that role. Once we see that roles are really sets of rules for behaviour, we can also understand that society will judge the performance of people in their various roles. When someone fulfills a particular role effectively, that person is likely to be commended by others. In contrast, people who fail to live up to the expectations of a role are likely to be judged negatively. In our society, then, we have good cops, good mothers, and good doctors. Unfortunately, we also have bad cops, bad mothers, and bad doctors. As we will see in the next sections, there are helpful roles that members of small groups can fulfill. There are also harmful roles that can hinder group efforts. In other words, group members — just like police officers, mothers, and doctors — can be good or bad at what they do.

HELPFUL AND HARMFUL ACTIONS AND ROLES

In this chapter, we will examine the important roles that members of small groups play within their groups. We will look at both functional roles and dysfunctional roles. **Functional roles** are the roles associated with being a good or helpful group member. **Dysfunctional roles** are those associated with negative and harmful behaviours that are detrimental to a group's unity and its productivity. Throughout the rest of chapter 1, we will focus on the role of group members in general. In chapter 2, we will examine specific roles, such as those of the group leader, reporter, and recorder. We will look at how you can be an effective group member and at specific actions that you can and should take to make your team more effective. In other words, we will study what is expected of an excellent team player.

functional role
behaviours associated with being a good or helpful group member

dysfunctional role
negative behaviours that cause an individual to become a harmful group member

TASK AND SOCIAL GOALS

Ideally, every group has two basic goals. The first is the **task goal**, the goal of getting the job done. The second is the **social goal**, the goal of building good relationships among group members. When a group functions as a team, members are productive; they get the job done. In addition, members respect one another and they develop a sense of oneness, a sense of belonging together. This sense of belonging is called **cohesion**. We will study much more about cohesion in chapter 7. For the moment, however, let's just note that the best teams are the ones that not only get the job done but also have members who appreciate one another. The team of investigators, for example, that gets the job done but also enjoys mutual respect among its members has functioned most effectively. They have been both productive and cohesive.

task goal
the goal of getting the job done

social goal
the goal of building relationships among group members

cohesion
a group's sense of oneness or togetherness

TASK AND SOCIAL ACTIONS

There are several simple, yet powerful, skills that you can develop to help your group achieve both its task goals and its social goals. These skills consist of six **task actions** and six **social actions**.[1] Each action is a skill that can be put into practice within any group. Learning and using these 12 skills is the key to becoming an excellent team player. Together, the six task actions constitute the task role of an effective group member, and they promote group productivity, the achievement of the group's task goals. The six social actions together define the social role of an effective group member. Fulfilling the social role effectively will contribute to building and maintaining a cohesive team. That, we have noted, is the social goal of an effective team. If you want to be an excellent team player, you will regularly use the six skills associated with the task role and the six skills associated with the social role. Let's now examine the six actions associated with the task role.

task action
an action by a group member that enables the group to get the task done

social action
an action by a group member that helps to build and maintain a cohesive team

YOUR TASK ROLE: SIX HELPFUL ACTIONS

The six helpful actions associated with the task role of an effective group member include sharing your ideas, asking others for their thoughts, suggesting directions

---

1   The concept of task actions and social actions has a long history. Benne and Sheats (1948, pp. 41–49) were among the first to discuss them, identifying 13 task roles, 8 social roles, and 8 harmful roles.

that your group might take, summarizing the progress of your group, checking to see that everyone understands an issue, and motivating members to get the job done.

1. Share Ideas

Do you readily share your ideas and views with others in your group? The most effective group members are the ones who contribute constructively to discussions. They regularly share their ideas about team tasks with fellow members. In this way, they help their teammates achieve the group's goals. The *Idea Sharer* is essential for team success. The most successful teams are those in which all members are Idea Sharers. The best way to have a good idea, said Nobel Prize winner Linus Pauling, is to have many ideas. When a group has many ideas, it has more possibilities for task success. If you want to be a helpful team member, let your team know what you think about the job at hand. Be an Idea Sharer.

2. Seek Ideas

Do you ask others in your group what they think the team should do to solve a problem or to achieve its goals? Effective group members want to hear what others have to say about an issue. They seek the opinions and views of others. They regularly ask others what they think. *Idea Seekers* are effective group members because they consciously seek information and opinions from other members of the group. They are convinced that the more ideas the group has to work with the better. They also believe that every member has a contribution to make. When one member is silent, for example, it is the Idea Seeker who will ask that person to share his thoughts. This is not a matter of forcing people to share or putting them on the spot. Rather, it is a genuine interest in knowing what others think about the issue in question. The silent member may be the one who has the best ideas. If you want your team to succeed, then regularly ask others for their thoughts. Be an Idea Seeker.

3. Suggest Directions

Do you suggest courses of action that your group might take as it seeks to accomplish its various tasks? Effective group members are ready, at any given time, to suggest directions that their team can take. The *Direction Suggester* offers ideas about the course of action that the team might take on a particular task. For example, the Direction Suggester might recommend that the group member with the most knowledge or skill take the lead on a particular task. Or, to provide another example, she might suggest that the team try option three before trying options one and two. Direction Suggesters aren't trying to boss others around. Rather, they see a possible course of action that they feel will be successful, and they suggest that the group go in that direction. You can contribute to your team's success by proposing that it proceed in certain ways to achieve its goals. Be a Direction Suggester.

4. Summarize Progress

Do you routinely take time in your group to summarize its progress on a particular task? Effective group members do so on a regular basis. Often when groups work on their tasks, members get confused and head in different directions. This, of course, can be frustrating and counterproductive. It is the *Progress Summarizer* who gets the group to stop and reflect on the progress being made. He attempts to pull together the various ideas and decisions of the group into a brief and clear summary, and he encourages others to clarify their thinking with respect to the group's task. Summarizing progress is a useful way of getting everyone back on track. If you regularly help your team to summarize its progress, you will make a most valuable contribution to your team's success. Be a Progress Summarizer.

5. Check Comprehension

In group meetings, do you try to ensure that everyone shares a common understanding of issues? Effective group members take the necessary steps to check that all members understand one another. If group members are interpreting things differently, then communication will fail and the team will waste time in confusion and misunderstandings. The *Comprehension Checker* is the team member who attempts to ensure that the group has a common understanding of an issue or task. Comprehension Checkers frequently use active listening skills, such as paraphrasing, to help their teammates understand a position or point of view. Paraphrasing involves restating a person's position in words different from those that person used. We'll examine listening and other valuable communication skills in chapter 5. Comprehension Checkers use the best communication skills available to help group members understand one another as they work to complete their tasks. Part of your task role is to ensure that members understand one another, to ensure that "everyone is on the same page." Be a Comprehension Checker.

6. Motivate the Group

Do you consciously and constructively try to motivate your group to get the work done? Among other things, effective group members are motivators. They are "movers and shakers" within the team. When undertaking a task, group members often have different levels of interest with respect to that task. In addition, it's not unusual for team members to get sidetracked. The *Group Motivator* is the person who encourages others to direct their energy to completing the task at hand. The Group Motivator may choose different strategies in an attempt to motivate the group, but she will always have task completion as the goal. She may, for example, crack a joke, make a serious comment, or lead by example to push others to get the job done. Groups form in order to get tasks accomplished. You can make a major contribution to your team's success by constructively motivating others to complete the team's tasks and achieve its goals. Be a Group Motivator.

Together, the six skills described in this section define the task role of an effective group member. As an individual, you may feel more comfortable doing some of these actions than others. Some of them, for example, may feel more natural to you than others do. As an ideal team member, however, you will want to do both the actions that you feel most comfortable doing and those actions that are less comfortable or less natural. The best team players are ready and willing to do all six of the task actions when and as appropriate. They regularly share their ideas, seek the opinions of others, suggest directions, summarize progress, check comprehension, and motivate their groups.

YOUR SOCIAL ROLE: SIX HELPFUL ACTIONS

Just as there are six skills that help a group to accomplish its task goals, so there are six skills that contribute to the achievement of social goals. These helpful actions include encouraging others to participate, supporting members when they contribute, facilitating communication, observing the group's emotional climate, relieving stress in the group, and mediating conflict when it arises.

1. Encourage Participation

Do you regularly invite other members of your group to participate in group deliberations? Effective group members encourage others to participate in group discussions and activities. The *Participation Encourager* is the person who tries to ensure that *all* members are involved in the efforts of the team. It is easy for some members to sit back and let others, perhaps the more vocal people, take the lead and make decisions. More passive members will tend to yield to the more assertive ones. When this happens, the group does not have the benefit of the ideas and the involvement of the quieter members. In addition, these members may feel left out or they may feel that their opinions don't count. If this occurs, the team's sense of cohesion will suffer. Encouraging all members to participate in discussion can be a powerful way to strengthen relationships among team members. Others will understand that you value their opinions and that they have influence within the group. Be a Participation Encourager.

2. Support Participants

When others contribute to team discussions, do you consciously support their participation? Effective group members support those who make contributions to the team's life. The *Participant Supporter* helps the group become a team by showing support for members who make contributions. A little praise, for example, can go a long way to motivate members to contribute more ideas and opinions. It makes the persons praised feel that they are worthwhile members of the team; it also enhances their sense of self-esteem and strengthens their sense of belonging. These positive feelings contribute to the team's cohesiveness. Even when you disagree with another member's ideas, you can support that member as a person. You might say, for example, "With all due respect, Larry, I don't think that your idea will work. Here's my thinking." In your remarks you have shown respect and support for Larry as a person while objecting to his idea, an idea that you think is weak. Whether others contribute good ideas or poor ones, support them as persons. Be a Participant Supporter. In so doing, you will make a major contribution to building and maintaining healthy relationships among the members of your team.

3. Facilitate Communication

In your team meetings, do you encourage others to share their feelings with the group? Effective group members facilitate the communication of feelings within the team. Earlier, we saw that the Comprehension Checker worked to ensure that members understood their jobs. In that case, communication skills were applied to task accomplishment. Here, we see communication skills being directed toward the group's social dimension. *Communication Facilitators* use their best communication skills to foster good relationships among the members of the team. They focus on the emotions and mood of the group in order to foster positive feelings among members. In so doing, they promote their team's social goals. In particular, the Communication Facilitator encourages the sharing of feelings in an honest but assertive way. This allows team members to communicate their frustrations as well as their enthusiasm. When members work on this aspect of communication, they encourage a supportive climate and a sense of togetherness. You will contribute to a positive team spirit in your group, if you facilitate the communication of feelings. Be a Communication Facilitator.

4. Observe Process

To be a good Communication Facilitator, you need to be a good observer of group process. In group meetings, are you attentive to the process that is going on? In other words, are you attentive to the group dynamics? Effective group members observe the dynamics within their group with a view to strengthening the relationships among members of the group. The *Process Observer* is always attentive to the interactions among group members as the group does its work. When frustrations, for example, threaten to lead to conflict, members who are observant can help to defuse a potentially harmful situation. When "good vibes" are being experienced, the Process Observer will feel them and reinforce them with appropriate words and actions. By being attentive to your group's dynamics, you can be a strong influence in the creation of a supportive, trusting environment. Be a Process Observer.

5. Relieve Stress

When members of your group are stressed, do you try to relieve the stress in helpful ways? Effective group members have, among other things, a calming effect on their teams. It's inevitable that people working together will experience stress and tension. Team success or failure depends, to a large degree, on the team's ability to manage this stress effectively. The *Stress Reliever* is the one who takes steps to reduce the tensions that groups inevitably experience. There are many different ways to relieve tension in a group. Sometimes all that's necessary is for someone to remind everyone to "lighten up." At other times, a joke can break the tension and put everyone in a more relaxed state of mind. Or, it may be best to call a timeout, suggesting that the group take a 10- or 15-minute break and then come back to work. The Stress Reliever is an essential member of a successful team. If you are prepared, when your group gets stressed, to contribute constructively to relieve the tension, you will make a valuable contribution to the achievement of your group's social goals. Be a Stress Reliever.

6. Mediate Conflict

When conflict arises in your group, do you attempt to mediate the conflict? When interpersonal problems occur, are you a part of the solution? Effective group members are ready and willing to help manage interpersonal conflict in constructive ways. The *Conflict Mediator* uses the best conflict management strategies to assist members to deal with the inevitable conflicts that arise between and among members of a group. The Conflict Mediator may, for example, use tactful private conversations with individuals to deal with interpersonal conflicts. Or, she may employ confrontation strategies with the whole group present to achieve a healthy resolution of a dispute. We'll examine conflict mediation and resolution in detail in chapter 6. One of the most important things that you can do for your group is to help mediate conflict when it arises. Be a Conflict Mediator.

Together, the six skills described in this section constitute the social role of an effective group member. Members may feel more comfortable doing some of these actions than doing others. However, the best team players will be ready and willing to do all six of the social actions when and as appropriate. They encourage others to participate, support them when they contribute, facilitate the communication of feelings, consciously observe the dynamics of the group, contribute to the relief of stress, and assist in mediating conflicts within their team.

SIX HARMFUL ROLES

Effective group members, as we have seen, are team players who fulfill their task role and their social role by skillfully using the six task actions and the six social actions that we have described above. It would be wonderful if group members always practised the six task actions and the six social actions. Unfortunately, in many groups this is not the case. All too often group members engage in counterproductive behaviours that result in poor group performance and strained relationships. These counterproductive actions are dysfunctional (harmful) because they prevent a group from functioning effectively. A number of harmful group member roles have been identified. Let's take a look at six that occur fairly frequently.[2]

1. The Free Rider

Free Riders don't contribute to the group's effort but expect to benefit from the group's work. They take a "free ride" on the work of others in the group. In school, for example, Free Riders will not do their share of the group project, but they will expect to get the same grade as the others on the team. This is unfair, of course, and often leads to hard feelings, which affect the team's cohesiveness. If Free Riders succeed, other members may well be less likely to work hard on the group's next project. Consequently, group productivity declines. Effective group members carry their fair share of the load and avoid being Free Riders. Free Riders may try to take a free ride on the work of others because of laziness, lack of commitment, overwork in other areas of life, or personal problems.

Healthy teams reduce the chances of free riding by establishing rules of conduct for the group, by stating clearly the penalties for violating those rules, and by enforcing the rules within the team. These expectations and penalties are often included in the team's written record, although they don't have to be. The key to preventing free riding lies in thorough and early discussion of the subject among all members of the group. In chapter 3 we will talk about the importance of group rules for all aspects of group life.

---

2   As noted in footnote 1, Benne and Sheats identified 8 dysfunctional roles. I discuss 6 harmful roles, using popular labels for each.

2. The Dominator

Dominators are at the opposite end of the contribution scale from the Free Rider. They take on excessive amounts of work, denying other members the opportunity to make their contributions. Often Dominators assume authority and make decisions independently. They may behave in this way out of a need to control others or to try to prove themselves in the group. Unfortunately, they offend others, who feel they are not respected for what they can and want to do on the team. In contrast to most members, Free Riders are happy to have a Dominator in the group.

As with the other harmful roles, effective teams confront offenders when they begin to engage in dysfunctional behaviour. This isn't always easy, but it is a skill that members need to develop to ensure that groups become real teams in the course of their lives. In chapter 6 we'll learn about constructive confrontation and its use in managing group conflict. In addition, we'll see in chapters 3 and 4 that groups that establish rules and goals that promote equality among team members dramatically reduce the chances of Dominators taking over.

3. The Rescuer

Rescuers are similar to Dominators in that they do an excessive amount of work, offer solutions prematurely, and make decisions independently. They do this particularly when the group is experiencing difficulties. They want to rescue the group from perceived disaster. The Rescuer is different from the Dominator in that the Rescuer is genuinely interested in the group. The Rescuer wants the team to be successful and tries to rescue the team out of concern for it. In other words, the Rescuer's motivation is not self-interest but group interest. Rescuers may, however, believe that they are more competent than others and that it is up to them to save the team. Again, such behaviour can damage team cohesiveness and, ultimately, be counterproductive.

Rescuers, like Dominators, must be confronted. While they have the group's best interests at heart, their actions are not consistent with healthy group dynamics. The energy of the Rescuer needs to be directed toward cooperative solutions to problems that the group faces. If the group is experiencing difficulties, everyone on the team needs to be involved in solving the problems. The group can't leave it to just one person to save the day. Once again, effective teams reduce or eliminate the need for Rescuers by ensuring that group norms (rules) foster accountability, cooperation, and mutual respect.

4. The Distracter

Distracters may take the group away from its task using a variety of techniques. For example, the Distractor may talk excessively, especially on irrelevant topics (the talker). Or, he may use humour to distract, incessantly cracking jokes (the clown). While an appropriate use of humour can be beneficial in helping to relieve stress in a group, it can also be harmful when used excessively and for other purposes. The Distracter is often trying to satisfy personal needs, especially the need for attention, and in so doing diminishes the group's effectiveness.

Healthy groups confront Distracters to ensure that the group gets its work done efficiently. Everyone's time is important and few people wish to waste their time. Worse yet is to have your time wasted by someone else. The Distracter is simply unfair to others, assuming that his actions are more important than the group's work. As with other problem behaviours, the solution lies in groups discussing their expectations, agreeing on what behaviours are acceptable, and insisting on adherence to established norms. In order for a team to succeed, the Distracter has to give up his penchant for attention just as others have to give up things that they would like to do. Group success almost always requires some individual self-sacrifice.

5. The Cynic

Cynics don't trust others, individually or in groups. They believe, for example, that the group's plans won't work, that some in the group will not carry their weight, or that group work in general is a waste of time. For the Cynic, nothing holds promise of success. Full of pessimism, Cynics regularly project their negativity onto new experiences, including those of the group. This negativity can affect other members, leading to the general view that the group's efforts are not worth it. Cynicism is detrimental, both to a team's task accomplishment and to its social development.

Because the Cynic's pessimism often derives from unhappy life experiences that have left a very deep and dark imprint on personality, it may be particularly difficult to alter the person's behaviour. With other dysfunctional behaviours, one can confront, establish rules and penalties, and attempt to alter behaviour through rewards and punishments. With the Cynic, these strategies may be less effective. Nevertheless, they should be employed with the hope of positive change. In addition, group members should counter the negativity of the Cynic with positive and optimistic attitudes and actions. Just as pessimism can be infectious, so can optimism. It is the positive attitudes of the members of your team that will help to counterbalance the negativity of the Cynic.

6. The Aggressor

Aggressors intimidate other group members, make negative judgments about them, and seek unhealthy confrontation. In some cases, the Aggressor may have a real or imagined grievance against other members of the group and may behave aggressively as a result. In other instances, anger he feels for people outside the group may be directed toward group members. Aggressors run the range from the more subtle passive-aggressive type to the less subtle active-aggressive type. Regardless of the degree of aggression and the reason for it, the intimidation experienced by group members will reduce productivity and overall cohesion. Members may bond together in a common defence against the Aggressor, but such cohesiveness is based on an unhealthy social situation that needs to be corrected.

The Aggressor is probably the most difficult person to deal with in group life. Fortunately, the overt aggressor is a fairly rare problem. If one appears in your group, he may have to be removed. Very few of us will tolerate his presence. If he doesn't leave, we very likely will. The group will not be able to function. More common in groups is the presence of the passive-aggressive personality. With this type of aggression, constructive confrontation is in order. In chapter 6, as noted earlier, we will examine strategies, like confrontation, that will help you to deal with members who try to intimidate others. It's unfortunate, but the reality is that there are difficult people in small groups just as there are such people in virtually all other areas of our lives. Fortunately, there are some helpful strategies available for dealing with difficult people.

We have now described six harmful roles that some people play within small groups. The roles of the Free Rider, the Dominator, the Rescuer, the Distracter, the Cynic, and the Aggressor are, obviously, roles that team players avoid. In contrast, effective team members use the six task actions and the six social actions described earlier to contribute to the success of their groups. Team players avoid the harmful roles and cooperate with others to eliminate the dysfunctional behaviours associated with those roles. Eliminating dysfunctional behaviour in your group is one of the most challenging aspects of working with people in groups. Since group work is essential in our world, we need to learn how to function effectively within groups. This chapter and the remaining chapters of this book are designed to help you do just that.

CHAPTER SUMMARY

We started our study of interpersonal and group dynamics by noting the importance of roles within our society and our lives. Just as society has certain expectations for the various roles that workers play, so there are expectations associated with the roles that members of small groups play. We expect police officers, for example, to do certain things and to avoid doing other kinds of things as they fulfill their roles. So too we expect certain things of the members of small groups. We noted that there are helpful and harmful roles within society, and that there are functional and dysfunctional roles within groups.

Next, we described six helpful actions that constitute the task role of an effective group member. The task role comprises the actions of the Idea Sharer, the Idea Seeker, the Direction Suggester, the Progress Summarizer, the Comprehension Checker, and the Group Motivator. With respect to the social role of an effective team player, we highlighted the actions of the Participation Encourager, the Participant Supporter, the Communication Facilitator, the Process Observer, the Stress Reliever, and the Conflict Mediator. We emphasized the fact that any member of a group can learn these 12 basic group skills and the fact that the best team players regularly use all of these skills.

Finally, we described six dysfunctional roles that occur from time to time within groups, causing them to be less productive and less cohesive. The roles of the Free Rider, the Dominator, the Rescuer, the Distracter, the Cynic, and the Aggressor are roles to be avoided. In each case, we offered some preliminary thoughts on how group members can deal with these dysfunctional behaviours when they occur.

In policing, effective teams are essential for the protection of society and the enforcement of the law. If you, as a future police officer, understand and practise the six task actions and the six social actions, you will contribute dramatically to the success of your future work teams. When you apply the same principles to the groups in your personal life, you will make a major contribution to the success of those groups as well.

KEY TERMS

cohesion   role

culture   social action

dysfunctional role   social goal

functional role   task action

norm   task goal

MASTERING THE MATERIAL

Now that you have read this chapter, use the following guides to ensure that you have mastered the material.

1. What is the difference between an actor's "playing" a role and your "living" a role?

2. Define *culture*.

3. Define *role*.

4. Define *norm*.

5. Helpful group member roles are called _____ roles, and harmful group member roles are called _____ roles.

6. Name and define the two basic goals of every group.

    a.   The name of the first basic goal is _____.

         Definition:

    b.   The name of the second basic goal is _____.

         Definition:

7. The six actions that help a group get the job done are called _____ actions, and the six actions that help a group build good relationships among group members are called _____ actions.

8. List, from memory, the six task actions that make up the task role.

    a.

    b.

    c.

    d.

    e.

    f.

9. List, from memory, the six social actions that make up the social role.

    a.

    b.

    c.

    d.

    e.

    f.

10. List, from memory, the six harmful or dysfunctional roles described in the chapter.

   a.

   b.

   c.

   d.

   e.

   f.

11. Name and describe the six helpful actions that make up the task role.

   a.

   b.

   c.

   d.

   e.

   f.

12. Name and describe the six helpful actions that make up the social role.

   a.

   b.

   c.

   d.

   e.

   f.

13. Name each of the six harmful roles and explain how to deal with each one.

   a.

   b.

   c.

   d.

   e.

   f.

APPLYING THE IDEAS IN POLICING

Scenario

You have been assigned by your police service to meet on a regular basis for a number of weeks with a small citizens' group. They want to improve the relationship between the community and your police service. Your service is eager to do the same. The group consists of five members of the community, but one person, the owner of a local shop, seems to dominate the initial meetings with his opinions. The other members are almost silent. They seem intimidated by both you and the shop owner.

Exercise 1.1

Using the scenario above, write some brief statements that you might make or questions that you might ask to help this group get the job done. In each case, identify the specific *task action* you are using.

Exercise 1.2

Using the scenario above, write some brief statements that you might make or questions that you might ask to help this group develop into a cohesive team. In each case, identify the specific *social actions* you are using.

Exercise 1.3

Using the scenario above, what harmful role(s) may the shop owner be performing? Identify the harmful role(s), and suggest constructive ways of dealing with them.

PRACTISING YOUR GROUP SKILLS

Purpose of This Section

The purpose of "Practising Your Group Skills" and the ultimate purpose of this book is to help you become a more effective participant in the groups to which you belong. This section is designed to provide opportunities for you and your fellow students to practise your group skills in a structured environment.

Team Responsibilities

A description of the team responsibilities for each of five different teams — the Executive Team, the Teaching Team, the Lesson Review Team, the Energizer Team, and the Evaluation Team — can be found in appendix A, pages 207–210. Your professor may have chosen to use from one to five of these teams to conduct the teaching and learning activities of the class. Units 2 and 3 of the Teacher's Guide provide your professor with additional information on the responsibilities of these teams.

Individual Role Responsibilities

A description of four individual role responsibilities — those of Leader, Recorder, Reporter, and Participant-Analyst — can be found in appendix A, pages 210–212. Your professor may have chosen to use from one to four of these roles within teams to give individuals experience leading, recording, reporting, and analyzing. Units 2 and 3 of the Teacher's Guide provide your professor with additional information on these individual role responsibilities.

Specific Team Assignments

Specific team assignments for this chapter appear immediately below. Specific team assignments for each of the subsequent chapters can be found in "Practising Your Group Skills" in each chapter.

CHAPTER 1 TEAM ASSIGNMENTS

The Executive Team

- *Executive Goal:* to provide leadership to your classmates for your class session on chapter 1.

- *Executive Objectives:* to facilitate the class session by (1) ensuring a good classroom setup, (2) welcoming the class, (3) introducing the lesson topic, (4) coordinating activities, and (5) bringing the session to a close.

- *Instructions:* Ensure that the classroom is set up to accommodate the class activities. Post an agenda for the session. Welcome people to class and announce the topic, "Member Roles: Participating Effectively in Your Group," in a creative and interesting way. Remind the class that the topic includes an examination of task actions, social actions, and harmful actions. Introduce and thank all speakers when appropriate. Coordinate the day's activities and bring closure at the end of the class. If necessary, return the classroom to its original configuration.

The Teaching Team

- *Teaching Goal:* to understand and demonstrate basic member participation skills in a small group setting.

- *Teaching Objectives:* to describe, explain, and demonstrate (1) the six task actions, (2) the six social actions, and (3) the six harmful actions.

- *Instructions:* As the Teaching Team, you have the freedom to choose how you will teach your lesson. You can be as creative as you wish, but you must achieve the teaching objectives. Your lesson consists of two parts. The first part is the experiential exercise, and the second part is your explanation of the chapter information.

  ❑ Your experiential exercise is called "Effective Participation" and you'll find it described fully in appendix B, pages 216–218. Make sure that you refer to "Effective Participation" when you teach and explain the task actions, social actions, and harmful actions.

  ❑ If time allows, you can also use exercises from the "Mastering the Material" and "Applying the Ideas in Policing" sections of chapter 1 in your lesson.

The Lesson Review Team

- *Review Goal:* to review (1) the professor's lesson or presentation from the previous class, or (2) good and bad experiences that classmates have had on teams in the past.

- *Instructions:* Since this is the first chapter of this book, there may be nothing to review from last class. However, if the professor did an introductory lecture in the last class session, the team can review the material from that presentation. Alternatively, the team can lead a brief discussion of the past experiences that classmates have had on teams. The discussion might focus, for example, on the best team experiences and the worst experiences that class members have had.

The Energizer Team

- *Energizer Goal:* to motivate your classmates by conducting an energizer activity.

- *Energizer Objectives:* to facilitate the energizing of your classmates by (1) planning an energizer activity and (2) implementing the plan at an appropriate time in the class session.

- *Instructions:* Your team doesn't have a specific, assigned activity to conduct. Rather, the team should remember its energizing purpose and conduct an activity that will provide a break in the class learning routine. Popular games like Simon Says, Heads Up Seven Up, and Murder Wink usually work well. So do various mixers and ice breakers. (Your professor's Teacher's Guide identifies a number of sources of energizer exercises.) Whatever you decide on, you must be prepared to give clear instructions and conduct the exercise effectively. When you lead the energizer, you are leading and directing the entire class. Plan well and execute professionally, even if the exercise is a "kid's game." Encourage everyone to get involved.

The Evaluation Team

As a member of the Evaluation Team, you need to review the information in chapter 10, pages 191–194, before you do anything else. There you will find helpful information on how to conduct your evaluation session. The most important thing to remember is that you are not to judge other people. Your role is to help the class make its own assessment of which practices worked well today and which didn't.

Note that the evaluation goal below is keyed to the content of this chapter. *If desirable or necessary, you can evaluate any other aspect of group experience.* Be sure, though, that you set the goal, develop appropriate objectives, and plan the evaluation session to achieve the goal and the objectives.

- *Evaluation Goal:* to assess group (or class) participation in today's class session.

- *Evaluation Objectives:* to (1) assess group (or class) member use of the six task actions, the six social actions, and the six harmful actions in today's class session and (2) identify practices in need of improvement.

- *Instructions:* Create an evaluation instrument based on the selected focus behaviours identified in the objectives. See chapter 10, pages 192–193, for information on creating evaluation instruments. Figure 10.1 provides an example. Solicit feedback from the class using the evaluation instrument. Use the feedback to discuss the class session with the purpose of identifying improvements that can be made to individual, group, and class performance in future class sessions. Conclude by noting the specific actions that need to be repeated or avoided to make improvements.

REFERENCES AND RECOMMENDED READINGS

Bales, R. (1950). *Interaction process analysis.* Reading, MA: Addison Wesley.

Benne, K.D., & Sheats, P. (1948). Functional roles of group members. *Journal of Social Issues, 4,* 41–49.

Bormann, E.G. (1990). *Small group communication: Theory and practice* (3rd ed.) (chapters 7 & 8). New York: Harper & Row.

Fiedler, F.E. (1964). A contingency model of leader effectiveness. In L. Berkowitz (Ed.), *Advances in experimental social psychology* (Vol. 1, pp. 149–190). New York: Academic Press.

Fiedler, F.E. (1967). *A theory of leadership effectiveness.* New York: McGraw-Hill.

Johnson, David W. (1991). *Human relations and your career.* Englewood Cliffs, NJ: Prentice-Hall.

Johnson, D.W., & Johnson, F.P. (2003). *Joining together: Group theory and group skills.* Boston: Allyn and Bacon.

Mouton, J.S., & Blake, R.R. (1984). *Synergogy: A new strategy for education, training, and development.* San Francisco: Jossey-Bass.

Leader Roles: Leading Effectively in Your Group

Chapter Objectives

After completing this chapter, you should be able to:

- Distinguish between a designated leader and an emergent leader.

- Explain the difference between a people-oriented leader and a task-oriented leader.

- Identify and describe three styles of leadership.

- Identify and describe different situations that require different leadership styles.

- Define the term *power*, and describe several different types of power.

- Identify and describe five characteristics of an effective leader.

INTRODUCTION

Some of you reading this chapter may aspire to being a leader in the policing field at some time in the future. Perhaps you have enjoyed leadership responsibilities in school, sports, or community activities. If you were successful in your leadership roles, you may be especially keen to take on leadership in the police service. Others may see leadership in a different way. Perhaps you'd rather let other people do the leading while you concentrate on being a good follower. Some people fear leadership. Whether you're in the first group and like the idea of being a leader, or whether you're in the second and don't enjoy leading, the concept of leadership is very important. Whether you serve as a sergeant or a constable, knowledge of leaders and leadership is invaluable. This chapter is intended to provide information about leadership to both future leaders and future followers. Let's look first at how people come to be leaders.

DESIGNATED LEADERS AND EMERGENT LEADERS

One way to become a leader is to be *designated* either *by* the group or *for* the group. **Designated leaders** are the official leaders of a group who occupy special roles that are vital to the success of the group. Police services, for example, needs chiefs, staff sergeants, and other designated leaders to coordinate and direct the members of the service. Similarly, the military needs commanders at various levels to give the orders that are carried out by other personnel. Likewise, cities need mayors and councillors to conduct the affairs of the community. In the first of these examples, a chief of police is hired by a community's police services board to command those who work under him and to direct the operations of the service. He is the service's official, designated leader.

designated leader
a leader chosen by or for a group

All large organizations and many small groups require a variety of designated leaders in order to function effectively.

While the titles (for example, chief, general, or mayor) of these designated leadership roles may differ from group to group, the basic leadership functions of all organizations are fairly constant. Both large organizations and small groups need members who are designated to serve as leaders, recorders, and reporters. The generic labels for these three essential functions are directing, keeping records, and communicating with people outside the group. Other designated roles may exist in different groups, but we will limit ourselves for the moment to these three basic role functions.

Leaders give direction to the group in various ways. *Recorders* keep a record of the decisions and important actions of the group so that an objective account of the group's activities is available for all to see. *Reporters* provide either members or outsiders with regular or occasional accounts of the group's work. Often these functions overlap, but the key point is that all groups need leadership in these three areas. For example, the chief and the chief's senior staff may make an important decision regarding the future direction of the department. Another person may function as a recorder during the deliberations of the senior administrative staff. A designated sergeant may then report the service's new policy to the public as the official communications officer of the service.

Later in this chapter we will examine the use of power by leaders. Make note that the forms of power most often associated with designated leadership are legitimate power, reward power, and coercive power. We'll return to these forms of power shortly.

A second way to become a leader is to possess and demonstrate some special knowledge or skill that the group needs at a particular time. **Emergent leaders** are group members who take on a temporary leadership role because of their special talents. In contrast to designated leaders, emergent leaders are usually unofficial leaders who bring their personal talents to bear on a particular issue.

emergent leader
a leader who assumes a temporary leadership role because of his or her special talents

For example, if a group is hoping to purchase a new computer system and one of its members is much more knowledgeable about computers than the other members, then she may emerge as a leader with respect to the computer purchase. Law enforcement officers, because of their knowledge, training, and experience, often emerge as unofficial leaders in both their police services and their communities. A constable with a high level of computer skills may, for example, emerge as an unofficial leader in a case involving computer crime. So, too, a constable who knows a lot about baseball may emerge as an unofficial leader in his community's invitational baseball tournament.

Emergent leaders exercise power that is based on their personal qualities or their personal expertise in a given area. Later in this chapter we'll examine the two forms of power most closely associated with emergent leadership. We'll study charismatic power and expert power.

Healthy groups need both designated leaders and emergent leaders to ensure that the group's tasks are accomplished and the relationships among members are strengthened. Interestingly, the basic skills necessary for effective leadership are the same for both designated and emergent leaders. These basic skills are the ones associated with the task role and the social role that we described in chapter 1.

Recall that there are six task actions that together make up the task role, and six social actions associated with the social role. The task actions include sharing ideas, seeking ideas, suggesting directions, summarizing progress, checking comprehension, and motivating the team. The social actions include encouraging participation, supporting participants, facilitating communication, observing process, relieving stress, and mediating conflict. These basic actions or skills can be learned by anyone, and they are essential to good leadership. In addition, those who become leaders have further expectations placed on them because of their designated or emergent responsibilities.

With regard to followers, those who understand their leaders can make a far greater contribution to a group's success than those who don't. Understanding the responsibilities of your leader can make you a better follower. For one thing, you are far less likely to follow blindly if you have a good grasp of your leader's rights, responsibilities, and approach to leadership. Both leaders and followers do well to understand leadership.

DIFFERENT LEADERS HAVE DIFFERENT GOALS

Some leaders tend to place more emphasis on task completion than they do on relationship development within a group. These **task-oriented leaders** are most interested in productivity; that is, getting the job done.[1] Their primary goal is to get the task completed. In contrast, other leaders tend to place more emphasis on building and maintaining a cohesive team. These **people-oriented leaders** see team building as the most important aspect of leadership. Their primary goal is to strengthen relationships among members. It is fair to say that both the task-oriented leader and the people-oriented leader go to extremes.

The most effective leader, in most circumstances, will be the one who strikes a healthy balance between task goals and social goals. The **ideal leader** is the one who places equal emphasis on both task completion and social relationships. He emphasizes the six task actions in order to get the job done, and the six social actions in order to build the team. Successful leaders in policing, as in every other field, are leaders who are attentive to both the task and the social dimensions of the groups they lead.

task-oriented leader
a leader who is most interested in productivity, or getting the job done

people-oriented leader
a leader who sees team building as the most important aspect of leadership

ideal leader
a leader who has equal respect for both task completion and social relationships

---

1   Fiedler (1964), using the concept of task and social goals, noted that some leaders are more oriented to task completion while others are more oriented to relationship development. Hence the terms *task-oriented leader* and *people-oriented leader*.

non-leader
a leader who places little or no emphasis on either task goals or social goals

In contrast to the ideal leader, the **non-leader** is one who places little or no emphasis on either task or social goals. If the non-leader is simply avoiding the responsibilities of leadership, the group will suffer as a result. Non-leaders of this type are a detriment to their teams. There is, however, another type of non-leader, one that we might call the *conscious* non-leader. If a non-leader recognizes that she is the leader of a very competent group of people, then she might consciously choose to let group members lead themselves. The French expression "laissez-faire" means "to leave alone" or "to let be." The non-leader who consciously allows a strong group to make its own decisions — leaves them alone or lets them be — is called a laissez-faire leader. We will say more about laissez-faire leadership in the next section. It can be a very effective approach to leadership under certain circumstances.

THREE STYLES OF LEADERSHIP

1. The Autocratic Leader

autocratic leader
a take-charge leader who tells others what to do and sees that they do it

Some leaders see leadership as a matter of telling others what to do, a matter of bossing others around. Such leaders are very directive and like to make most, if not all, decisions. They look to group members to carry out their directives or orders, and their style of leadership is like that of a dictator or autocrat. The **autocratic leader** is a take-charge person who tells others what to do and sees that they do it.[2] Autocratic leaders often place the greatest emphasis on task completion, and are thus similar to the task-oriented leader described above. Autocratic leadership is often criticized for its less-than-democratic approach to group life. Many people find this style offensive and an insult to group members. Consequently, they react with feelings of anger and alienation.

There are many situations, however, in which autocratic leadership is the most effective form of leadership and, in fact, may be absolutely necessary. For example, one may have to be autocratic with little children to protect them from danger. Sometimes leaders need to be autocratic with adult followers as well. In emergency situations, for instance, someone often has to take charge. So, too, in the military in wartime, there is often no time for democratic decisions. For survival and victory, someone has to give the orders, and others have to follow them. Obviously, many situations in policing also require the autocratic approach. The very nature of policing requires this directive approach in order to serve and protect. In the many dangerous situations that police officers face in the course of their work, leaders must take an authoritarian approach.

2. The Democratic Leader

democratic leader
a leader who involves all members of a group in discussion of issues and decisions

For many situations, the democratic leader is the most effective leader. The **democratic leader** involves all members of the group in discussion of issues and decisions that have to be made. Because the democratic leader places trust in the members of the group, members feel that they can influence the group's action, and this can be a rewarding experience. For example, a group of staff sergeants doing strategic

---

2   Lewin, Lippitt, and White (1939) were among the first to describe the autocratic, democratic, and laissez-faire leadership styles that appear commonly today in the literature on group dynamics.

planning will usually have a chairperson who functions as a democratic leader, encouraging members' participation and drawing out their various points of view. Members of democratic groups tend to have far less hostility than do members of autocratically run groups. If time permits discussion and the group reaches a consensus on a decision, then members are much more likely to be committed to implementing that decision.

A drawback of the democratic style is that discussion and consensus building take time. Members may become frustrated if there is insufficient time to reach a decision, or if trivial matters are constantly brought forward by the democratic leader. Democratic leaders have high regard for the contributions of all group members. This high regard is the result of the leader's emphasis on the social dimension of the group's life. Equally, though, the democratic leader values task completion. Frequently, the democratic leader is the ideal leader described earlier in this chapter.

3. The Laissez-Faire Leader

As noted above, the non-leader sometimes adopts the non-leader approach to avoid the responsibilities of leadership. In contrast, the **laissez-faire leader** consciously adopts the non-leader approach with a specific purpose in mind. For example, knowing that the group consists of very responsible and self-motivated individuals, a leader may deliberately sit back and let the group direct itself. This can be a wise strategy because it recognizes and respects the competence of group members. In contrast, if the leader takes an autocratic approach with a group of very knowledgeable and highly skilled people, they may feel alienated and frustrated. The sergeant who takes the autocratic approach regularly in daily briefings with front-line constables might be effective in getting the job done using that approach. The same sergeant might decide to use the laissez-faire approach in a meeting of peers and be very effective in doing so. Thus, leadership requires a clear understanding of the group's membership and circumstances. At times, the laissez-faire style of leadership is the most effective style.

laissez-faire leader a leader who consciously adopts the non-leader approach with a specific purpose in mind

Effective group members, whether they are leaders or not, understand these three different styles of leadership, and function more effectively in their groups than members who don't have this understanding. The police officer who can read a situation and see the need for one approach over another has a distinct advantage over the officer who does not have this ability.

Now, let's take a closer look at three different situations that require different approaches to leadership.

DIFFERENT SITUATIONS, DIFFERENT APPROACHES

We noted earlier that different styles of leadership are appropriate in different situations.[3] There is a place for autocratic leadership, a place for democratic leadership, and a place for laissez-faire leadership. The most appropriate style of leadership to use in any given case depends on the level of maturity of the members of your

---

3   One of the best-known approaches to situational leadership is that of Hersey and Blanchard (1977). The description of different leadership styles for different maturity levels (different situations) presented here is based on their important work.

group maturity
a group's achievement orientation, level of responsibility, and expertise

group. **Group maturity** comprises three elements: a group's commitment to achievement, its level of responsibility, and its degree of expertise. When a group is composed of members who are not very responsible, have a low desire to achieve, and are not very knowledgeable, the group has a *low level of maturity*. In contrast, a group whose members are very responsible, highly achievement-oriented, and very knowledgeable is a group that has a *high level of maturity*. A group whose members have a moderate degree of responsibility, self-direction, and expertise is a group that has a *moderate level of maturity*.

Autocratic leadership is most effective with a group that has a low level of maturity. For example, when a group has little initiative, lacks responsibility, and is inexperienced, the leader needs to take a directive approach to help the group succeed. In contrast, when faced with a group that is keen to achieve, takes responsibility seriously, and has knowledgeable and skilled members, the leader needs to respect the talent of the group. In such situations, the laissez-faire style is likely to be most effective. When a group has a moderate level of maturity, the democratic style is most likely to succeed. The democratic leader can, for example, help to nurture a team's sense of responsibility, promote its interest in achievement, and develop its knowledge and skills. Recognizing the individual talents within a moderately mature group, the democratic leader works to maximize the benefits of those talents through a true team effort.

One of the key characteristics of successful leaders is their knowledge of both people and situations. They know when to use the various leadership styles. As a leader you need to know when to be autocratic, when to be democratic, and when to be laissez-faire. Before we examine further traits of successful leaders, let's say a few words about leadership and power.

LEADERSHIP AND POWER IN GROUPS

power
the ability to influence a situation in desired directions

Power is the ability to influence a situation in a desired direction. Notice that power, as defined here, is neither good nor bad in itself. It is neutral. Often, however, people see power as negative, and there is no doubt that power can be used inappropriately in ways that harm group members. Despite this common view, power is not necessarily bad. It can be a force for good, a positive force for getting the job done and building a team. In this section of the chapter, we will focus on the positive and necessary aspects of power in groups, recognizing that power can be abused on occasion. Let's now examine five different forms of power that exist within most groups.[4]

1. Legitimate Power

legitimate power
power that flows from the designated positions within a group

The first form is called **legitimate power**, and it is the power that accompanies a designated leadership role within a group or an organization. The Prime Minister of Canada, for example, has certain powers that come with the office. He can call elections, sign bills into law, and do many other things that no other Canadian has the power to do. Whenever a person occupies a designated leadership role, she has a certain amount of power by virtue of being the designated leader. Promotion to

---

4 French and Raven (1981, p. 317) have examined the basis of power in small groups and provided an excellent review of the subject.

the rank of staff sergeant, for example, gives the person promoted new powers, those associated with the role of staff sergeant.

More generally, any team leader usually has the power to call meetings, propose agendas, and speak to outsiders on behalf of the group. A recorder, too, will have a certain power associated with shaping and keeping the official records of the group. Other designated leaders will also have some special power associated with their positions in the group. The reason for this form of power within groups is that individuals need these special powers to carry out the responsibilities of their designated positions. Legitimate leadership roles require legitimate power in order to be fulfilled effectively.

Included in the legitimate leadership roles of some groups, particularly formal work groups, are powers to reward and to punish members of the group. These rewards and punishments are called **sanctions**. In policing, for example, there are punishments for insubordination. Policing and other organizations have punishments such as suspension or dismissal to control the behaviour of members of the organization. Policing also offers rewards to its members. In addition to the reward of a paycheque, there are special service awards for bravery and conduct above and beyond the call of duty. Other organizations also reward good behaviour with promotions, bonuses, and other benefits. Sanctions are sometimes referred to as sticks and carrots. You can get an animal, for example, to do what you want it to do in two ways. You can beat it with a stick (punishment) or entice it with a carrot (reward).

sanctions
powers to reward or punish members of a group

2. Reward Power

A second form of power, then, is called **reward power**, and it is the power to give benefits to members who display appropriate or exemplary behaviour within a group. We can see reward power at work in many groups in society, including family groups. Parents, for example, may increase a child's allowance because the child has done an exceptional job of doing household chores. In small groups, however, rewards are rarely of the monetary variety. In small groups, reward usually comes in the form of praise from others. Exemplary performance may also be rewarded with a promotion to a leadership role that brings increased status. Similarly, on sports teams, certain players are rewarded with the captain's "C" or the assistant captain's "A." In school work groups, rewards may take the form of bonus marks.

reward power
power resulting from the use of rewards to influence conduct

3. Coercive Power

A third form of power is **coercive power**, the power to punish inappropriate behaviour. To coerce someone is to force the person to do what you want, and the threat of punishment is one form of coercive power. Officers who violate the code of conduct of the Ontario *Police Services Act*, for example, may be faced with a variety of punishments that are intended to deter violations of that code. Reprimands, suspensions, and dismissals are all examples of coercive power within a police service. Families "ground" errant children, sports teams "bench" players, and teachers lower grades of students. Each of these practices illustrates the use of coercive power, which might just as well be called punishment power.

coercive power
power resulting from the use of punishment to influence conduct

4. Charismatic Power

charismatic power
power resulting from
a leader's personal
qualities

A fourth form of power is called **charismatic power**, a type of power that results from an individual's personal qualities. Legitimate power, reward power, and coercive power are, as noted above, associated with designated leadership positions. Charismatic power, in contrast, is associated with emergent leadership. Sometimes people emerge as leaders because of their personal qualities. For example, it may be that an individual is well spoken, trustworthy, and charming. Such an individual, we say, has charisma, a word that comes from the Greek language and means gifts. The student who is intelligent, well spoken, thoughtful, and fair may well emerge as an unofficial leader within a school work group.

Charismatic power can be combined with legitimate power, and often is. Former Canadian prime minister Pierre Elliott Trudeau is a good example of a leader who had both charismatic power and legitimate power. Similarly, the constable who is respected as an officer of the law but who is also admired for personal qualities — friendliness, good humour, and integrity, for example — has both charismatic power and legitimate power as she relates to members of the community. The most popular leaders are those who possess both forms of power. That doesn't mean, of course, that a person has to be charismatic to be a good leader. It just means that charisma can be an added advantage for a leader.

5. Expert Power

expert power
power resulting from
particular knowledge
or skill

A fifth and final form of power is also associated with emergent leadership. **Expert power** is the power that results from having special knowledge and skill that is required by a group. When an individual knows something or possesses a skill that is needed by a group, that individual has power. In this case, the power comes not from a designated office (legitimate power) or from the individual's personal charm (charismatic power), but from his or her expertise. For example, the seasoned detective who has vast first-hand experience in criminal investigation is likely to exercise expert power regardless of rank. His knowledge and skill are forms of expert power that are extremely valuable to the policing agency. However, a person's expertise doesn't necessarily translate into power within the group. Members gain expert power only when their expertise is needed by the group to accomplish its purposes. At the annual police–firefighter tug-of-war contest, the seasoned detective may be useless to the team. Knowledge and skill in investigative procedure mean nothing in a test of brawn.

In this section, we have noted five forms of power common in small group life. Legitimate power, reward power, and coercive power are more closely associated with designated leadership, while charismatic and expert power are more commonly associated with emergent leadership. We have tried to point out, however, that these forms of power are not mutually exclusive. That is to say, a good leader can possess all of them, and the best leaders usually do. When you assume positions of leadership within your small groups, your knowledge of these five forms of power and the appropriate use of them will contribute to your success as a leader. We'll now move on to examine certain characteristics that are typical of the most effective leaders.

CHARACTERISTICS OF AN EFFECTIVE LEADER

Our review of leadership roles in this chapter is somewhat general. This review is intended to examine leadership in ways that will help you as you provide leadership in small groups both in school and in the workplace. It is not intended, however, to provide all the fine detail necessary for senior leadership within large organizations. For example, exercising effective leadership at the rank of staff sergeant requires knowledge of the basic concepts studied in this chapter, but it also requires much more specific knowledge of the responsibilities associated with that position. It also requires experience working at different levels of the organization. Further, achieving leadership responsibilities in a policing agency is hard work, the result of giving leadership in many different situations over a long period of time.

Senior leadership positions may be a part of your future. For the moment, though, we need to examine five general traits or characteristics that are essential to good leadership in the present. What traits or characteristics do effective leaders possess? Many studies have investigated the qualities associated with successful leadership, and the list of desirable characteristics is quite long. Rather than attempt to identify all the traits that have been studied by researchers,[5] we will limit ourselves to five key characteristics of the effective leader. If you develop these five characteristics in your own life, you will have the essentials of successful leadership for both the present and the future.

1. Knowledge

Successful leaders are *knowledgeable*. First, and most importantly, they have a good understanding of group dynamics. They know how people in groups tend to interact, and they also know the essentials of working effectively with people in groups. Their knowledge includes an understanding of the two basic goals, the task goal and the social goal. Moreover, they understand the six actions that facilitate the achievement of the task goal, and they understand the importance of the six actions that contribute to the achievement of social goals. These basics of group dynamics were, of course, the subject of chapter 1. Effective leaders also understand the fundamentals of good leadership as discussed in the current chapter. Their knowledge extends to the various topics that will be studied in the remainder of this book; namely, the importance of group norms, goals, communication, conflict resolution, cohesion, critical discussion, problem solving, decision making, and performance evaluation.

Some people think that good leaders must also know everything that their group is dealing with at any given time. For example, some people think that the leader of a group working on a physics project must be very knowledgeable about physics. While knowledge of physics may be very helpful, it may not be absolutely necessary. If the leader isn't acquainted with the subject under consideration, she can research the topic and become more knowledgeable about it. The leader need

---

5   Stogdill (1981, pp. 63–68), Shaw (1981, pp. 324–325), and Kenney and Zaccuro (1984, pp. 678–685) are only a few of many researchers who have examined the characteristics of effective leaders. The list of traits associated with leadership is very long. For the purpose of this book, the list has been reduced to five key characteristics.

not become an expert on the matter in question, however, if she possesses a solid understanding of group processes.

Successful leaders know how to work with people regardless of the subject area that a group is dealing with. Cabinet ministers in the federal government provide us with a good example of the point that we are making. They are often given new portfolios within the government — a switch from finance to health, for example — not because they know the area of responsibility in great detail. Rather, they are given different responsibilities because they know how the system works and they can adapt to new circumstances and begin to learn about the new responsibilities. To succeed as a leader, you will want to have a good understanding of interpersonal and group dynamics.

2. Communication

Successful leaders are good *communicators*, skilled at both *speaking* and *writing*. In addition, they are active listeners who employ the best *listening* skills. Effective leaders also give helpful *feedback* to others and they use assertive communication when dealing with conflict within a group. As noted in chapter 1, every member of a group should be a Progress Summarizer and a Comprehension Checker, because these actions involve good communication that contributes to successful task completion. In addition, we noted that the group's social goal is more likely to be reached if members are Communication Facilitators and Conflict Mediators, functions that employ communication skills. Effective leaders are excellent communicators who regularly employ these and other important communication skills personally and encourage all group members to do the same.

You will have an opportunity to examine the key communication skills — speaking, listening, and giving feedback — in chapter 5. There we will review several rules for sending oral messages effectively, listening actively, and providing constructive feedback. As in all human relationships, communication skills are critical for maximizing the benefits of those relationships. Communication skills are also the key to resolving interpersonal disputes when they occur. In chapter 6, we'll study assertive communication and the resolution of conflict. The most effective leaders are skilled communicators who apply their skills to the dynamic relationships among group members. To become a good leader, you will need to learn to communicate with excellence.

3. Task Orientation

Have you ever worked for a slave driver? While the image underlying this question comes from a sad world — the world of slave ownership — it describes perfectly those leaders who pursue the completion of tasks with no concern for the feelings of people. Perhaps it was a boss, a teacher, or a coach who, in your experience, seemed fixated on tasks and oblivious to people. The extreme task-oriented leader is, of course, a leader who fails to balance task completion with a healthy respect for the feelings of people. Extremist leaders of this type are also referred to as dictators or despots. To succeed as a leader, you will need to avoid this overemphasis on task completion.

Effective leaders are, however, clearly *task-oriented*. They know what has to be done and they keep the group's task goals clearly in focus. However, they do not emphasize task completion at the expense of relationships among group members. When groups meet, they usually have work to do, tasks to complete. Effective leaders know what that work is, and they try to ensure that it is done as efficiently as possible. To this end, they employ all six task actions regularly, and they encourage group members to do the same. But, good leaders balance this concern for task completion with a sensitivity to the social needs of group members. Because of this balance, they are ideal leaders. Your success as a leader will come, in large part, from your ability to strike a balance between the social needs of people and the need to be productive.

4. People Orientation

You have, no doubt, met leaders who pay little or no attention to the job that has to be done. These leaders often enjoy socializing and may do a good job of cultivating team spirit. If, however, they always socialize and the group doesn't complete its tasks, such leaders will fall out of favour with members. In the rough and ready world of competitive business, they are not likely to be around for very long if productivity suffers. The boss will fire them. In the world of groups outside the workplace, they may last longer, but they may also incur the disfavour of group members who get frustrated when tasks go uncompleted and valuable time is wasted. Effective leaders refrain from going to this extreme. To succeed as a leader, you will need to balance concern for people with a concern for getting the job done.

Effective leaders, then, are *people-oriented*. They do not, however, focus on social goals to the exclusion of task goals. They are ideal leaders who understand the importance of both task goals and social goals. Good leaders are empathetic and sensitive to the feelings of group members, and they constantly monitor the emotional climate of the group. They balance this concern for people, however, with a healthy regard for the work that needs to be accomplished.

5. Flexibility

Earlier in this chapter, we distinguished among three different styles of leadership — autocratic, democratic, and laissez-faire. We noted that each type has its place depending on the circumstances of a given situation. We pointed out that autocratic leadership is effective when a group is immature. Democratic leadership, we said, was effective when a group is moderately mature. When faced with a mature group, we noted that laissez-faire leadership is often most effective.

Effective leaders are *flexible* with respect to leadership style. They understand when a laissez-faire approach is appropriate and adopt that approach when required; they also know when an autocratic approach is appropriate, and change their leadership style accordingly. When circumstances require a democratic approach, the good leader shifts to that mode of leadership. This flexibility allows the good leader to adjust to changing circumstances, while less effective leaders remain locked into their preferred style or fail to recognize and adjust to new realities. As a present and future leader, you will need to have the flexibility to demonstrate leadership in different ways depending on the situations that you face.

CHAPTER SUMMARY

In this chapter, we first distinguished between designated and emergent leaders. Designated leaders, we said, are the official leaders chosen by a group or for a group. In contrast, emergent leaders rise to temporary, unofficial positions of leadership because they have the special expertise that a group needs or because they are gifted persons whose personal qualities are valued by the group. We then pointed out that different leaders may emphasize different goals, causing some leaders to be task-oriented, others to be people-oriented, and still others to be ideal leaders who balance concern for task with concern for people. We went on to describe autocratic, democratic, and laissez-faire approaches to leadership and drew attention to the situations in which each is most effective. Then, after examining the relationship between leadership and power — particularly, legitimate power, reward power, coercive power, expert power, and charismatic power — we proceeded to describe five qualities that are typical of successful leaders. Effective leaders, we noted, understand group dynamics, communicate clearly, ensure that tasks are completed, empathize with members, and adjust to new circumstances. They are knowledgeable, communicative, task-oriented, people-oriented, and flexible.

KEY TERMS

autocratic leader

charismatic power

coercive power

democratic leader

designated leader

emergent leader

expert power

group maturity

ideal leader

laissez-faire leader

legitimate power

non-leader

people-oriented leader

power

reward power

sanctions

task-oriented leader

MASTERING THE MATERIAL

Now that you have read this chapter, use the following guides to ensure that you have mastered the material.

1. Define *designated leader*.

2. Name the three designated leader roles that are common in many groups.

3. Define *emergent leader*.

4. Give an example of an emergent leader within a group.

5. A leader who places emphasis on getting the job done is called a(n) _____-oriented leader.

6. A leader who places emphasis on the social aspects of the group is called a(n) _____-oriented leader.

7. A leader who equally balances concern for productivity with concern for people is called a(n) _____ leader.

8. A leader who places little or no emphasis on either task accomplishment or team building is called a(n) _____-leader.

9. Describe the characteristics of the autocratic leader.

10. Describe the characteristics of the democratic leader.

11. Describe the characteristics of the laissez-faire leader.

12. Identify the three components of the concept of group maturity.

13. In terms of group maturity, when is it best to adopt the autocratic style of leadership?

14. In terms of group maturity, when is it best to adopt the laissez-faire style of leadership?

15. In terms of group maturity, when is it best to adopt the democratic style of leadership?

16. Define *power*.

17. What are sanctions?

18. What is legitimate power?

19. What is reward power?

20. What is coercive power?

21. What is expert power?

22. What is charismatic power?

23. Name and describe the five characteristics of an effective leader.

    a.

    b.

    c.

    d.

    e.

APPLYING THE IDEAS IN POLICING

Exercise 2.1

Briefly describe three situations in a police officer's work life in which an *autocratic leadership approach* is likely to be the best strategy.

    1.

    2.

    3.

Exercise 2.2

Briefly describe three situations in a police officer's work life in which a *democratic leadership approach* is likely to be the best strategy.

1.

2.

3.

Exercise 2.3

Briefly describe three situations in a police officer's work life in which a *laissez-faire leadership approach* is likely to be the best strategy.

1.

2.

3.

Exercise 2.4

Briefly describe three situations in a police officer's personal life in which an *autocratic leadership approach* is likely to be the best strategy.

1.

2.

3.

Exercise 2.5

Briefly describe three situations in a police officer's personal life in which a *democratic leadership approach* is likely to be the best strategy.

1.

2.

3.

Exercise 2.6

Briefly describe three situations in a police officer's personal life in which a *laissez-faire leadership approach* is likely to be the best strategy.

1.

2.

3.

PRACTISING YOUR GROUP SKILLS

Purpose of This Section

The purpose of "Practising Your Group Skills" and the ultimate purpose of this book is to help you become a more effective participant in the groups to which you belong. This section is designed to provide opportunities for you and your fellow students to practise your group skills in a structured environment.

Team Responsibilities

A description of the team responsibilities for each of five different teams — the Executive Team, the Teaching Team, the Lesson Review Team, the Energizer Team, and the Evaluation Team — can be found in appendix A, pages 207–210. Your professor may have chosen to use from one to five of these teams to conduct the teaching and learning activities of your class. Units 2 and 3 of the Teacher's Guide provide your professor with additional information on the responsibilities of these teams.

Individual Role Responsibilities

A description of four individual role responsibilities — those of Leader, Recorder, Reporter, and Participant-Analyst — can be found in appendix A, pages 210–212. Your professor may have chosen to use from one to four of these roles within teams to give individuals experience leading, recording, reporting, and analyzing. Units 2 and 3 of the Teacher's Guide provide your professor with additional information on these individual role responsibilities.

Specific Team Assignments

Specific team assignments for this chapter appear immediately below. Specific team assignments for each of the subsequent chapters can be found in "Practising Your Group Skills" in each chapter.

CHAPTER 2 TEAM ASSIGNMENTS

The Executive Team

- *Executive Goal:* to provide leadership to your classmates for your class session on chapter 2.

- *Executive Objectives:* to facilitate the class session by (1) ensuring a good classroom setup, (2) welcoming the class, (3) introducing the lesson topic, (4) coordinating activities, and (5) bringing the session to a close.

- *Instructions:* Ensure that the classroom is set up to accommodate the class activities. Post an agenda for the session. Welcome people to class and announce the topic, "Leader Roles: Leading Effectively in Your Group," in a creative and interesting way. Remember that the topic includes autocratic, democratic, and laissez-faire styles of leadership. Introduce and thank all speakers when appropriate. Coordinate the day's activities and bring closure at the end of the class. If necessary, return the classroom to its original configuration.

The Teaching Team

- *Teaching Goal:* to understand and demonstrate leadership skills in a small group setting.

- *Teaching Objectives:* to describe, explain, and demonstrate (1) three leadership styles and the situations in which they are effective and (2) five characteristics of an effective leader.

- *Instructions:* As the Teaching Team, you have the freedom to choose how you will teach your lesson. You can be as creative as you wish, but you must achieve the teaching objectives. Your lesson consists of two parts. The first part is the experiential exercise, and the second part is your explanation of the chapter information.

  ❑ Your experiential exercise is called "Leadership Styles" and you'll find it described fully in appendix B, pages 218–219. Make sure that you refer to "Leadership Styles" when you teach and explain the autocratic, democratic, and laissez-faire leadership styles, and the five characteristics of an effective leader.

  ❑ If time allows, you can also use exercises from the "Mastering the Material" and "Applying the Ideas in Policing" sections of chapter 1 in your lesson.

The Lesson Review Team

- *Review Goal:* to review chapter 1, "Member Roles: Participating Effectively in Your Group."

- *Review Objectives:* to provide a review of (1) the experiential exercise, (2) the six task actions, (3) the six social actions, and (4) the six harmful actions.

- *Instructions:* As the Lesson Review Team, you have the freedom to choose how you will do the review. You can be as creative as you wish, but you must achieve the review objectives. Remember that your time is very limited, so don't try to re-teach last chapter's lesson.

The Energizer Team

- *Energizer Goal:* to motivate your classmates by conducting an energizer activity.

- *Energizer Objectives:* to facilitate the energizing of your classmates by (1) planning an energizer activity and (2) implementing the plan at an appropriate time in the class session.

- *Instructions:* Your team doesn't have a specific, assigned activity to conduct. Rather, the team should remember its energizing purpose and conduct an activity that will provide a break in the class learning routine. Popular games like Simon Says, Heads Up Seven Up, and Murder Wink usually work well. So do various mixers and ice breakers. (Your professor's Teacher's Guide identifies a number of sources of energizer exercises.) Whatever you decide on, you must be prepared to give clear instructions and conduct the exercise effectively. When you lead the energizer, you are leading and directing the entire class. Plan well and execute professionally, even if the exercise is a "kid's game." Encourage everyone to get involved.

The Evaluation Team

As a member of the Evaluation Team, you need to review the information in chapter 10, pages 191–194, before you do anything else. There you will find helpful information on how to conduct your evaluation session. The most important thing to remember is that you are not to judge other people. Your role is to help the class make its own assessment of which practices worked well today and which didn't.

Note that the evaluation goal below is keyed to the content of this chapter. *If desirable or necessary, you can evaluate any other aspect of group experience.* Be sure, though, that you set the goal, develop appropriate objectives, and plan the evaluation session to achieve the goal and the objectives.

- *Evaluation Goal:* to assess leadership skills within the group (or class) in today's class session.

- *Evaluation Objectives:* to (1) assess group (or class) member use of autocratic, democratic, and laissez-faire leadership practices and (2) identify practices in need of improvement.

• *Instructions:* Create an evaluation instrument based on the selected focus behaviours identified in the objectives. See chapter 10, pages 192–193, for information on creating evaluation instruments. Figure 10.1 provides an example. Solicit feedback from the class using the evaluation instrument. Use the feedback to discuss the class session with the purpose of identifying improvements that can be made to individual, group, and class performance in future class sessions. Conclude by noting the specific actions that need to be repeated or avoided to make improvements.

REFERENCES AND RECOMMENDED READINGS

Fiedler, F.E. (1964). A contingency model of leader effectiveness. In L. Berkowitz (Ed.), *Advances in experimental social psychology* (Vol. 1, pp. 149–150). New York: Academic Press.

French, J., & Raven, B. (1981). The basis of social power. In D. Cartwright & A. Zander (Eds.), *Group dynamics: Research and theory.* New York: McGraw-Hill.

Hersey, P., & Blanchard, K. (1977). *Management of organizational behavior: Utilizing human resources* (3rd ed.). Englewood Cliffs, NJ: Prentice Hall.

Kenny, D., & Zaccuro, J. (1984). An estimate of variance due to traits in leadership. *Journal of Applied Psychology, 68,* 678–685.

Kottler, J.A. (1994). *Advanced group leadership.* Pacific Grove, CA: Brooks/Cole.

Lewin, K., Lippitt, R., & White, R. (1939). Patterns of aggressive behavior in experimentally created "Social Climates." *Journal of Social Psychology, 10,* 271–299.

Portnoy, R.A. (1986). *Leadership!* Englewood Cliffs, NJ: Prentice Hall.

Shaw, M. (1981). *Group dynamics* (3rd ed.) (pp. 324–325). New York: McGraw-Hill.

Stogdill, R. (1981). *Handbook of leadership: A survey of theory and research* (pp. 63–82). New York: McGraw-Hill.

White, R., & Lippitt, R. (1960). Leader behavior and member reaction in three social climates. In D. Cartwright & A. Zander (Eds.), *Group dynamics: Research and theory* (2nd ed.) (pp. 527–553). Evanston, IL: Row, Peterson.

Norms: Establishing Effective Rules in Your Group

Chapter Objectives

After completing this chapter, you should be able to:

- Describe the difference between a culture and a society.
- Identify and describe several elements of culture.
- Describe the difference between imposed norms and developed norms.
- Identify and describe five basic moral principles.
- Describe three key factors in the development of effective group norms.
- Identify and explain nine areas of group life that require norms.

INTRODUCTION

Police officers are agents selected by society to ensure its rules are followed by its members. No society can tolerate the breaking of its rules; this would lead it into chaos. Therefore, every society chooses from its members those who are sworn to uphold the law and maintain social order.

Only brief reference to the rules of society will be made in this chapter. Our primary focus will be on the examination of the rules that contribute to the success of small groups. Large groups and small groups alike need rules to guide and control the actions of group members. As we learned in chapter 1, the written or unwritten rules of a group are called *norms*.

All groups of people who want to get along in a civilized fashion develop norms for their members. We need rules of conduct in order to work together for common purposes. The most important *societal norms* are expressed in the form of laws. Societies value the order and stability that laws protect, and they cannot abide the disorder and instability that lawbreaking creates.

Just as societies have rules, so do the various organizations within a society. The most important *organizational norms* take the form of policies and procedures. For example, employees who flagrantly defy the rules of their organization are likely to find themselves unemployed. The police service could not carry out its responsibilities within a community if its officers did not follow its own very specific rules and regulations.

Norms are also an important part of family life. *Family norms*, the "rules of the house," may differ from family to family, but all families have their rules. Families, like societies and organizations, require a degree of order if people are to live together in harmony under the same roof.

When people break the rules of a society, an organization, or a family, they can expect to be punished. The rewards for keeping the rules of a group, and the punishments for breaking them, are called *sanctions*. Notice that sanctions can be positive (rewards) or negative (penalties). More often than not, however, when we refer to sanctions we mean punishments. We highlighted norms and sanctions, you will recall, in our examination of coercive power in the last chapter. Norms and sanctions are essential elements in the culture of all societies.

In Canada, for example, legislators make the laws (norms), the police enforce them, the courts establish guilt and assign penalties (sanctions), and the corrections system administers them. At a societal level, in Canada and elsewhere, we refer to the system that maintains the most important norms and sanctions of society as the criminal justice system.

To function harmoniously, societies need rules, as do small groups. In this chapter, we will focus on norms within small groups. We'll examine the social context in which small-group norms exist, and we'll look at the kinds of rules that are essential for effective group performance. Let's start with the broader social context and review the ways that norms are established and the role they play in society.

SOCIETY AND CULTURE

society
a large, identifiable community of individuals who fulfill a variety of differing and interdependent roles

A **society** is a large, identifiable community of individuals who fulfill a variety of differing and interdependent roles. Canada, for example, is a large community that can be identified by geographical boundaries, unique historical events, and a distinctive culture. Our country is made up of millions of citizens, each of whom has role responsibilities within our society.

When we study the distinctive ways that a particular society meets the needs of its members, we are examining that society's culture. In chapter 1, you will remember, we looked briefly at the concept of culture as we discussed the various roles that people play in societies and in small groups. There we emphasized that the concept of **culture**, which we defined as the way of life of people in a given society or group, can be applied to both large and small groups. Societies have cultures, and so do organizations and work groups. Our primary interest in this book and this chapter is the culture of small groups.

culture
the way of life of people in a given society or group

subculture
a smaller culture within a larger culture

Many cultures have subcultures within them. A **subculture**, of course, is a smaller culture within a larger culture. Canadian culture is often described as a mosaic of subcultures. If English-speaking and French-speaking communities are viewed as dominant cultures in the Canadian mosaic, then subgroups like the Chinese, the

Italians, and the Germans — where members live together in sufficient numbers — are considered to be subcultures.

Like societies, the cultures of large organizations often have subcultures. Policing provides a good example. Within the mainstream culture of large police services, we often find a subculture that operates with values, principles, and rules that are different from those of the mainstream. Some of these police subcultures have become a serious problem within various societies. In the worst cases, the subculture has adopted values and principles that run contrary to those of the main culture. The so-called blue wall of silence, in which officers remain silent about crimes when they should be speaking out, is a good example of a troublesome aspect of an institutional subculture.

In the course of your policing studies, you will have the opportunity to study Canada's culture and some of its important subcultures, including subcultures within policing. It is important for you to have a good understanding of the concepts of culture and subculture. Let's look at the key components of such cultures and subcultures.

COMPONENTS OF GROUP CULTURES AND SUBCULTURES

Cultures are complex. When you think of the way of life of any group of people — a society, an organization, or a family, for example — you recognize how complex cultures are. Social scientists who study the complexities of culture have identified several things that are common to all cultures. These elements or components of culture include language, knowledge, technology, and the arts.

Language, of course, refers to the symbol systems used to communicate within a group. In Canada, for example, we have two official languages, French and English. These languages are systems of words and symbols that Canadians use to communicate with one another. There are, of course, many other languages that are spoken within Canadian subcultures. Language is one important component of culture.

A second important component of culture is knowledge. *Knowledge* refers to the body of information commonly known within a group. As a developed society, Canadians have a great deal of knowledge of a great many things. We share in the scientific discoveries of a modern world and this scientific knowledge is critically important for our health and welfare. Note, however, that a primitive jungle tribe also has knowledge as a part of its culture. While the tribe might not understand our scientific knowledge, it has much knowledge that we do not possess. The tribe has, for example, knowledge of poisonous substances and dangerous insects of which the average Canadian is ignorant. Every society has its distinctive knowledge of certain subjects.

A third component of culture is technology. *Technology* refers to a group's tools and the proper use of those tools. In Canada, for example, we use hammers, cars, robots, and thousands of other tools in our daily lives. The jungle tribe, too, has its technology. It uses bamboo spears, fish hooks made of bone, and many other tools unfamiliar to us. Every society uses its special tools to do the work necessary for its survival. Every society has its technology.

The *arts* are a fourth component of culture common to all groups. The arts refer to a group's creative ways of expressing its thoughts and feelings, and creative ways in which members enjoy themselves. Paintings, music, and dance are examples. While there is no single form of dance that all Canadians enjoy, many different forms of dance are prevalent within our society. In the jungle, too, tribal members paint themselves, make music, and dance. They, like us, have arts as part of their culture. While each of these four components — language, knowledge, technology, and the arts — is an extremely important aspect of culture, we will concentrate on three additional components that are more important for our present purposes. The following components of culture have particular relevance to the rules that govern groups of people. Let's now take a look at values, principles, and norms.

1. Values

If you value something, it is important to you. For example, your health, your family, and your education are probably very important aspects of your life. We say that you value them, or that they are among the many things that you value. **Values**, then, refer to whatever is of importance or worth to an individual or a group. If others value the same things that you do, we then speak of shared values or common values. For example, since virtually everyone values personal safety and security, it is not surprising that safety and security are values that we hold in common with many others. They are shared values.

As we are engaged in a study of small group dynamics, our discussion will focus primarily on shared values and the rules associated with those values. Now groups, like individuals, tend to value many different things. The totality of a group's values is called the group's *value system*. Group values and value systems refer to those things that are important to the members of a group.

As we have already noted, our values are reflections of our feelings. They are a very important part of our affective or emotional makeup. To use the language of poetry, values are "things of the heart." Because we feel so strongly about safety and security, we develop rules that are designed to keep us safe and secure. Laws of the road and laws governing sewage disposal are only two examples of rules that have been generated by our values. When we discuss, debate, and communicate our values with others, we call our most important values *principles*.

2. Principles

In any area of life, we refer to our basic ideas as principles. There are, for example, principles of mathematics, physics, hygiene, policing, and virtually every other area of our lives. When we drive on the roads, to give a more specific example, we are supposed to wear seat belts, stop at stop signs, and keep within the speed limit. These specific rules of the road are based on the principle of safety. Because we value our well being, we adhere to the principle of safety when we develop our traffic laws.

Principles, then, are basic ideas that are used as standards to evaluate or judge a course of action. If a proposed traffic law, for example, violates the principle of safety, it should not be passed. The principle of safety is a basic idea or standard that we use to evaluate the proposed law. Principles of any kind are a part of our cognitive or thinking side. If, as we said above, values are "things of the heart," then principles are "things of the head." Values and principles are much like two sides

values
whatever is of importance or worth to an individual or a group

principles
the standards by which a group evaluates a course of action

of the same coin, the emotional side and the intellectual side. Together, they generate the rules of conduct within all groups, large or small.

A group that values fairness and individual responsibility, for example, will use the principles of equality and individual accountability to establish rules that require individual members to carry their own weight and to do their fair share of the group's work. Guided by these principles, the group will prohibit free riding and establish penalties for those who try to take a free ride. In this example, the group feels that fairness and responsibility are important (values), and it uses the basic ideas of equality and accountability (principles) to create rules (norms) that forbid free riding.

3. Norms

All group norms are generated by the values and principles held by the group's members or by the values and principles of a higher authority. **Norms**, you will recall from chapter 1, are the written or unwritten rules of a group. If a group values human life, for example, it establishes laws against killing. If it values private property, it establishes laws against theft. Values, principles, and norms are intimately connected within all cultures, subcultures, and small groups.

> **norm**
> a written or unwritten rule of a group

Before distinguishing among different types of norms, we should note that police officers bear a heavy responsibility in their communities. They are required to have a good understanding of the fundamental values, principles, and norms of Canadian society, and also of the province and the municipality in which they serve. In addition, they need to understand some of the basic values, principles, and norms of a variety of subcultures within the broader society. Finally, in order to function effectively within a great variety of small groups, officers need to understand the values, principles, and norms operating within those groups. To help prospective officers, especially with small-group culture, let's explore a variety of different norms.

TYPES OF NORMS

There are three basic types of norms with which you should be familiar: folkways, mores, and roles.

1. Folkways

Among the most important values of any group are its standards of conduct — that is, its expectations regarding the behaviour of group members. Social scientists distinguish between two different types of norms in group life. A group's least important norms are called **folkways**.[1] These are trivial rules, often unwritten, for conduct in certain areas of our lives. Clothing fashions, for instance, might fall into this category. A person who dresses out of fashion may be teased for being out of touch. The emotions aroused by breaking folkways are minimal, however, and so are the sanctions. Laughter and teasing are punishments of sorts, but they are not severe punishments.

> **folkways**
> the least important norms of a group

---

1   The terms *folkways* and *mores* are somewhat unusual words. They have a long history in the field of social research, where they were first introduced by Sumner (1940).

2. Mores

mores
the most important norms of a group

A group's most important norms are called **mores** (pronounced "more-rays"). Because the mores of a given society are so important, they are almost always written down in the society's legal code. The *Criminal Code* provides a good example. Our most important values — life, safety, security, and property, for example — are protected by the laws of that code. In religious communities, too, certain rules are part of the religious mores of the community, directing members to do this or to avoid that, possibly with heaven or hell as the potential sanctions. Mores also appear as rules in institutional policy manuals that spell out acceptable conduct for members of the organization. When mores are violated, people become very upset. In addition, the punishments for breach of these most important rules of a group are usually very severe. In Canada, for example, the penalty for murder in the first degree is life in prison.

3. Roles

In addition to the many folkways and mores that we have in our culture, the roles that we discussed in chapter 1 constitute another type of norm. *Roles*, you will recall, are sets of expectations regarding specific responsibilities within a group. For example, we expect police constables to conduct themselves in certain ways and not in others; so, too, for sergeants, staff sergeants, inspectors, and chiefs, whose specific role responsibilities are detailed in the law, in departmental regulations, and in codes of professional ethics. In our society, we also expect fathers and mothers to behave in certain ways and to abide by the rules of good parenting. We believe that they should protect, care for, and ensure that their children are educated. Because good parenting is so important to our society, we put many of the rules of good parenting into law.

When we examined the role of an effective group member in chapter 1, we identified six task actions that are part of that role. We also noted six social actions that are expected of a good team player. These expectations function as a set of rules for being an effective group member. In addition, in chapter 2, we noted many of the qualities that are expected of a group leader. These expectations form a set of norms for the role of leader. For example, a group expects its leader to be autocratic only if appropriate. Otherwise, members expect their leader to be democratic or laissez-faire, depending on circumstances.

ORIGINS OF NORMS

Norms originate in one of two ways. Either they are imposed upon a group by a higher authority or the group itself generates its own norms. An understanding of the importance of both imposed and developed norms is critical for an understanding of group dynamics. We'll discuss both imposed norms and developed norms, but we'll devote more time to developed norms, the rules that groups create for themselves.

1. Imposed Norms

imposed norm
a rule established by an authority outside the group

As members of particular groups in society, we have many norms imposed on us by various authorities. An **imposed norm** is a rule established by an authority outside the group. The *Criminal Code,* for instance, applies to all residents of

Canada, including students working in groups in a college course. Assault is an offence under that code, whether it occurs on the streets or in a classroom. In addition, norms established by the college are also binding on the student; for example, smoking may not be permitted in college buildings. Further, certain rules of conduct and the academic standards for a particular course are established by the professor. In each of these cases, norms are imposed upon the individual and the group by some authority beyond the group. We all live our lives in a social context that includes many imposed norms.

2. Developed Norms

In addition to the many norms imposed upon a group, most groups will develop further rules for their members. A **developed norm** is a rule created by the members of a group to govern behaviour within their group. As noted in the sections above on values, principles, and norms, members of a group may develop rules to prevent or minimize free riding within the group. If outside authorities, like professors in a college setting, don't impose rules forbidding free riding on a college work group, then the students are likely to develop the rules themselves. As we'll see, members of small groups need to develop their own rules or sets of expectations in order to function at an optimal level. The norms that work groups develop are usually norms associated with basic moral values and principles such as goodness, equality, justice, truth, and freedom. These values and principles are, in fact, the same ones that underlie the mores of society. They are the fundamental principles of civilized life.

developed norm
a rule established by a group to govern behaviour within the group

ETHICS, SMALL GROUPS, AND THE LAW

Any group that wants its members to cooperate willingly in a civil way must establish rules of conduct based on fundamental ethical principles. Adherence to these principles is essential for harmony and cooperation within any group. These same principles are the ethical standards for societal laws. The principles described below are the minimum required to allow people to work cooperatively within a civilized community. They are extremely important for reasoning in ethics and for establishing societal laws. What are these principles?

The first basic moral principle is **goodness**, the principle that requires you to do good to others in the group and to refrain from harming them. The basic rule that is derived from this principle says: "Do good and don't harm." The second principle, **equality**, requires you to treat others in your group as equals. This principle, expressed as a norm, says: "Treat others as equals and don't discriminate for or against them." Equality, of course, is the basic principle that promotes mutual respect among group members. **Justice**, also called the *fairness* principle, is the third of the basic moral principles. Sometimes being just or fair means giving people what they have earned (merit), while at other times it means giving everyone involved an equal share of something (equity). At still other times, it means meeting the special needs of a group member (need). The principle of justice stated as a rule says: "Be fair to others, not unfair." The principle of **truth** requires you to have personal integrity by being truthful and trustworthy. Expressed as a rule, this principle says: "Tell the truth, be honest, and have integrity." Finally, the principle

goodness
the moral principle of doing good to others and not doing harm

equality
the moral principle of treating each member of a group equally

justice
the moral principle of fair dealing among group members

truth
the moral principle of mutual integrity and trustworthiness

freedom
the moral principle of
mutual respect for group
members' choices

of **freedom** requires you to respect the choices that others make, especially when you disagree with their choices. It is also the principle that protects your right to make your own choices. As a rule, this principle says: "Respect the choices of others; don't force others."

Large groups, like societies, also base their laws on these ethical principles. Those who serve society as police officers need to be especially familiar with these principles and their application in law. The law, of course, is the official set of rules that a particular society is prepared to enforce at a particular time. Laws change from time to time because values shift, and the basic principles need to be applied in new circumstances.

With these basic moral principles in mind, let's take a closer look at the ways in which an individual can contribute to the development of effective norms within a group.

DEVELOPING NORMS WITHIN YOUR GROUP

You will have many opportunities in both your personal and professional life to contribute to the development of group norms. There are three important points to remember when developing the rules of your group. The three "Cs" for developing effective rules within your group are consistency, critical discussion, and consensus. Let's look at each one in turn.

1. Consistency

consistency
being in agreement with

To be **consistent** means to be in agreement with. The developed norms of your group, for example, must be *consistent* with imposed norms. That is to say, the rules of your small group must agree with the laws of society and the rules of any other organizations within which your group exists. If a college forbids smoking on campus, for instance, a student work group within that college mustn't allow smoking. It mustn't establish rules or practices that disagree with those of the institution. Of course, criminals and other deviants don't accept this premise. They knowingly break the laws of society for their personal gain. However, since most of us are not criminals, we will want to ensure that the rules that we develop within our groups will benefit our groups, while remaining consistent with imposed societal and institutional norms. As your group develops its rules, make sure that your rules are consistent with those of your broader social context.

2. Critical Discussion

critical discussion
the healthy exchange
of differing views on
an issue

When developing group norms, everyone in your group should participate in the discussion and the discussion should be conducted in an open, critical, and constructive manner. **Critical discussion** is a healthy exchange of differing views on a given issue. If all members of your group participate in the discussion, then all points of view can be considered. In chapter 8, we will study the process of *critical discussion* in detail. For the moment, we can describe it as a win–win approach in which participants criticize ideas but support persons. It's the opposite of win–lose approaches in which one person tries to beat or defeat another, as is the case in a formal debate. Rather, critical discussion involves the presentation of different and sometimes opposing ideas so that group members can identify the best ideas on which to base their decisions.

Critical discussion is the opposite of *groupthink*, an ineffective and uncritical approach to discussion and decision making that we will examine in chapter 8. In groupthink, members do not challenge one another's ideas, and poor decisions often result. When a group uses critical discussion, everyone has a better chance of ending up a winner because the group is much more likely to make informed decisions. When your group develops its norms, you should insist upon a critical discussion of the proposed rules.

3. Consensus

Group norms should be established by *consensus* whenever possible. **Consensus** means unanimous agreement. In other words, everyone in the group agrees on the decision. Note that consensus is not the same as majority vote. When a decision is made by majority vote, it usually takes only 51 percent to decide an issue. If 51 percent of a group, for example, are in favour of establishing a particular rule, that leaves 49 percent opposed. In circumstances like this, it can be very difficult to get the losers to abide by the decision. When establishing the rules of conduct for members, groups will want everyone to be in agreement if at all possible. Consensus achieves that. Majority vote does so only rarely. We will look at both consensus and majority vote in detail when we study decision making in chapter 9. As your group members share their expectations of one another, strive to get consensus on the norms that you will want everyone to live by.

consensus
unanimous agreement within a group

GAINING SUPPORT FOR YOUR GROUP'S NORMS

If you use the three Cs — consistency, critical discussion, and consensus — when developing norms within your group, you will gain support for the rules for three reasons. First, your group's norms will not contradict those of a higher authority and your members will, consequently, be free of challenges from outside your group. Second, the use of critical discussion will ensure that all points of view are considered. All group members can have their say. Third, getting consensus means getting unanimous agreement about the rules. With consensus, everyone on your team will be a winner and there will be no losers. By observing the three Cs, you will maximize **commitment** to the rules that you develop. Compliance with the norms should follow easily.

commitment
a willingness to stick with things over the long term

ENSURING YOUR GROUP'S SUCCESS

If you want your group to succeed, to become an effective team, then you have to develop norms in several key areas of your group's life. To achieve both your task goals and your social goals, ensure that your group has clearly stated expectations for its members in each of these key areas. Remember, as we proceed in this section, that expectations are just another type of rule or norm. In each of the areas below, your group should develop rules that require members to deal with matters in the most effective way possible. Your teammates should expect certain things of one another in each of the following areas.

1. Accountability

Your team should expect that all its members will be accountable for their actions within the group and on behalf of the group. Individual team members must fulfill their respective roles responsibly. Individual *accountability* is very important in this regard. If your group establishes norms that require individuals to be accountable for their respective role responsibilities, then dysfunctional behaviours will be minimized. The norms of your group should also foster cooperation among its members. Members must understand that they swim or sink together. That is, the success of your team depends on individual accountability and mutual cooperation.

2. Cooperation

Your team should establish rules that require your members to cooperate in order to achieve their goals. Establish *cooperative* goal structures whenever possible. When setting task goals and social goals, a group can pit one member against another by establishing *competitive* goal structures. It is also possible to establish *individualistic* goal structures, whereby the work of the group is accomplished by individuals who work independently on different aspects of the group's task. In contrast, the goals of the group can be *cooperatively* structured so that members have to work together to achieve the group's goals. Cooperative goal structures promote group cohesion and are superior to competitive goal structures in most instances. Chapter 4 examines goals and goal setting in greater detail.

3. Communication

Establish norms for your group that require two-way communication among members. Two-way *communication* involves sending messages, receiving messages, and giving feedback. It consists of active speaking and listening that engages members in ongoing dialogue that fosters healthy working relationships. In contrast, one-way communication is a monologue that is frequently detrimental to group life. We will examine several rules for effective communication in chapter 5. For the moment, let's just say that successful groups expect their members to communicate effectively when critically discussing issues, making decisions, solving problems, and managing interpersonal conflict.

4. Confrontation

Your group should develop rules that require conflicts to be resolved through constructive *confrontation*. Team members must use the best conflict resolution strategies available. Conflict between individuals in a group occurs frequently and strikes at the cohesiveness of the team. It should not be avoided. Rather, it should be confronted and dealt with skillfully. Successful teams require their members to practise assertive confrontation when dealing with interpersonal conflict. You and your teammates need to ensure that disputes, when they arise, are dealt with openly and effectively. We'll explore the conflict resolution process in chapter 6.

5. Support

Members of successful teams expect *support* from their teammates, and they get it. You and your teammates need to create a supportive climate in which all members are free to give their very best. While the achievement of task goals is critical, equally important is the achievement of social goals, especially group cohesion. The norms of your group should promote teambuilding, the development of a supportive climate in which group members can excel in their roles and meet their responsibilities. When group members respect and support one another, team productivity and cohesion will result. Cohesion is the subject of chapter 7, and in that chapter we'll provide details on how your group can build itself into a team.

6. Evaluation

Make sure that your team creates norms that require frequent *evaluation* of its performance. The members of your group should regularly assess your group's achievements. For a group to improve, it must measure its performance in an objective way. The task goals and social goals that the group has established are critical for performance evaluation. By determining whether its goals are being met, a group can rate its performance. Good performance will motivate the team to do more of the same. Poor performance will motivate it to change in ways that will achieve its objectives. Effective groups evaluate their performance on an ongoing basis. In chapter 10 we'll examine the details of this important group activity.

7. Discussion

As we saw earlier in this chapter, when developing its rules your team should include norms that require ongoing critical and constructive *discussion* of issues. Your group should routinely engage in critical discussion whenever there are decisions to be made and problems to be solved. Critical discussion involves exploring ideas with the hope of coming to the best decisions. When you challenge the ideas of another person in your group, avoid attacking the person. Critical discussion involves criticizing ideas, not people. You and your fellow members can learn to criticize ideas while remaining supportive of the person who presented them. Critical discussion is examined in chapter 8.

8. Decisions

Because your group will make *decisions* on a regular basis, you should have norms that require members to know and use the best decision-making strategies possible. Effective decision-making strategies are crucial when deciding issues. Consensus, we noted earlier in this chapter, is the ideal way for groups to decide an issue. It requires full participation of members and results in maximum support for the decision arrived at. However, because consensus is not always possible, it is important for teams to use other decision-making strategies as appropriate. Majority vote can be a legitimate method under certain circumstances, and there are several other ways of making group decisions that are also appropriate in different situations. Effective groups will require their members to understand and use the best decision-making method for each circumstance. In chapter 9, we'll study several methods by which groups can arrive at decisions.

9. Solutions

The rules of your group should include the requirement to seek *solutions* to problems in a systematic way. Modern science has proved extremely successful in understanding human problems and finding solutions to them. The field of health care provides us with many excellent examples, from immunizations to heart transplants. So, too, other areas of science have enjoyed great successes. These successes can be attributed to the basic scientific method. The problem-solving process, described in chapter 9, is based on that powerful method. Your group should employ the problem-solving process whenever it works at solving problems.

CHAPTER SUMMARY

At the beginning of this chapter we distinguished between societies and cultures and proceeded to describe several components of culture. In particular, we examined the close connection between values, principles, and norms. We went on to note the differences between mores, the most important norms of a group, and folkways, the least important rules. We then pointed out that rules can be imposed upon a group or developed by the group itself. Whether imposed or developed, norms are based on fundamental ethical values and principles; namely, goodness, equality, justice, truth, and freedom. Next, we presented the three Cs for developing group norms — consistency, critical discussion, and consensus — and showed how they lead to maximum support of a team's norms. Finally, we underscored the importance of developing norms or expectation statements for each of several key areas of group life. Specifically, we said that groups should have rules to ensure individual accountability, member cooperation, two-way communication, team-building, performance assessment, critical discussion, effective decisions, and regular use of the problem-solving method.

KEY TERMS

consensus   imposed norm

commitment   justice

consistency   mores

critical discussion   norm

culture   principles

developed norm   society

equality   subculture

folkways   truth

freedom   values

goodness

MASTERING THE MATERIAL

Now that you have read this chapter, use the following guides to ensure that you have mastered the material.

    1. Define *norm*.

    2. The most important rules of a society are called _____.

    3. The most important rules of an organization are part of the organization's _____.

    4. Define *sanctions*.

    5. Define *society*.

    6. Define *culture*.

7. Identify the seven components of culture.

8. What are values?

9. What are principles?

10. Give three examples of societal norms.

11. What are folkways?

12. What are mores?

13. What are roles?

14. Distinguish between imposed norms and developed norms.

15. Identify and describe the five basic ethical principles.

    a.

    b.

    c.

    d.

    e.

16. When developing group norms, what are the three Cs? Explain each of them.

    a.

    b.

    c.

17. Identify and explain the nine key areas of group life that require norms.

    Area #1:

    Area #2:

    Area #3:

    Area #4:

Area #5:

Area #6:

Area #7:

Area #8:

Area #9:

APPLYING THE IDEAS IN POLICING

Exercise 3.1

In this chapter, seven components of group culture were identified: language, knowledge, technology, the arts, values, principles, and norms. Consider the police service to be a subculture, and give one or two examples from that subculture of each of these components. If possible, provide examples that are unique to the police subculture. Examples of *language* from the police subculture might be "cruiser," "MO," "nightstick," or "jumper."

Language:

Knowledge:

Technology:

The arts:

Values:

Principles:

Norms:

Exercise 3.2

In this chapter, a *role* was defined as a set of expectations regarding specific responsibilities within a group. Police officers have a role to play within local communities, and members of local communities have expectations of their police officers. List six important expectations that you feel citizens commonly have with respect to police officers.

    1.

  2.

  3.

  4.

  5.

  6.

Exercise 3.3

Imagine that you have recently been hired as a constable with a regional police service. List six things that you would expect of the sergeant who supervises you.

  1.

  2.

3.

4.

5.

6.

Exercise 3.4

Imagine that you have recently been hired as a constable with a regional police service. List six things that you would expect of the constables with whom you work.

1.

2.

3.

4.

5.

6.

PRACTISING YOUR GROUP SKILLS

Purpose of This Section

The purpose of "Practising Your Group Skills" and the ultimate purpose of this book is to help you become a more effective participant in the groups to which you belong. This section is designed to provide opportunities for you and your fellow students to practise your group skills in a structured environment.

Team Responsibilities

A description of the team responsibilities for each of five different teams — the Executive Team, the Teaching Team, the Lesson Review Team, the Energizer Team, and the Evaluation Team — can be found in appendix A, pages 207–210. Your professor may have chosen to use from one to five of these teams to conduct the teaching and learning activities of the class. Units 2 and 3 of the Teacher's Guide provide your professor with additional information on the responsibilities of these teams.

Individual Role Responsibilities

A description of four individual role responsibilities — those of Leader, Recorder, Reporter, and Participant-Analyst — can be found in appendix A, pages 210–212. Your professor may have chosen to use from one to four of these roles within teams to give individuals experience leading, recording, reporting, and analyzing. Units 2 and 3 of the Teacher's Guide provide your professor with additional information on these individual role responsibilities.

Specific Team Assignments

Specific team assignments for this chapter appear immediately below. Specific team assignments for each of the subsequent chapters can be found in "Practising Your Group Skills" in each chapter.

CHAPTER 3 TEAM ASSIGNMENTS

The Executive Team

- *Executive Goal:* to provide leadership to your classmates for your class session on chapter 3.

- *Executive Objectives:* to facilitate the class session by (1) ensuring a good classroom setup, (2) welcoming the class, (3) introducing the lesson topic, (4) coordinating activities, and (5) bringing the session to a close.

- *Instructions:* Ensure that the classroom is set up to accommodate the class activities. Post an agenda for the session. Welcome people to class and announce the topic, "Norms: Establishing Effective Rules in Your Group," in a creative and interesting way. Remind the class that norms are rules and that groups need norms to function effectively. Introduce and thank all speakers when appropriate. Coordinate the day's activities and bring closure at the end of the class. If necessary, return the classroom to its original configuration.

The Teaching Team

- *Teaching Goal:* to understand and demonstrate the role of group norms in a small group setting.

- *Teaching Objectives:* to describe, explain, and demonstrate (1) the relationship among values, principles, and norms, and (2) the three "Cs" for developing effective group norms.

- *Instructions:* As the Teaching Team, you have the freedom to choose how you will teach your lesson. You can be as creative as you wish, but you must achieve the teaching objectives. Your lesson consists of two parts. The first part is the experiential exercise, and the second part is your explanation of the chapter information.

  - ❑ Your experiential exercise is called "Mutual Expectations" and you'll find it described fully in appendix B, pages 219–220. Make sure that you refer to "Mutual Expectations" when you teach and explain values, principles, norms, and the three "Cs" for developing effective norms.

  - ❑ If time allows, you can also use exercises from "Mastering the Material" and "Applying the Ideas in Policing" in your lesson.

The Lesson Review Team

- *Review Goal:* to review chapter 2, "Leader Roles: Leading Effectively in Your Group."

- *Review Objectives:* to provide a review of (1) the experiential exercise, (2) the three leadership styles, and (3) the five characteristics of an effective leader.

- *Instructions:* As the Lesson Review Team, you have the freedom to choose how you will do the review. You can be as creative as you wish, but you must achieve the review objectives. Remember that your time is very limited, so don't try to re-teach last chapter's lesson.

The Energizer Team

- *Energizer Goal:* to motivate your classmates by conducting an energizer activity.

- *Energizer Objectives:* to facilitate the energizing of your classmates by (1) planning an energizer activity and (2) implementing the plan at an appropriate time in the class session.

- *Instructions:* Your team doesn't have a specific, assigned activity to conduct. Rather, the team should remember its energizing purpose and conduct an activity that will provide a break in the class learning routine. Popular games like Simon Says, Heads Up Seven Up, and Murder Wink usually work well. So do various mixers and ice breakers. (Your professor's Teacher's Guide identifies a number of sources of energizer exercises.) Whatever you decide on, you must be prepared to give clear instructions and conduct the exercise effectively. When you lead the energizer, you are leading and directing the entire class. Plan well and execute professionally, even if the exercise is a "kid's game." Encourage everyone to get involved.

The Evaluation Team

As a member of the Evaluation Team, you need to review the information in chapter 10, pages 191–194, before you do anything else. There you will find helpful information on how to conduct your evaluation session. The most important thing to remember is that you are not to judge other people. Your role is to help the class make its own assessment of which practices worked well today and which didn't.

Note that the evaluation goal below is keyed to the content of this chapter. *If desirable or necessary, you can evaluate any other aspect of group experience.* Be sure, though, that you set the goal, develop appropriate objectives, and plan the evaluation session to achieve the goal and the objectives.

- *Evaluation Goal:* to assess group (or class) conduct in today's class session.

- *Evaluation Objectives:* to (1) assess group (or class) member compliance with school, classroom, and individual team rules and (2) identify practices in need of improvement.

- *Instructions:* Create an evaluation instrument based on the selected focus behaviours identified in the objectives. See chapter 10, pages 192–193, for information on creating evaluation instruments. Figure 10.1 provides an example. Solicit feedback from the class using the evaluation instrument. Use the feedback to discuss the class session with the purpose of identifying improvements that can be made to individual, group, and class performance in future class sessions. Conclude by noting the specific actions that need to be repeated or avoided to make improvements.

REFERENCES AND RECOMMENDED READINGS

Asch, S. (1952). *Social psychology*. New York: Prentice Hall.

Bjorkquist, B.D. (2002). *The principles of ethical reasoning: Ethics and policing in a civil society*. Toronto: Prentice Hall.

Clarke, R.R., & Mouton, J.S. (1981). *Productivity: The human side*. New York: AMACOM.

Deutsch, M. (1949). A theory of cooperation and competition. *Human Relations, 2,* 129–152.

Deutsch, M. (1949). An experimental study of the effects of cooperation and competition upon group process. *Human Relations, 2,* 199–231.

Drews, E.M., & Lipson, L. (1971). *Values and humanity*. New York: St. Martin's Press.

Facione, P.A., Scherer, D., & Attig, T. (1978). *Values and society*. Englewood Cliffs, NJ: Prentice Hall.

Festinger, L. (1954). A theory of social comparison processes. *Human Relations, 7,* 117–140.

Gilligan, C. (1982). *In a different voice: Psychological theory and moral development*. Cambridge, MA: Harvard University Press.

Gilligan, C., Ward, J., Taylor, J., & Barbige, B. (1988). *Mapping the moral domain*. Cambridge, MA: Harvard University Press.

Hurka, T. (1999). *Principles: Short essays on ethics*. Toronto: Harcourt Brace.

Johnson, D.W. (1970). *The social psychology of education*. New York: Holt, Rinehart, & Winston.

Mappes, T.A., & Zembaty, J.S. (1992). *Social ethics*. New York: McGraw-Hill.

Sherif, M. (1936). *The psychology of group norms*. New York: Harper.

Stevenson, C.S. (1963). *Facts and violence*. New Haven, CT: Yale University Press.

Sumner, W.G. (1940). *Folkways*. Boston: Ginn.

Goals: Setting Clear Targets for Your Group

Chapter Objectives

After completing this chapter, you should be able to:

- Define the term *goal*.

- Distinguish between long-term and short-term goals.

- Explain the difference between a goal and an objective.

- Explain how to develop measurable objectives.

- Identify and describe five characteristics of effective objectives.

- Identify and describe five benefits of effective objectives.

INTRODUCTION

It is common for people in our society to talk about goals. One person, for example, says that he has the goal of losing five pounds. Another says that her goal is to save a thousand dollars for a new computer. Yet another has the goal of becoming a police officer. Goal setting seems to be a common practice in today's world. But what, exactly, is a goal?

A **goal** is a desired state of future affairs. In simpler terms, it is a target, something aimed for. In our example above, the dieter desires a future in which he will be five pounds lighter. The prospective computer owner wants a future world that includes a new computer. Both the dieter and the prospective computer owner intend to live their lives in ways that will bring about the desired future state. If they are sincere about their goals, they will do a variety of things, like eating less and saving more, that are designed to achieve their stated goals. The would-be police officer will do the same. She'll take steps now that she hopes will ensure her future in policing. She's aiming to be a police officer. Her target, we say, is policing.

Individuals set goals and so do organizations and small groups. In fact, the best organizations and teams are the ones that set clear goals and work toward the achievement of those goals in a systematic, calculated manner. While the concept of a goal is itself a relatively simple one, goal setting in small groups requires

> **goal**
> a desired state of future affairs, a target; goals are expressed in general, rather than specific, terms

attention to many specifics. Goal setting is more complex and more demanding than one might expect at first glance. In this chapter, we'll examine a variety of important aspects of group goal setting. We'll also explain why clear goals are so important for the success of your group. Before doing so, however, let's consider the importance of goals within a typical police service.

The most important goals of a police service are set by its senior administrators. If, for example, the goal is to reduce common assaults by at least 20 percent in the coming year, the chief of police, working with officers from various levels in the organization, will establish the target and the practices necessary to hit the target. The practices, in our example, might include increasing foot patrols, lobbying the city for better lighting, and other actions that are likely to help the service achieve its goal.

To achieve this goal, and any others that the service sets, it is imperative that the senior administrative officers know how to set clear goals for the future. It is also essential that officers at lower levels in the organization understand goal setting. A good understanding of goal setting at lower levels is important because it is at these levels of the organization that the practices designed to achieve the goals will be implemented. Moreover, since policing is a team effort, members at all levels of the service will contribute more readily to the success of the service if they understand the importance of goal setting and the best ways to go about it. Let's now look at some of the most important aspects of goal setting.

LONG-TERM AND SHORT-TERM GOALS

long-term goal
a target that requires planning and strategies implemented over an extended period of time

short-term goal
a target that requires planning and strategies implemented over a brief period of time

The word "goal" may apply to **long-term** as well as short-term targets. For example, a hockey team sets the long-range goal of winning the league championship. But to achieve that goal, they must also set and accomplish many **short-term** goals. For instance, the team must win enough games to make the playoffs. Further, to win the first game of the season (a short-term goal), they may have to set and achieve several even shorter-term goals, such as "shutting down" the opposition's high scorer by close checking and "solving" the goaltender who led the league in shut-outs last season. So, too, the student who has the long-term goal of becoming a police officer must achieve many short-term goals along the way. Success in classes, on tests, on assignments, and many other short-term tasks are essential for overall success in long-term goal achievement.

GOALS AND OBJECTIVES

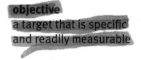

objective
a target that is specific and readily measurable

In the field of group dynamics, we often make a distinction between *goals* and *objectives*. The distinction is simple but important. When targets are stated in *general terms*, we refer to them as goals. In our earlier examples, losing weight, buying a computer, and becoming a police officer are goals. They are targets, but they are expressed in very general terms. In contrast, when we state our targets in *specific terms* that include measurable standards, we call our targets operational goals or **objectives**. This distinction is a useful one because it highlights the importance of specifying our targets very precisely. That is, we need to identify specific objectives that will, when achieved, lead to the accomplishment of our more general goals.

For example, the goal of getting a college education is accomplished only by achieving many specific objectives that ultimately lead to that goal. The long-term goal of becoming a police officer is achieved by reaching many shorter-term objectives. The student who aspires to being a police officer will have to set and achieve many specific objectives in his pursuit of that goal. One of the many objectives might be expressed as follows: to complete the first year of the police foundations program at the end of the current school year by attending all classes, dedicating a minimum of three hours to study per day, and achieving an "A" average in all subjects. Notice how specific this objective is compared with the general goal of passing the first year.

In this objective, we know precisely *what* the target is; namely, to complete year one with an "A" average. We also know precisely *when* the objective will be achieved; namely, by April of this year. We know, further, precisely how the objective will be achieved; namely, by dedicated study and regular class attendance. We also know, although it isn't stated, precisely who is responsible for the achievement of the objective; namely, the student. In contrast to general goals, objectives identify the specifics. Objectives include the "what," "when," "how," and "who" of reaching the target.

When we state our targets in the language of objectives, then, we need to identify precisely *what* the target is, *when* we will know that it has been reached, *how* it will be achieved, and *who* is responsible for its achievement. Consider another example. A group might state as one of its goals: "Our group will raise money to give to charity." This worthy but very general goal needs to be restated as a specific objective. The objective might be: "Under the leadership of Bradley Brown, by May 1 of this year our group will raise $500 for the Red Cross through weekly car washes." In this specific objective, we can see who has the lead responsibility, what amount of money has been targeted, when the target is to be reached, and how the money is to be raised.

Several problems are likely to arise if your group fails to set clear objectives. First, if members aren't clear on your group's objectives, your group will lack *direction*. Second, your group is likely to lack *motivation* because success in achieving objectives will not be easily determined. Third, your *communication* is likely to suffer because members are uncertain about your group's focus or purpose. Fourth, this uncertainty is likely to generate unnecessary *conflict*. Finally, your group will lack the standards necessary for effective *evaluation* of its performance. In the last section of this chapter we will examine the benefits that come to groups that have clear goals and specific objectives. Before discussing those benefits, let's look at a process for developing well-crafted objectives within your group.

DEVELOPING OBJECTIVES IN YOUR GROUP

As with the development of group norms, effective groups use critical discussion and consensus to develop their goals and objectives. Critical discussion, you will recall from chapter 3, is a process that encourages not only an exchange and critique of ideas but also support of those who offer their ideas. Consensus is unanimous agreement, and it fosters maximum commitment from members to the decisions of the group. Through critical discussion and consensus, effective teams establish their more general goals and their very specific objectives.

In your group, for example, one member may adopt a particular point of view and argue for it, offering as many good reasons in support of it as possible. Other members should offer their criticisms of that position and suggest alternatives. They, too, must provide reasons for their positions. All of this is done in a mutually supportive manner. The object is not to criticize people but ideas. Because it involves a criticism of ideas, not people, critical discussion is sometimes called *conceptual conflict*, a battle of ideas. "Concept," of course, is just another word for "idea."

When your group has considered all reasonable points of view, it should then set its goals or objectives by consensus; that is, by unanimous agreement among the members of the group. When all your members have offered their points of view and all have agreed to an objective, your team's commitment to achieving that objective should be very high. Also, the conceptual conflict that you have engaged in should produce a very clear objective.

CHARACTERISTICS OF EFFECTIVE OBJECTIVES

There are five important characteristics that your team's objectives should include. If your group ensures that its objectives have the five characteristics described below, it should enjoy the benefits that derive from having clear and measurable targets to work toward. Let's now take a look at each of the characteristics.

1. Start with Task and Social Goals

First, effective objectives should reflect the fact that your group has two types of goals to achieve, its task goals and its social goals. Successful groups get their work done, regardless of what that work may involve. In other words, they achieve their task goals. In addition, effective groups build themselves into teams. They develop a sense of cohesiveness, a sense of togetherness among their members. They achieve their social goals. When your team sets its objectives, the objectives should contribute to the achievement of your fundamental task and social goals. When you set your objectives, then, always consider your task and social goals. Your objectives will identify the specific steps that your group will take to accomplish these goals. At any time, your group should be able to identify its task-related objectives as well as its relationship-related objectives. In sum, effective objectives will be ones that lead to the achievement of both the task goals and the social goals that your team establishes.

2. Include Individual and Group Needs

Second, your group should set objectives that take into account both individual needs and group needs. Your group, like all groups, is composed of individuals with unique needs. Effective objectives take this fact into consideration. If individual needs are not addressed, the group will suffer. This is not to suggest, however, that your group can cater to each individual's every wish. When joining a group, we usually have to give up some of our personal goals in order to help the group reach its goals. This is the compromise of group life. Effective objectives, however, will be set up with both individual and group interests in mind. Your team should strive to establish objectives that meet group needs while accommodating, as much as possible, the needs of individual group members.

3. Build in Cooperation

Third, your group should build member cooperation into its objectives. *Cooperatively structured* objectives, you will recall from chapter 3, require that members work together to achieve the objective. They require positive interaction and interdependence among members; thus, they build cohesion. In contrast, *competitively structured* objectives pit one member against another. This approach tends to create a win–lose atmosphere that can be very detrimental to team spirit.

It is also possible to create *individualistically structured* objectives. With individualistic structures, group tasks can be completed by individual members working on their own. As with competitive goal structures, this approach should be used sparingly because it does not promote interdependence and cohesion among members. When setting its objectives, your team should create objectives that build in cooperation.

Some examples may help you understand the differences among these approaches. Any team sport — for example, football, hockey, or baseball — requires that members cooperate and work closely together to achieve the team's objectives. Sports teams build cooperation into their objectives. Everyone must work together to win. In contrast, many car dealerships build competition into dealership objectives. The dealership tries to achieve a particular objective — higher monthly sales, for instance — by giving bonus incentives to individual sales personnel. In this case, one salesperson can make more money by taking sales from another. The prospect of a personal bonus is an incentive to compete with others on the sales team. Finally, the auto factory provides a good example of individualistic structures. In the factory setting, the company sets objectives in which the windshield installer neither cooperates with nor competes with the fuel-tank installer. Each works independently of the other, as the company achieves its production objectives.

4. Set Realistic Objectives

Fourth, your team should set realistic goals for itself. Research shows that groups that set realistic objectives are more likely to achieve their objectives. If your group is overly enthusiastic and sets objectives that are beyond its capacity to achieve, members will be frustrated and morale will likely decline. In contrast, if your group sets objectives that are achievable with little effort, it will likely become stagnant. The high jumper, for example, who has repeatedly jumped 1.5 metres with maximum effort will, no doubt, be frustrated if the bar is set at 2.0 metres. The same jumper will be bored with the bar at 1.0 metre. A realistic objective for our jumper might be 1.6 metres. The best course of action is to set realistic objectives that provide sufficient challenge to your members to motivate them to achieve those objectives. The successful achievement of realistic objectives will be a rewarding motivator for future achievements.

5. State Objectives in Measurable Terms

Fifth, your team should express its objectives in clearly measurable terms. We made this point earlier in this chapter when we emphasized that an objective must include the "what," "when," "how," and "who" questions. By specifying *what* is to be done, *when* it is to be done by, *how* it is to be done, and *who* is responsible for getting it done, we state our objective in measurable terms. In other words, we can measure our success in accomplishing the objective. Putting the point differently, we can determine exactly when we have achieved the objective. Precisely stated objectives also provide clear direction for group efforts. As we'll see in the next section, one of the benefits of clear objectives is precisely the direction that they provide to teams.

BENEFITS OF EFFECTIVE GOALS AND OBJECTIVES

If your team sets clearly measurable objectives, it can expect to gain five benefits that will contribute to the success of your team. Let's look at each benefit in turn.[1]

1. Direction

First, clear objectives will give your group direction for its activities. Measurable objectives provide a guide for planning and coordinating group efforts. If the objectives of your group are unclear or non-existent, then your group will tend to flounder and waste its time. When this happens, members will become frustrated and lose interest. In contrast, when objectives are clear, they become the targets toward which group energy can be directed. Members will understand why the group exists, and they will know where it is heading. Instead of feeling that energy is being wasted, your members will feel productive. Their efforts will be rewarded as each objective is achieved.

2. Motivation

Second, clear objectives will increase the motivation of the members of your group. The old expression "Nothing succeeds like success" expresses this point well. When your group members see that meaningful objectives have been met, they will experience a sense of accomplishment. This sense of achievement is a powerful motivator. Groups that succeed in achieving their short-term objectives are motivated toward the achievement of their long-term goals. Clear objectives stated in measurable terms will benefit your team by motivating members to higher levels of achievement.

3. Communication

Third, clear objectives will improve communication among the members of your group. When objectives are clearly stated in measurable terms, then the group has a focus for communication. When members function as Idea Seekers and Idea Sharers, the team's objectives determine what information is relevant and what is not. Clear objectives have the same effect on the other task actions that we studied in chapter 1; namely, the Direction Suggester, the Progress Summarizer, the Comprehension Checker, and the Group Motivator. What applies to the task actions also applies to the social actions that we examined in the first chapter. The Participation Encourager, the Participant Supporter, the Communication Facilitator, the Process Observer, the Stress Reliever, and the Conflict Mediator all find communication easier when objectives

---

1   Four of the five benefits presented here are based on Johnson and Johnson's work (1997, p. 78). I have added the third benefit, communication.

are clear. To improve its communication, your team should develop clear and measurable objectives.

4. Conflict Resolution

Fourth, clear objectives will facilitate conflict resolution among the members of your group. Often, conflicts arise out of different member perceptions of what the group is supposed to be doing. These differing perceptions may have an unfavourable effect on the climate of the group. If the group's goals and objectives are clear, however, the group has a way of bringing disputing members back to the agreed-upon goals and objectives. If the group's objectives have not been identified clearly, it is difficult or impossible to employ them in conflict resolution. Among the social actions that define the social role of an effective group member is that of the Conflict Mediator. Among other things, she uses clear objectives to help resolve conflict within the group. Your team will experience benefits in the area of conflict resolution if it sets clear objectives for itself. Fewer conflicts are likely to arise, and those that do arise will be easier to handle.

5. Performance Evaluation

Fifth, clear objectives will benefit your group by providing standards for performance evaluation. When an archer shoots an arrow at a clear target, it is easy to see whether the target has been hit or missed. If the archer sees that her shot has gone up and to the right of the bull's eye, she can adjust her next shot downward and to the left. She can adjust her performance in the direction of success. Similarly, when your group has well-defined targets, your members can measure their performance by reference to the team's objectives and adjust their performance in the direction of success. If the group has fallen short of the target, it can establish new strategies or revive old ones to achieve its objective.

CHAPTER SUMMARY

In the introduction to this chapter, we defined a goal as a desired future state of affairs. After noting the difference between long-term goals and short-term goals, we proceeded to distinguish between goals that are quite general targets and objectives that are very specific targets. As specific targets, objectives include information about what is to be done, when it is to be done by, how it is to be done, and who has responsibility for getting it done by. Next, we emphasized the importance of setting group objectives by critically discussing them and reaching consensus about them. Then, we went on to describe five characteristics of a good objective. We said that a good objective will reflect the task and social goals of the group, that it will include both individual member needs and team needs, that it will require the cooperative efforts of members, that it will be realistic, and that it will be stated clearly in measurable terms. We concluded our examination of goals and objectives by summarizing the benefits that accrue to teams that have clearly stated objectives. These benefits include direction for the team, motivation for members, improved communication, more effective conflict resolution, and standards for assessing team performance.

KEY TERMS

goal

long-term goal

objective

short-term goal

MASTERING THE MATERIAL

Now that you have read this chapter, use the following guides to ensure that you
have mastered the material.

1. Define *goal* in three different ways.

   A desired state of future affairs, a target; goals are expressed in general rather than specific, terms.

2. Define *objective*.

   A target that is specific and readily measurable

3. Goals that are to be achieved in the near future are called
   Short term goals, and those that are to be achieved in the more
   distant future are called *Long term* goals.

4. Some writers refer to objectives as *Operational* goals.

5. Targets that are stated in general terms are called *goals*.

6. Targets that are stated in specific, measurable terms are called
   objectives.

7. Groups should develop their objectives through *Concensus* and
   discussion.

8. Rewrite the following goal in the form of an objective: "Our goal is to
   improve police services in our community."

9. If a group target is stated as an objective, then the statement will answer four questions. What are the four questions?

   a.

   b.

   c.

   d.

10. Identify and explain each of the five characteristics of an effective objective.

   a.

   b.

   c.

   d.

   e.

11. Identify and explain the five benefits of clear and measurable objectives.

   a.

   b.

   c.

   d.

   e.

APPLYING THE IDEAS IN POLICING

Exercise 4.1

Imagine that the senior administration of the regional police service for which you work has set the following goal for the service: *to reduce crime in our community*. You have been asked to devise three objectives that will, if met, contribute to the achievement of the stated goal. Write the objectives below.

   1.

   2.

   3.

Exercise 4.2

Imagine that a group of citizens has established the following goal for itself: *to make our community safer*. Because you are a respected officer in the community, the citizens have approached your supervisor asking that you serve on one of their committees. Your supervisor has agreed and assigned you to that special task. The citizens' group wants you to devise three objectives to help them achieve their goal. Write the objectives below.

     1.

     2.

     3.

Exercise 4.3

Imagine that you have been chosen captain of your precinct's baseball team. After several losing seasons you are in a position to help your team achieve its main goal: *to win the league championship next season*. Write three objectives that will, if achieved, contribute to your team's goal of winning the league championship next season.

     1.

     2.

     3.

PRACTISING YOUR GROUP SKILLS

Purpose of This Section

The purpose of "Practising Your Group Skills" and the ultimate purpose of this book is to help you become a more effective participant in the groups to which you belong. This section is designed to provide opportunities for you and your fellow students to practise your group skills in a structured environment.

Team Responsibilities

A description of the team responsibilities for each of five different teams — the Executive Team, the Teaching Team, the Lesson Review Team, the Energizer Team, and the Evaluation Team — can be found in appendix A, pages 207–210. Your professor may have chosen to use from one to five of these teams to conduct the teaching and learning activities of the class. Units 2 and 3 of the Teacher's Guide provide your professor with additional information on the responsibilities of these teams.

Individual Role Responsibilities

A description of four individual role responsibilities — those of Leader, Recorder, Reporter, and Participant-Analyst — can be found in appendix A, pages 210–212. Your professor may have chosen to use from one to four of these roles within teams to give individuals experience leading, recording, reporting, and analyzing. Units 2 and 3 of the Teacher's Guide provide your professor with additional information on these individual role responsibilities.

Specific Team Assignments

Specific team assignments for this chapter appear immediately below. Specific team assignments for each of the subsequent chapters can be found in "Practising Your Group Skills" in each chapter.

CHAPTER 4 TEAM ASSIGNMENTS

The Executive Team

- *Executive Goal:* to provide leadership to your classmates for your class session on chapter 4.

- *Executive Objectives:* to facilitate the class session by (1) ensuring a good classroom setup, (2) welcoming the class, (3) introducing the lesson topic, (4) coordinating activities, and (5) bringing the session to a close.

- *Instructions:* Ensure that the classroom is set up to accommodate the class activities. Post an agenda for the session. Welcome people to class and announce the topic, "Goals: Setting Clear Targets for Your Group," in a creative and interesting way. Remind the class that goals and objectives are essential if groups are to function effectively. Introduce and thank all speakers when appropriate. Coordinate the day's activities and bring closure at the end of the class. If necessary, return the classroom to its original configuration.

The Teaching Team

- *Teaching Goal:* to understand and demonstrate the role of goals and objectives in a small group setting.

- *Teaching Objectives:* to describe, explain, and demonstrate (1) the difference between goals and objectives, (2) the correct way to write an effective objective, and (3) the five benefits of effective objectives.

- *Instructions:* As the Teaching Team, you have the freedom to choose how you will teach your lesson. You can be as creative as you wish, but you must achieve the teaching objectives. Your lesson consists of two parts. The first part is the experiential exercise, and the second part is your explanation of the chapter information.

  ❏ Your experiential exercise is called "Writing Clear Objectives" and you'll find it described fully in appendix B, pages 221–222. Make sure that you refer to "Writing Clear Objectives" when you teach and explain the difference between goals and objectives, the correct way to write an objective, and the five benefits of clear objectives.

  ❏ If time allows, you can also use exercises from "Mastering the Material" and "Applying the Ideas in Policing" in your lesson.

The Lesson Review Team

- *Review Goal:* to review chapter 3, "Norms: Establishing Effective Rules in Your Group."

- *Review Objectives:* to provide a review of (1) the experiential exercise, (2) values, principles, and norms, and (3) the three "Cs" for developing group rules.

- *Instructions:* As the Lesson Review Team, you have the freedom to choose how you will do the review. You can be as creative as you wish, but you must achieve the review objectives. Remember that your time is very limited, so don't try to re-teach last chapter's lesson.

The Energizer Team

- *Energizer Goal:* to motivate your classmates by conducting an energizer activity.

- *Energizer Objectives:* to facilitate the energizing of your classmates by (1) planning an energizer activity and (2) implementing the plan at an appropriate time in the class session.

- *Instructions:* Your team doesn't have a specific, assigned activity to conduct. Rather, the team should remember its energizing purpose and conduct an activity that will provide a break in the class learning routine. Popular games like Simon Says, Heads Up Seven Up, and Murder Wink usually work well. So do various mixers and ice breakers. (Your professor's Teacher's Guide identifies a number of sources of energizer exercises.) Whatever you decide on, you must be prepared to give clear instructions and conduct the exercise effectively. When you lead the energizer, you are leading and directing the entire class. Plan well and execute professionally, even if the exercise is a "kid's game." Encourage everyone to get involved.

The Evaluation Team

As a member of the Evaluation Team, you need to review the information in chapter 10, pages 191–194 before you do anything else. There you will find helpful information on how to conduct your evaluation session. The most important thing to remember is that you are not to judge other people. Your role is to help the class make its own assessment of which practices worked well today and which didn't.

Note that the evaluation goal below is keyed to the content of this chapter. *If desirable or necessary, you can evaluate any other aspect of group experience.* Be sure, though, that you set the goal, develop appropriate objectives, and plan the evaluation session to achieve the goal and the objectives.

- *Evaluation Goal:* to assess group (or class) members' goal-setting practices.

- *Evaluation Objectives:* to (1) assess the degree to which individuals and groups consciously set goals and objectives and achieve them and (2) to identify practices in need of improvement.

- *Instructions:* Create an evaluation instrument based on the selected focus behaviours identified in the objectives. See chapter 10, pages 192–193, for information on creating evaluation instruments. Figure 10.1 provides an example. Solicit feedback from the class using the evaluation instrument. Use the feedback to discuss the class session with the purpose of identifying improvements that can be made to individual, group, and class performance in future class sessions. Conclude by noting the specific actions that need to be repeated or avoided to make improvements.

REFERENCES AND RECOMMENDED READINGS

Engleberg, I.N., & Wynn, D.R. (1997). *Working in groups: Communication principles and strategies.* New York: Houghton Mifflin.

Frey, L.R., & Barge, K.J. (Eds.). (1997). *Managing group life: Communicating in decision-making groups.* New York: Houghton Mifflin.

Harris, T.E., & Sherblom, J.C. (1999). *Small group and team communication.* Needham Heights, MA: Allyn & Bacon.

Johnson, D.W., & Johnson, F.P. (1997). *Joining together: Group theory and group skills* (6th ed.). Needham Heights, MA: Allyn & Bacon.

Robbins, S.P., & Hunsaker, P.L. (1996). *Training in interpersonal skills.* Upper Saddle River, NJ: Prentice Hall.

Wilson, G.L. (1999). *Groups in context: Leadership and participation in small groups* (5th ed.). Boston: McGraw-Hill.

Messages: Communicating Effectively in Your Group

Chapter Objectives

After completing this chapter, you should be able to:

- Describe a model of the oral communication process.
- Explain the difference between an *encoder* and a *decoder*.
- Define the term *message*, and identify the two dimensions of a message.
- Distinguish between verbal and non-verbal communication.
- Identify and describe three different types of noise.
- Describe the characteristics of a two-way message.
- Explain what a feedback message is.
- State and explain six rules for sending a message effectively.
- State and explain three rules for receiving a message effectively.
- State and explain four rules for giving effective feedback.

INTRODUCTION

In policing, as in virtually all areas of human experience, effective communication is critically important. During the daily briefing session in which assignments are made, at the time of the questioning of a driver pulled over for speeding, or at a post-operation debriefing, police officers need the very best communication skills to do their jobs effectively. Officers regularly have important conversations with superiors, peers, and members of the public. Clear and effective communication is an extremely valuable skill in policing just as it is in all professions.

Communication takes place in many settings, and some of those settings have special protocols with respect to the communication process. Protocols are particular procedures that must be followed in extraordinary circumstances. For example, the chief of police who speaks to a large gathering of officers may engage in one-way communication; that is, communication with little or no opportunity for feedback from the listeners. The size of the audience and the purpose of the meeting may impose limitations on the communication process. In other words, a special protocol is in effect for that situation.

There are many different situations that require special communication protocols that we will not address in this chapter. We'll focus instead on communication in small group settings, those situations most commonly experienced by police and others. Developing communication skills for these ordinary settings will prepare you for most kinds of interpersonal communication, both professional and personal. Any additional skills or rules associated with special protocols — for instance, those associated with a hostage taking — will have to be addressed elsewhere by the reader as the need arises.

In this chapter we'll examine the process of spoken or oral communication. We'll focus our attention on the skills required to send and receive spoken messages effectively. The rules for speaking effectively differ from the rules for writing effectively. The skills and rules described in this chapter, then, do not necessarily apply to writing skills. Let's examine the oral communication process. What are some of the factors that influence our spoken messages in a group setting? How can we do the best job of speaking effectively to our teammates?

A MODEL OF THE ORAL COMMUNICATION PROCESS

Before we look at specific rules for clear oral communication, we'll examine a model of the communication process itself. A model is a simplified description of a process that is expressed in a diagram (see figure 5.1). The model presented in this chapter is called an explanatory model because it attempts to explain all the elements of the oral communication process, both the positive features and the negative ones. This explanatory model, for example, includes noise and explains what it is. Noise is a common but negative feature in oral communication. Good communicators will know what noise is, and they will attempt to eliminate it from their communication.

As we begin to examine our model, take note that **communication** occurs when there is a successful exchange of information or feelings between members of a group. In other words, communication happens only when the receiver of a message understands it in the way that the sender intended. Our model of the oral communication process includes a message *sender*, the *message* itself, a *receiver* of the message, and a *feedback* message (figure 5.1). Imagine, now, two people in a conversation. If we carefully analyze their communication, we'll see that communication is a very complex process. First of all, someone has to start the process. This happens when one person is motivated to send a message to another person.

Sender and Receiver

The **sender** first has an idea or a feeling (or both) that she wants to communicate to the other person, the **receiver** of the message (see figure 5.1, phase 1). The

communication
the successful exchange of information and feelings between people in a group

sender
the person who begins the communication process by expressing thoughts and feelings in words

receiver
the person in the communication process who interprets the sender's words

FIGURE 5.1   A Model of the Oral Communication Process

Communication includes a sender, a receiver, a message, and a feedback message. Noise (physical, physiological, or psychological) can interfere with communication at a number of points in the process.

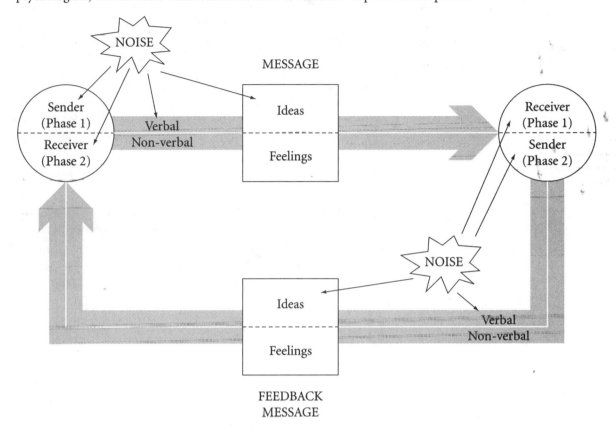

sender must then put these thoughts and feelings into words and say the words to the other person. Putting the message into words is called **encoding**, and the sender can be called the encoder. If the sender's words are well chosen and understood by the receiver, the receiver will interpret the message accurately. In other words, the receiver understands what the sender intended to say. Interpreting the message accurately is called **decoding** the message, and the receiver is sometimes called the decoder. As noted earlier, effective communication occurs only when the receiver understands the sender's message in the way that the sender intended.

encode
to express a message in spoken or written words

decode
to interpret a spoken or written message accurately

The Message

The **message** is *what* the sender communicates to the receiver. Messages are generally of two kinds. They are about the sender's ideas or about the sender's feelings. Often, a single message conveys both ideas and feelings. Because human beings are thinking beings, we frequently communicate our ideas, thoughts, and opinions to one another. Psychologists refer to this thinking or intellectual side of our human nature as our *cognitive dimension*. We are, however, much more than thinkers. We also have feelings and we experience moods. Psychologists call this feeling side of our nature the *affective dimension*. Good communicators learn to express both their thoughts and their feelings clearly so that others are easily able to understand their messages.

message
the thoughts and feelings communicated by a sender, whether verbally or non-verbally

Verbal and Non-Verbal Communication

What we communicate to others is different from *how* we communicate to others. What we communicate is the message; *how* we communicate is the method of sending our messages. When we use words to convey our ideas and feelings to others, we use **verbal communication**. "Verbal" means "in words" and includes both written and spoken words. We use the word "oral" specifically to designate spoken words, and the word "written" to designate scripted words. This chapter, as noted above, focuses on the process of oral communication.

When we convey a message to others without using words, we use **non-verbal communication**. "Non-verbal" means "without words." Non-verbal communication includes gestures, eye contact, and body posture. In recent years, much has been written on the subject of non-verbal communication. These studies have helped us understand the importance of non-verbal messages.

Non-verbal messages, however, are easily misunderstood, because they are not based on a universal grammar or set of rules. Verbal messages are more likely to communicate effectively because they are based on a grammar that is widely accepted, even if not universally understood. Both types of messages, verbal and non-verbal, can be effective methods of communication. When they are used in combination to complement one another, then the messages they convey become stronger.

Noise

In our model of the oral communication process, anything that interferes with the communication of a message from a sender to a receiver is called **noise**.[1] Noise, we need to note, takes three distinctly different forms. As communicators, we need to be familiar with each form, recognize each form when it occurs, and do our best to eliminate it. The three types of noise are physical noise, physiological noise, and psychological noise. To explain and illustrate each type, we'll use the example of a police officer questioning a driver at the side of a busy road on a very windy day.

The first form of noise is *physical* noise. By physical noise we mean loud and disturbing sounds. In our example, the roar of passing engines, the singing of tires, the blaring of horns, and the howl of the wind are all physical noises. They are loud sounds that interfere with communication between the officer and the motorist. When we think of noise, we usually think of physical noise.

A second form of noise is *physiological* noise. The adjective "physiological" has the same language roots as the noun "physiology," which refers to the study of bodies. Human physiology, of course, studies the human body. Physiological noise, then, refers to interferences to communication that result from disorders of the body. Poor eyesight and hearing difficulties are examples. A person unable to hear is restricted to reading lips or written messages. A person who cannot see doesn't have the benefit of seeing non-verbal cues sent by a speaker. While physiological noise is relatively rare, it creates unique communication challenges when it does occur. Imagine the added communication difficulty in our example, if the driver of the car is hearing-impaired.

Sometimes noise is neither physical nor physiological, but psychological in nature. Psychological noise is the third form of noise that we need to be familiar with.

verbal communication
a message expressed in words (speech or writing)

non-verbal communication
a message expressed without the use of words, by gestures, eye contact, or body posture

noise
any physical, physiological, or psychological interference that impedes communication

---

1   Wilson (1999, p. 14) provides an excellent review of the varieties of noise that can affect communication in groups. This summation is based on his categories.

Psychological noise is communication interference that stems from a heightened emotional state, usually a negative one. Sometimes people use words that anger and upset us so much that our emotions interfere with our ability to communicate effectively. We begin, for example, ranting and raving rather than speaking clearly in a rational manner. Our psychological upset can also keep us from listening effectively.

Our anger, the psychological noise, can interfere with the entire communication process. Police officers and other professionals must learn to control their emotions and, thereby, reduce psychological noise when communicating with others. If the motorist in our example calls the police officer a pig, the officer may react angrily, contributing to the psychological noise. Or, he may react calmly, eliminating some of the interference. Sexist, racist, and similar remarks usually create noise that disrupts the communication process.

Two-Way Communication

Our model of the communication process indicates that communication is a two-way process in which a message goes from a sender to a receiver and back again. Two-way communication is the ideal way to communicate in a small group. Occasionally, however, two-way communication is replaced by one-way communication. This shift is often a sign that there are problems within the group.

If, for example, someone in your group isn't open to the ideas and feelings of others and doesn't really listen to them or give them feedback, then two-way communication isn't occurring. If the situation persists, the group will suffer. Unhealthy one-way communication also occurs when one or two members dominate the group's discussions. If a member, for instance, is vocal and convinced that his ideas are the only good ones in the group, then one-way communication will dominate, especially if other members tend to be passive.

Two-way communication is the ideal within small groups and should be encouraged and expected. As in many areas of life, good communication is essential for success. Later in this chapter, we'll study several rules for effective two-way communication. Before examining those rules, however, we'll review the nature of feedback messages. They are an essential aspect of healthy two-way communication.

Feedback Messages

Two-way communication occurs when the receiver of a message becomes the sender of a return message (see figure 5.1, phase 2). This return message is called a **feedback message**, and it is a natural part of ordinary conversation. Your group should work to encourage constructive feedback between and among members. Only when there is open, two-way communication within a group can it achieve its basic task goals and social goals.

Notice that all the elements of the communication process that have been discussed thus far are involved in feedback messages. In the feedback stage, the original receiver becomes the new sender, and the original sender becomes the new receiver. The new sender can use both verbal and non-verbal communication to convey both her thoughts and her feelings to the new receiver. It is also possible that the feedback message will be corrupted by noise of one kind or another. All the things that hindered or helped the original message may also be at work in the feedback message. Good communicators work to ensure that their feedback messages are

feedback message
a return message sent by a receiver to the original sender

clearly understood by others. As the conversation continues, this cycle of two-way communication continues also.

RULES FOR EFFECTIVE COMMUNICATION

Let's now examine some rules for effective communication using the sender, the receiver, and the feedback message as the basis of our study. In the sections that follow, we'll present rules for sending messages effectively, rules for receiving messages effectively, and rules for giving effective feedback.

Sending Messages Effectively

There are six rules to follow when sending oral messages to members of your group.[2] If you follow these rules in your discussions, you will help to ensure that the communication in your group is both two-way and effective.

RULE #1: USE FIRST-PERSON PRONOUNS IN YOUR MESSAGES

In grammar the words "I," "me," and "mine" are called first-person pronouns. We use these words to refer to ourselves without continually repeating our name. If we use these pronouns, we can indicate clearly to others what we are thinking or feeling. By using first-person pronouns we take responsibility for our thoughts and feelings. Others will know what we think and feel.

Consider the following statement: "Some people get angry when they are continually interrupted." When the speaker uses the expression "some people," it is not clear to listeners whether the speaker includes himself among the "some people" or not. Now consider this statement: "I get angry when I am continually interrupted." In this case, we know exactly what the speaker feels. By using the first-person pronoun "I," he has taken responsibility for both his feelings and the communication of those feelings to others.

Use "I," "me," and "mine" to communicate your thoughts and ideas to others. By using the first-person pronouns, you can enhance your communication skills.

POOR: "*Some people* get angry when *they* are continually interrupted."

BETTER: "*I* feel angry when *I* am continually interrupted."

POOR: "Our team has decided to support the college fund raiser."

BETTER: "I have decided to support the college fund raiser and so has my team."

RULE #2: CONVEY YOUR FRAME OF REFERENCE, AND KNOW THE RECEIVER'S FRAME OF REFERENCE

frame of reference
the context from which a
person speaks or listens

The expression **frame of reference** refers to the social and psychological context from which a person is speaking or listening. In any conversation, there are at least two frames of reference: the sender's and the receiver's. In common language, this second rule might be stated: "Tell the other person where you're coming from, and find out where the other person's coming from." When speaking in a conversation, you should help your listener to know your frame of reference. Likewise, as a listener

---

2   Johnson and Johnson (1997, p. 144) present eight guidelines for sending messages effectively. I
    include five in this section, adding rule #3 on communicating ideas.

in a conversation, an understanding of the speaker's context will be a tremendous help to you in understanding his message.

A speaker who communicates the context from which he is speaking helps the listener to understand his message. In the two examples of poor communication below, the listener has no indication of the speaker's frame of reference. In the examples of better communication, the listener learns the frame of reference.

POOR: "I don't want to study with you today." [Providing no context]

BETTER: "I've had a really rough day, so I'm not up to studying with you." [Providing a context]

POOR: "Let's go for a coffee. I'm sure you've got time." [Assuming a context]

BETTER: "How's your day going? Do you have time for a coffee?" [Seeking the context]

RULE #3: PRESENT YOUR IDEAS CLEARLY AND CONCISELY

Messages, you will recall, may convey our ideas, our feelings, or both. This rule addresses the communication of our ideas, thoughts, and opinions. It is about our cognitive messages and tells us to convey our ideas clearly and concisely. While the rule itself is straightforward, keeping it is often difficult. Following this rule requires the skillful use of words and correct use of grammar.

The skillful use of words requires a good vocabulary. Obviously, a good vocabulary is an asset in both spoken and written communication. The more words we have to communicate our ideas, the better we can become at sending messages to others. Reading good books and listening to skilled speakers are two ways that you can improve vocabulary. Unfortunately, acquiring a good vocabulary is not an easy thing to do. It takes a great deal of time and effort. Developing a repertoire of words is an ongoing task in life, and good communicators are always trying to find the best words by which to convey their ideas.

Correct use of grammar is also critical to effective communication. Grammar, of course, is the structure of a language. It involves the order of presentation of our words, the sequencing of words, in ways that reflect the logical processes of the mind. It is grammar that determines the meaning or sense of the statements that we use. Consider the following sentences:

- The blue bird flew away.
- The bird with blue feathers flew away.
- The bird which has blue feathers flew away.

Each of these sentences conveys exactly the same meaning. The first sentence is obviously the briefest, the most concise. Though different in a number of ways, each sentence makes the same statement. We recognize that the statements are equivalent because we understand the meaning of the words (vocabulary) and we comprehend the structure of the words (grammar).

Now consider the following statements:

- The flew bird away blue.
- Flew feathers blue with away bird the.
- Which the flew blue has bird away feathers.

Each one is confusing and essentially meaningless. These three collections of words do not observe grammatical structures of the English language. Consequently, they lack meaning despite the fact that we understand each individual word. In your spoken communication, you should use words accurately and present them in a logical order. You should communicate your ideas clearly and briefly using good vocabulary and proper grammatical construction. The examples below show how poor communication of an idea can be improved by using fewer words and proper grammar.

> POOR: "John, eh, you know, like asked his dad, like if he could, you know, make the use of his dad's wheels, eh, so like his dad says, 'ya man,' so like, that's cool, eh?"

> BETTER: "Isn't it great that John's dad loaned him the car?"

> POOR: "Like it was so boss, like him, eh, like his new wardrobe, eh, like it was, like, so him. Like, you know what I mean?"

> BETTER: "He looked really good in his new suit, didn't he?"

Clarity and conciseness require study and practice. Improving your communication skills is a lifelong project.

RULE #4: DESCRIBE YOUR FEELINGS; DON'T EXPRESS THEM

The previous rule gave guidance on the communication of *ideas*. Rule #4 addresses the communication of *feelings*. We can communicate our feelings in two ways: We can express them, and we can describe them. The word "express," as used here, means "to let the emotions spill or burst out." If you're angry, you may yell and shout. If you're sad, you may weep. If you're happy, you may laugh or giggle. Often, we can express our feelings and no harm is done, particularly when the feelings are happy ones. Sometimes, however, the expression of emotion can be disastrous. Anger, in particular, can cause problems if expressed rather than described.

Powerful emotions, like anger, can be communicated most effectively through description. When you describe your angry feelings, you let the other person know what you are experiencing emotionally, but you avoid the negative repercussions of an emotional outburst. There are two helpful ways to describe your emotions.

- One way to describe your feelings is to *name* them. Just as we need a good vocabulary for communicating ideas, so we need a good vocabulary for describing our feelings. Developing a vocabulary of feelings can be a challenge. Many of the helping professions make use of "feeling" words, but learning to use them appropriately requires a lot of practice. As with rule #3, adhering to this rule is a lifelong project. Over time, however, you can improve your communication skills by developing a vocabulary that allows you to name the feelings that you experience.

- A second way to describe feelings is to use *comparisons*. In language studies, we have two forms of comparison — similes and metaphors. Both make comparisons between two things. A *simile* uses the words "like" or "as," and makes a direct comparison. For example, "Joe ran *like* the wind" directly compares Joe's running to the movement of the wind. A *metaphor* is an indirect comparison that is more subtle than a simile. For example, "The ship plowed through the sea" indirectly compares the ship's movement through the water to a farmer's plow turning over the soil. Both similes and metaphors can be used to describe our emotions.

> POOR: "@**&@**, I don't give a #%**@ whether I ever see you again!!! You *%##@* me off with your *&%%##@* attitude." [Expressing anger]

> BETTER: "When you talk to me that way, I get really angry." [Describing anger by naming]

> BETTER: "When you talk to me that way, I feel like a pit bull in a leg trap." [Describing anger by simile]

> BETTER: "When you talk to me that way, my blood starts to boil." [Describing anger by metaphor]

RULE #5: DESCRIBE THE BEHAVIOUR; DON'T JUDGE THE PERSON

When people do things that we disagree with or disapprove of, a natural reaction is to make a judgment about the person. For example, if a person in your group has been late for several meetings in a row and has also left early each time, you may assume that she doesn't care about the group. Such assumptions imply judgments about the personality or character of the other person. In effect, you are attributing a flaw or weakness to that person's character; you are questioning her motives.

Making personal judgments can be detrimental to the group. Personal judgments are not a very helpful communication practice as they are inappropriate and often inaccurate. For example, the individual who repeatedly arrives late may care very much about the group, but she may be facing unavoidable circumstances that are causing the late arrivals and early departures.

Rather than making judgments, you should restrict your comments to a description of the other person's behaviour. Sticking with the facts and avoiding judgments about others allows them to tell us what is happening in their lives. There may be perfectly good reasons for their behaviour. Jumping to judgmental conclusions about others will only impede communication by fostering bad feelings. Even when others are uncommitted or lazy, we should confront them constructively without making judgments about their character. We'll study constructive confrontation in chapter 6 where we examine conflicts and how best to deal with them. Here are two possible approaches to the person who arrives late and leaves early.

> POOR: "You're always late and you always leave early. It's obvious that you're not committed to our group. Or, is it that you're just plain lazy?" [Judging the person]

> BETTER: "You've arrived late and left early several times. Have we scheduled our meetings at a bad time?" [Describing behaviour]

RULE #6: REQUEST FEEDBACK, AND DON'T IGNORE IT

It's a good practice to request feedback from others. First of all, it allows you to see whether the other person has understood your message. If the receiver has understood your message, you can let him know that he has. If he hasn't understood it, you have a chance to clarify your position. Second, requesting feedback gives you an opportunity to understand what the other person feels about what you have said. In other words, you have an opportunity to check out his emotional reaction to what you've said. Finally, feedback can give you a chance to adjust your views or your behaviour in light of the views of others. Sometimes, but not always, that may be an important thing to do.

> POOR: "I think that we should buy the IBM computer. It's got everything we need. My mind's made up." [Taking a position but not requesting feedback]

BETTER: "I think that we should buy the IBM computer. It's got everything we need. What do you think? Have I missed anything here?" [Taking a position but requesting feedback]

Asking for feedback but then ignoring the feedback that you get is not very helpful. For one thing, you're not likely to get feedback in the future. In effect, ignoring feedback will probably cut you off from valuable perceptions that others have of you. Further, you're more likely to repeat your mistakes or ineffective practices in the future. One of the great values of feedback is that it gives us a chance to adjust our views and alter our behaviour. Feedback can help all members of your team improve their performance.

POOR: "Well, I'm happy with the way I did that. If I had to do it again, I'd do exactly the same thing." [Ignoring feedback]

BETTER: "Well, I thought I had done a pretty good job. In light of what you've said, however, I can see an even better way to do it next time. Thank you." [Acting on feedback]

Receiving Messages Effectively

The six rules we studied for sending messages are designed to help us do a better job of *speaking* more effectively. Now, we turn our attention to *listening* more effectively. **Active listening** is the name that we give to a three-fold process that includes the skills of expressing intention, listening with your whole person, and paraphrasing the messages of others. To be a good listener, you need to use all of these active listening skills. The rules that follow are designed to help you to employ these skills in your communication with others. Here, then, are three important rules for listening effectively.

active listening
the conscious use of cognitive, affective, and behavioural cues to encourage and clarify communication between and among people

RULE #1: COMMUNICATE YOUR INTENTION TO LISTEN

The first step in active listening is to let the speaker know that you want to hear her message and that you intend to listen.[3] You can communicate your intention in two ways. First, you can express your intention in words. This can be done simply by saying, for example, "I'm really interested in what you have to say about this issue. Please tell me what you think." In this example, you tell the speaker that you want to hear her views. You clearly communicate your intention to listen. When you, the listener, express your intention to listen and support your verbal expression with appropriate body language, then you let the speaker know that you have every intention to listen. Since body language is such an important part of active listening, we'll say more about it in rule #2 below.

A second way of communicating your intention to listen is to ask inviting questions or to make inviting statements. *Inviting questions* are questions that encourage the speaker to elaborate on her views and feelings. Generally speaking, inviting questions cannot be answered with a single word, such as "yes" or "no." Instead, they are designed to elicit a more detailed response. If, for example, I ask, "Would you please tell me all about yourself?" I am inviting you to disclose yourself

---

3 Johnson and Johnson, 1997, p. 145.

to me in a way that encourages more than a one-word response. Similarly, by using *inviting statements* I can show you that I intend to listen to you and assure you that I think that your ideas are worth hearing. I might say, for instance, "I would love to hear your thoughts about the government. I'll bet that they are very interesting." These statements invite you, the speaker, to share your thoughts in some detail. Our statements and our questions, when expressed sincerely, show others that we intend to listen and that we are genuinely interested in what they have to say.

RULE #2: LISTEN WITH YOUR WHOLE PERSON

Listening is often considered a matter of simply perking up one's ears. Active listening, however, involves much more than just your ears. To listen effectively, you need to involve your whole person — your ears, your head, and your heart. That is, good listening involves your body, your mind, and your feelings.

Active listening, it has been said, starts with your feelings, not your ears. Empathy is a special kind of feeling that motivates active listening. **Empathy** means "feeling what another person feels" or "feeling with another person." A feeling, empathy, helps us to engage our minds in a conversation with another person. In other words, an emotional connection leads to a cognitive connection. In effect, when we listen with our heart, then we also listen with our head. In addition, we will be much more inclined to make eye contact and to lean toward the speaker. This *behavioural listening*, or "listening with the body," is the natural result of affective and cognitive engagement with another person. For example, when you watch an exciting movie that has captured your attention, you naturally lean forward to watch and listen; you are fully engaged. This is exactly how active listeners listen to other people. To be an active listener, listen with your whole person.

empathy
feeling what another person feels; feeling with another person

RULE #3: PARAPHRASE THE FEELINGS AND IDEAS OF THE SENDER

To **paraphrase** is to restate in different words what another person has said. This part of the communication process is extremely important and is often neglected in conversation. Paraphrasing is a key skill in providing feedback, and when you paraphrase the sender's message, you allow the sender to confirm that you have understood him correctly. If you have misunderstood, the sender can immediately clarify his message. We noted this important skill above in rule #6 for sending messages effectively. Communication experts call this exchange between sender and receiver "negotiation." They say that the two parties are *negotiating* for meaning; they are ensuring that they understand one another.

paraphrasing
the skill of accurately restating another's position in words different from the original

Since messages convey both ideas and feelings, active listeners paraphrase both aspects of the sender's message.[4] When this occurs, both parties in the communication process "stay tuned" to each other at the level of emotions (affectively) and at the level of ideas (cognitively). The negotiation of meaning is made easier when both parties are attuned to each other. Active listening involves listening for both thoughts and feelings. It also requires paraphrasing both kinds of message, cognitive and affective.

---

4 Johnson and Johnson, 1997, pp. 145–146.

Giving Feedback Effectively

In our model of communication (figure 5.1), there are two phases in the process. In phase 1, there is a sender and a receiver. In phase 2, the original sender and receiver reverse roles. In two-way communication, we are always switching between the roles of sender and receiver. It should not be surprising, then, to find that the six rules for sending messages presented earlier in this chapter apply to the giving of feedback. In addition to those rules, however, there are four rules that are specific to giving feedback.[5]

RULE #1: DON'T FORCE FEEDBACK ON OTHERS

Effective groups create supportive climates in which members can give and receive feedback freely and comfortably. Not all groups develop supportive climates, however, so it is important to note that you shouldn't force feedback on others. Rather, you and the other members of your group should work on creating and maintaining an environment in which feedback occurs naturally without threat or fear, so that everyone can benefit from it. We'll explain how to build a supportive climate in your group in chapter 7.

Note, now, that there are two exceptions to rule #1. Two situations require that feedback be given, whether people welcome the feedback or not.

- First, in a performance review, your supervisor will give you feedback whether you want it or not. This is a necessary part of supervising others.

- Second, in the management of group conflict, it may be necessary to give feedback to a member even when the person does not want it. Constructive confrontation is an essential part of conflict resolution.

RULE #2: FOCUS FEEDBACK ON BEHAVIOUR, NOT PERSONALITY

It is natural to become defensive when we feel that our character or our motives are being questioned or attacked. That is exactly what happens when feedback focuses on judgments about personality rather than descriptions of behaviour. A defensive climate develops, and communication becomes more difficult or even impossible.

As we noted in the rules for sending messages effectively (rule #5), good communicators *describe* the actions of others without imputing motives to others, or making personal judgments about them. By sticking to an accurate description of behaviour (for example, "You have arrived late for the last couple of meetings"), you can give feedback without making a judgment about the other person's character (for example, "You're not committed to this group. If you were, you wouldn't be late all the time"). By avoiding judgments, you help to ensure that healthy, two-way communication will continue.

RULE #3: TARGET SPECIFICS, NOT GENERALITIES

Good feedback zeroes in on specifics. Because the information is focused, it is more useful to the original sender. When you provide feedback to others, identify specific things that may be helpful to the other person, things that they can identify and change. For example, rather than saying that someone's overhead presentation wasn't helpful, tell the presenter exactly what made the presentation weak. Perhaps

---

5   Johnson (1993, pp. 38–39) presents eight rules. Four of those form the basis of this summary.

there was too much information on each slide or maybe the font was too small. Possibly he chose a colour of font that was washed out when projected on the screen. If you give constructive feedback on specifics, the other person can benefit more readily from your feedback.

> POOR: "Sometimes when you speak to the group you tend to pause quite a lot and that interrupts your flow of thought." [Feedback too general]

> BETTER: "I noticed that you said 'uh' and 'you know' several times during the course of your remarks, and each time I was distracted from your topic." [Feedback very specific]

The information in the second statement is more useful because the speaker learns precisely what aspects of his speech need work.

RULE #4: OFFER OPTIONS, NOT ADVICE

Many of us love to tell others what to do. It may be that we get some kind of ego boost from this or it may reflect a need, on our part, to control others, or both. In our conversations with others, all too often we give advice. If advice is specifically requested, it may be appropriate to offer some. However, unsolicited advice can inhibit communication. When advice is not specifically asked for, you should focus on describing the other person's options as you see them. By highlighting the options, you can help others to see their situation more clearly. You avoid telling them what to do, but you help them identify their choices. In the process, you will help them to make better choices for themselves. In effect, offering options is a way of showing respect to others.

> POOR: "I think you're crazy if you don't buy the Civic. There's no other choice." [Unsolicited advice]

> BETTER: "For that money, you can get a Civic, a Neon, or a Focus. Have you done a comparison?" [Offering options]

CHAPTER SUMMARY

After emphasizing the importance of communication for both our professional and personal lives, we presented a model of the oral communication process. The model included the basic ideas of a sender, a receiver, a message, and feedback. The message, we noted, can be about ideas or feelings or both, and it can be delivered both verbally and non-verbally. Next, we examined noise, pointing out three forms of noise that interfere with the process of oral communication. Physical noise, physiological noise, and psychological noise all interfere with communication. Then we described the nature of two-way communication and underscored the importance of feedback messages. Next, keying on the sender, we presented six rules for sending messages effectively. These rules emphasized the importance of using "I" messages, providing frames of reference, conveying ideas clearly, describing feelings, avoiding judgments, and asking for feedback. Turning to the receiver, we reviewed three rules for active listening. These rules emphasized the importance of communicating intention, listening with the whole person, and paraphrasing the messages of others. Finally, focusing on feedback, we presented four rules for giving constructive feedback. These rules highlighted the importance of not forcing feedback on others, focusing on the behaviour of others, providing specific feedback, and avoiding the giving of unsolicited advice.

KEY TERMS

active listening

communication

decode

empathy

encode

feedback message

frame of reference

message

noise

non-verbal communication

paraphrasing

receiver

sender

verbal communication

MASTERING THE MATERIAL

Now that you have read this chapter, use the following guides to ensure that you have mastered the material.

1. Identify the four main parts of the communication model presented in the text.

    a. A sender

    b. A receiver

    c. A message

    d. A feedback message

2. Putting a message into words is called __Encode__.

3. Interpreting a message accurately is called __Decode__.

4. Message senders are sometimes called __Encoder__ because they put their thoughts and feelings into words.

5. Message receivers are sometimes called __Decoder__ because they interpret the sender's message.

6. Name the two types of message that people normally send to one another.

    a. Verbal Communication

    b. Non Verbal Communication

7. Psychologists call the thinking side of our nature the _____ dimension.

8. Psychologists call the feeling side of our nature the _____ dimension.

9. The word "verbal" means _____ and includes both _____ words and _____ words.

10. Define *noise*.

11. Identify and explain the three different kinds of noise described in the chapter.

    a.

    b.

    c.

12. Give an example of one-way communication, and an example of two-way communication.

    a.

    b.

13. What is a feedback message?

14. List, from memory, the six rules for sending messages effectively.

    Rule #1:

    Rule #2:

    Rule #3:

    Rule #4:

Rule #5:

Rule #6:

15. List, from memory, the three rules for receiving messages effectively.

    Rule #1:

    Rule #2:

    Rule #3:

16. List, from memory, the four rules for giving feedback effectively.

    Rule #1:

    Rule #2:

Rule #3:

Rule #4:

APPLYING THE IDEAS IN POLICING

Exercise 5.1

Imagine that you and your partner have arrived at the scene of a major accident at a main intersection of a large city. Give three examples of *physical noise* that might inhibit communication in that setting.

1.

2.

3.

Exercise 5.2

Imagine that you and your partner are at the scene of a domestic dispute. A husband is accusing his wife of cheating on him and he's been threatening her. Three children under seven years of age are cowering in a corner of the room. Give three examples of *psychological noise* that might inhibit communication in this setting. Give one example for each of the following: your partner, the wife, and the husband.

1. Partner:

2. Wife:

3. Husband:

Exercise 5.3

Imagine that you are a constable who has come home late from a very hectic and somewhat dangerous day at work. You are rattled and tired. Your spouse greets you at the door and reminds you that you have to be at your daughter's school play in 45 minutes. You know your daughter is counting on you to be at the play. So is your spouse. You feel you should go, but you don't really want to. Write what you might say to your spouse to convey your thoughts and feelings in these circumstances. Remember to observe the rules for sending messages effectively.

Exercise 5.4

You and your shift partner are having coffee. You notice that he is unusually agitated and on the verge of crying. Your partner begins to say something about his marriage falling apart and his wife walking out on him. Remembering the rules for *active listening*, what would you do and what would you say to your partner as an initial response?

1. What would you do?

2. What would you say?

Exercise 5.5

Imagine that you have a new shift partner who has repeatedly made derogatory, racist, and ethnic comments and jokes about people you see as you cruise the streets of a major city. She doesn't do this outside the cruiser so no one else hears her remarks. You believe that it's wrong to do this, and feel that you have to say something. Since you are likely to be working with this person for some time, however, you do not want to make life miserable for yourself. Observing the rules of effective communication, what could you say to communicate your thoughts and feelings about your partner's comments and jokes? Try to give two different examples of an effective response.

1.

2.

PRACTISING YOUR GROUP SKILLS

Purpose of This Section

The purpose of "Practising Your Group Skills" and the ultimate purpose of this book is to help you become a more effective participant in the groups to which you belong. This section is designed to provide opportunities for you and your fellow students to practise your group skills in a structured environment.

Team Responsibilities

A description of the team responsibilities for each of five different teams — the Executive Team, the Teaching Team, the Lesson Review Team, the Energizer Team, and the Evaluation Team — can be found in appendix A, pages 207–210. Your professor may have chosen to use from one to five of these teams to conduct the teaching and learning activities of your class. Units 2 and 3 of the Teacher's Guide provide your professor with additional information on the responsibilities of these teams.

Individual Role Responsibilities

A description of four individual role responsibilities — those of Leader, Recorder, Reporter, and Participant-Analyst — can be found in appendix A, pages 210–212. Your professor may have chosen to use from one to four of these roles within teams to give individuals experience leading, recording, reporting, and analyzing. Units 2 and 3 of the Teacher's Guide provide your professor with additional information on these individual role responsibilities.

Specific Team Assignments

Specific team assignments for this chapter appear immediately below. Specific team assignments for each of the subsequent chapters can be found in "Practising Your Group Skills" in each chapter.

CHAPTER 5 TEAM ASSIGNMENTS

The Executive Team

- *Executive Goal:* to provide leadership to your classmates for your class session on chapter 5.

- *Executive Objectives:* to facilitate the class session by (1) ensuring a good classroom setup, (2) welcoming the class, (3) introducing the lesson topic, (4) coordinating activities, and (5) bringing the session to a close.

- *Instructions:* Ensure that the classroom is set up to accommodate the class activities. Post an agenda for the session. Welcome people to class and announce the topic, "Messages: Communicating Effectively in Your Group," in a creative and interesting way. Remind the class that the topic includes rules for sending messages effectively, receiving messages effectively, and providing effective feedback to others. Introduce and thank all speakers when appropriate. Coordinate the day's activities and bring closure at the end of the class. If necessary, return the classroom to its original configuration.

The Teaching Team

- *Teaching Goal:* to understand and demonstrate effective oral communication skills in a group setting.

- *Teaching Objectives:* to describe, explain, and demonstrate (1) six effective practices (rules) for sending oral messages, (2) three effective practices (rules) for active listening, and (3) four effective practices (rules) for giving constructive feedback.

- *Instructions:* As the Teaching Team, you have the freedom to choose how you will teach your lesson. You can be as creative as you wish, but you must achieve the teaching objectives. Your lesson consists of two parts. The first part is the experiential exercise, and the second part is your explanation of the chapter information.

❏ Your experiential exercise is called "One-Way and Two-Way Communication" and you'll find it described fully in appendix B, pages 222–223. Make sure that you refer to "One-Way and Two-Way Communication" when you teach and explain the rules for sending messages, the rules for receiving messages, and the rules for giving feedback.

❏ If time allows, you can also use exercises from "Mastering the Material" and "Applying the Ideas in Policing" in your lesson.

The Lesson Review Team

* *Review Goal:* to review chapter 4, "Goals: Setting Clear Targets for Your Group."

* *Review Objectives:* to provide a review of (1) the experiential exercise, (2) the difference between goals and objectives, (3) the correct way to write an effective objective, and (4) the five benefits of effective objectives.

* *Instructions:* As the Lesson Review Team, you have the freedom to choose how you will do the review. You can be as creative as you wish, but you must achieve the review objectives. Remember that your time is very limited, so don't try to re-teach last chapter's lesson.

The Energizer Team

* *Energizer Goal:* to motivate your classmates by conducting an energizer activity.

* *Energizer Objectives:* to facilitate the energizing of your classmates by (1) planning an energizer activity and (2) implementing the plan at an appropriate time in the class session.

* *Instructions:* Your team doesn't have a specific, assigned activity to conduct. Rather, the team should remember its energizing purpose and conduct an activity that will provide a break in the class learning routine. Popular games like Simon Says, Heads Up Seven Up, and Murder Wink usually work well. So do various mixers and ice breakers. (Your professor's Teacher's Guide identifies a number of sources of energizer exercises.) Whatever you decide on, you must be prepared to give clear instructions and conduct the exercise effectively. When you lead the energizer, you are leading and directing the entire class. Plan well and execute professionally, even if the exercise is a "kid's game." Encourage everyone to get involved.

The Evaluation Team

As a member of the Evaluation Team, you need to review the information in chapter 10, pages 191–194, before doing anything else. There you will find helpful information on how to conduct your evaluation session. The most important thing to remember is that you are not to judge other people. Your role is to help the class make its own assessment of which practices worked well today and which didn't.

Note that the evaluation goal below is keyed to the content of this chapter. *If desirable or necessary, you can evaluate any other aspect of group experience.* Be sure, though, that you set the goal, develop appropriate objectives, and plan the evaluation session to achieve the goal and the objectives.

- *Evaluation Goal:* to assess group (or class) members' oral communication practices.

- *Evaluation Objectives:* to (1) assess the speaking skills, the listening skills, and the feedback skills within the group (or class) and (2) identify practices in need of improvement.

- *Instructions:* Create an evaluation instrument based on the selected focus behaviours identified in the objectives. See chapter 10, pages 192–193, for information on creating evaluation instruments. Figure 10.1 provides an example. Solicit feedback from the class using the evaluation instrument. Use the feedback to discuss the class session with the purpose of identifying improvements that can be made to individual, group, and class performance in future class sessions. Conclude by noting the specific actions that need to be repeated or avoided to make improvements.

REFERENCES AND RECOMMENDED READINGS

Burley-Allen, M. (1995). *Listening: The forgotten skill* (2nd ed.). New York: John Wiley & Sons.

Engleberg, I.N., & Wynn, D.R. (1997). *Working in groups: Communication principles and strategies.* New York: Houghton Mifflin.

Frey, L.R., & Barge, J.K. (Eds.). (1997). *Managing group life: Communicating in decision-making groups.* Boston: Houghton Mifflin.

Harris, T.E., & Sherblom, J.C. (1999). *Small group and team communication.* Needham Heights, MA: Allyn & Bacon.

Johnson, D.W. (1993). *Reaching out* (5th ed.). Needham Heights, MA: Allyn & Bacon.

Johnson, D.W., & Johnson, F.P. (1997). *Joining together: Group theory and group skills* (6th ed.). Needham Heights, MA: Allyn & Bacon.

Nichols, M.P. (1995). *The lost art of listening.* New York: Guilford.

Wilson, G.L. (1999). Groups in context: Leadership and participation in small groups (5th ed.). Boston: McGraw-Hill.

Wolvin, A.D., & Coakley, C.G. (1996). *Listening* (5th ed.). Madison, WI: Brown & Benchmark.

Conflict: Resolving Disputes in Your Group

Chapter Objectives

After completing this chapter, you should be able to:

- Define the term *conflict*.
- Describe four different types of conflict.
- Describe conceptual conflict and explain its importance.
- Describe five different conflict styles.
- Explain the differences among passive, aggressive, and assertive communication.
- Identify and explain six rules for managing conflict effectively.

INTRODUCTION

Police officers regularly face conflict. Domestic disputes, violent demonstrations, fights between gangs, and many other situations put officers in the midst of conflict. The management of some conflicts, especially where violence is highly likely, requires special knowledge and skills on the part of officers. Use of force, for instance, involves knowledge and skills that are developed over time through professional training. So, too, the conflict resolution skills necessary to manage a hostage-taking incident are high-level skills. These kinds of conflict resolution are beyond the scope of this book.

Officers, however, will find themselves in many conflict situations that are of a more ordinary variety than those mentioned above. It is conflict resolution in these less dramatic, but no less important, circumstances that we will address in this chapter. Disputes arise between people both in the home and on the job. Here police officers are much like others, regardless of occupation. It is conflict resolution in these more ordinary, everyday circumstances that is the subject of this chapter. We'll examine the nature of conflict and offer some practical strategies for dealing with conflict, whether it arises in the home or on the job.

It is not uncommon for disputes to arise between members of small groups. Group dynamics are complex, and it isn't surprising that the interests of one member will conflict with those of others from time to time. These interpersonal disagreements are to be expected, as they are a natural part of group life. However, if conflict is not managed constructively by group members, it can be destructive. When disagreements surface, it's important for all members to function as Conflict Mediators in order to deal with disputes in ways that will resolve issues and strengthen relationships among group members. In chapter 1 we noted briefly the important role of the Conflict Mediator. Now it's time to look at this function in greater detail. We'll begin by taking a look at four common types of conflict.

TYPES OF CONFLICT

conflict
an interpersonal dispute between or among members of a group

Conflict within small groups can be defined as an interpersonal dispute between or among group members. Such disputes or disagreements occur for a variety of reasons. In this section, we'll discuss four types of conflict that can, if not dealt with appropriately, seriously harm relationships among group members. If unresolved, these forms of conflict are detrimental to group life. Then, in the next section, we'll examine a fifth type of conflict, one that is helpful to groups and needs to be encouraged. Later in the chapter, we'll learn how to deal with conflicts when they arise. Let's now look at four harmful types of conflict.

1. Resource Conflict

When a group lacks resources to do its work, and disagreements arise as a result, the dispute is called *resource conflict*. When resources are scarce, group members are often forced to compete with one another for the available resources. Suppose there are only three computers for a group of five people, and each person needs one. It is easy to see how conflicts might arise. Resource conflict often occurs in large organizations, such as police services, when one part of the organization gets a "better deal" than another. Resource conflict can, however, occur in small groups as well.

In our example, even if members try to share the use of the existing computers, you can see how easily disputes might occur. Mary, for example, thinks that her assignment has higher priority than Joe's, and that she, therefore, deserves the only available computer. Joe sees the situation very differently. He thinks that he needs it first. If Mary gets access to the computer before him, Joe may well accuse Mary of hogging it. Or, he may keep pressuring her to hurry up and finish. This kind of behaviour is typical of group members who have to compete for scarce resources.

The obvious solution in this example is for the organization to buy more computers. While institutions are often to blame for inadequate resources, the interpersonal disputes that result need resolution at the personal level. Mary and Joe have to work together. They can't stop working until the company supplies them with another computer, so they need to resolve their disputes and get on with their jobs in the best way possible, given the lack of resources. They need to resolve their disputes constructively to maintain a good working relationship. Hopefully, the company will also purchase more computers.

2. Power Conflict

Sometimes people engage in power struggles in an attempt to gain control of a group. Two people, for example, keenly want to be leader of the group. They want to have the greatest influence among its members and, consequently, they get into disputes with one another as to who should be in charge. They may also try to court other members to gain their support against the rival. Such *power conflicts* often arise within political parties and large organizations. However, power struggles can occur in every kind of group, including small groups. Someone has to provide leadership in a group, and members often disagree over who that person should be.

Even though a police service is organized hierarchically, with authority clearly defined, power conflict can and does arise in the many small groups, both formal and informal, that form in such large organizations. Moreover, within police associations, union members frequently compete for positions of power within the association. Sometimes this simply reflects healthy competition in a democratic organization. At other times, it degenerates into unhealthy personal conflict. Psychologists, no doubt, have theories to explain why people engage in power struggles. Those theories, however, are not our immediate interest. Rather, we need to understand the practical steps that need to be taken to resolve power conflicts when they occur. Regardless of *why* power conflicts occur, we need to know *how* to deal with them.

3. Status Conflict

Status conflict occurs when members of a group compete for recognition within the group. Status conflict is not the same as power conflict, although they do often occur together. If Jack, for example, wants to exercise control over others in his group, then he may engage in a power conflict to achieve his goal. In contrast, if he simply wants to be recognized by others to satisfy his ego — wants to be seen as a "somebody" — then he may compete for status, without competing for power. Of course, Jack may be interested in both status and power. To distinguish between power conflict and status conflict, remember that the former is about control and the latter is about recognition.

As with power conflict, status conflict can and does arise in hierarchical organizations such as police services. Unfortunately, some officers with higher rank are prone to flaunt their status, creating unnecessary conflict with junior officers. Rookies sometimes experience the brunt of this unprofessional conduct. At the same time, rookies may engage in conflict among themselves with the hope of receiving recognition from more senior officers. Status conflict also occurs in police associations and in other groups within policing services. As with the other types of conflict, most important for us is the acquisition of skills that allow us to mediate and resolve conflicts when they occur.

4. Personality Conflict

Conflict that is rooted in the differing personality traits of group members is called *personality conflict.* Perhaps one member is very easy-going while another is a hard-driving Type A personality. Ted, for example, may want to relax and enjoy the social aspects of the group meeting. In contrast, Moira feels strongly that the group is lazy and not as productive as it should be. Ted and Moira may clash because of their differing personalities.

Since this form of conflict stems from differing personality traits, it is particularly difficult to manage. How do you get people to change their personalities? And in a conflict, who should do the changing? Despite the fact that it's impossible to get a leopard to change its spots, it is still possible to manage the leopard's behaviour. While this analogy may be a weak one, it still makes a point. Personality conflicts, like other conflicts, need to be managed constructively for the sake of the group.

If personality differences lead to conflict that is not managed well, it is easy to see how this can negatively affect a team's performance. In contrast, effective conflict management within small groups can lead to more harmonious and effective group performance and make life on the job more enjoyable. Indeed, when conflicts are resolved fairly and effectively, relationships often become stronger. Much of your time is spent with others in groups and, as noted in chapter 1, you need to be an effective Conflict Mediator on your team. Doing so can be an extremely rewarding experience, both for you personally and for those you help.

CONCEPTUAL CONFLICT

As noted, the four types of conflict above are potentially damaging to a group if they are not managed properly. The goal in any group is to eliminate such conflicts through effective conflict resolution strategies. We now turn our attention to a fifth type of conflict, one that deserves to stand apart from the four that we have just discussed. This type of conflict is beneficial to groups and it is absolutely necessary if your team is to excel. This form of conflict should be promoted and encouraged, not eliminated or discouraged.

We call this positive form of conflict *conceptual conflict*. The adjective "conceptual" derives from the word "concept," which means "idea." Conceptual conflict, then, refers to a battle of ideas. Because this type of conflict is about competing ideas, it is also called *ideational conflict*. The adjective "ideational" comes from the noun "idea." Here again we have the notion of a battle between ideas. Finally, we should note that this type of conflict is also called *constructive controversy*.

When group members engage in conceptual conflict, they critically challenge one another's ideas and thinking. Note, especially, that they are involved in a criticism of ideas, not an attack on persons. Monica can criticize Andy's ideas without criticizing Andy as a person. Effective decision making and problem solving depend on the critical analysis of ideas. Conceptual conflict is designed to identify a group's best ideas. The best ideas should lead to the best decisions and solutions to problems. Successful teams create an atmosphere in which members feel comfortable not only challenging the ideas of others but also receiving criticism of their own ideas from others.

Before we leave this topic, take careful note of a real danger associated with constructive controversy. Unfortunately, many of us take the criticism of our ideas personally. We think that a criticism of our suggestion is an attack on us. All too often, we take things much too personally. We seem to be unable to differentiate our ideas from our personalities. When group members take criticism of their ideas as personal affronts, then conceptual conflict can degenerate quickly into personality conflict. One of the biggest challenges in group life is to receive criticism of your ideas without taking the criticism personally. It requires a certain maturity and confidence to detach yourself from your ideas. It also requires maturity to criticize the ideas of others without making the criticism personal. We'll return to these important ideas in our examination of critical discussion in chapter 8.

CONFLICT STYLES

Now that we have defined conflict and noted several different types of conflict, let's take a look at **conflict styles**, typical ways that people behave when they have disputes with others. Figure 6.1 represents a variety of conflict styles. The horizontal axis measures the degree to which individuals will fight for their personal goals. The extreme left (0) indicates little concern for one's own personal goals; the extreme right (10) indicates maximum concern for one's own goals. The vertical axis measures the degree to which the same individuals value their relationships with the person(s) with whom they are in conflict.[1] The bottom of the vertical line (0) marks the point of little or no interest, while the top (10) marks maximum interest in the relationship. By using this grid, we can plot five distinctly different conflict styles.

conflict style
the manner in which a group member typically engages in disputes with others

1. The Turtle

Some people don't like to engage in conflict at all. They place low value on both the achievement of their personal goals (horizontal axis) and also on the maintaining of the relationship (vertical axis) with their disputants. In the most extreme case, these individuals would be at 0,0 on the grid. This conflict style is characterized by *withdrawing* from conflict. Just like a turtle, these people pull in their heads to avoid danger. *Turtles* avoid conflict at any cost. Their withdrawing behaviour is also called *avoidance behaviour*.

At one time or another, we are all Turtles, and sometimes it is wise to be so. If, to take an extreme example, you are accosted by a mugger wielding a knife, withdrawal and avoidance may be perfectly in order. In ordinary circumstances, however, regular turtle-like behaviour reflects an unhealthy and overly passive approach to interpersonal relationships. Turtles lack the assertiveness that is essential for mature relationships. Moreover, a group of turtles is not likely to get much done and will never become an effective team.

2. The Shark

Some people will fight to the finish to accomplish their personal goals and, in the process, care little or nothing about their relationship with the other party. In the extreme, these individuals would be at 10 on the horizontal axis and 0 on the vertical axis. They adopt a win–lose approach to conflict, and intend to be the winners. Like a shark moving in for the kill, these individuals apply force to come out on top. *Sharks* will engage in this *forcing behaviour* in an attempt to win at all costs.

---

1   Blake and Mouton (1964) introduced the distinction between the value one places on one's own goals and the value one places on the relationship. Using this distinction, Thomas and Killman (1974) discuss "avoiding," "competing," "accommodating," "compromising," and "collaborating." I follow Johnson and Johnson (1997, pp. 340–341) and employ the animal designations.

FIGURE 6.1   Conflict Styles

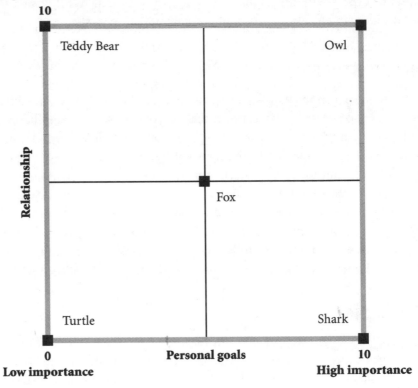

Source: Johnson and Johnson (1997, p. 284). Reprinted by permission.

We can all be Sharks at times, but some people regularly adopt this approach. They are ready at any time to eat up the opposition. Sharks are aggressive when it comes to conflict, and they can be very detrimental to a group. We first met the Shark when we studied harmful roles in chapter 1. There, you will recall, we described the harmful effects of the Dominator and the Aggressor. A group full of sharks will try to destroy one another and they will never become a team. At times being a Shark may be necessary, but regular aggression causes serious problems.

3. The Teddy Bear

Some people value relationships more highly than the achievement of their personal goals. Such people will try to preserve the relationship at all costs, giving up their goals in order to keep the relationship harmonious. In the extreme case, these individuals will be at the 0,10 position on the grid. They try to smooth out the bumps in their relationships. *Teddy Bears* are known for their *smoothing behaviour*.

As with the other conflict styles, most of us will be Teddy Bears at one time or another. Sometimes, for example, more will be accomplished in a relationship if you "pour oil on troubled waters." That is, more will be gained by temporarily setting aside your personal goals for the sake of the relationship. For some people, however, smoothing is their typical approach to conflict. Such passive behaviour is not healthy, either for one's group or for oneself. A group of Teddy Bears may be reasonably good at superficial socializing, but they are not likely to develop mature relationships that result in team productivity.

4. The Fox

Some people are willing to compromise — that is, to give up something in order to get something in return. The other person in the dispute does the same. Because each gives up some personal goals, this approach could be described as a lose–lose approach; but since both parties also gain something, it is equally appropriate to call this a win–win situation. In our presentation, we'll emphasize this more positive view. *Compromising behaviour* is essential if the disputing parties are to deal reasonably with their conflict. *Foxes* compromise in order to resolve interpersonal conflicts.

Once again, most of us are Foxes at one time or another, taking the 5,5 position on the conflict grid. Some individuals, however, make this their typical style. Foxes are neither aggressive nor passive. In contrast to the Shark and the Teddy Bear, Foxes are rationally self-interested when in conflict with others. This means that they calculate their possible gains and losses, and then act in their own self-interest. A group full of foxes may become an effective team, but they will likely fall short in the area of team spirit and cohesion. Nevertheless, engaging in conflict like a Fox is generally good, but there is an even better way to deal with conflict.

5. The Owl

The ideal conflict style involves achieving one's own goals, achieving the other's goals, and strengthening the relationship between the two persons in conflict. This style requires *confronting behaviour* that leads to an ideal solution. If disputants can confront each other and resolve their conflict by having both parties achieve their personal goals and by improving the relationship, then both parties have been very wise indeed. *Owls* wisely confront to achieve a true win–win solution. Owls take the 10,10 position on the grid.

Ideally, we should all be Owls all the time. In reality, however, such wise solutions occur too infrequently. Nevertheless, there is nothing to keep us from trying to resolve our interpersonal problems in this way! Owls are assertive rather than aggressive and recognize both their own rights and the rights of others. In addition, they are altruistic, showing genuine concern for others, yet egoistic, seeking their own self-interest. A group of Owls will become a true team, practising constructive confrontation and collaboration. They will get the job done and have mutual respect for one another.

Different situations require different approaches to conflict, and different individuals have different conflict styles. To be an effective group member, you need to understand withdrawing, forcing, smoothing, compromising, and confronting behaviours, and consciously choose the style most appropriate to the circumstances. Throughout, however, you should strive to be the wise, confronting owl.

CONFLICT, RESPECT, AND ASSERTIVE COMMUNICATION

When you are in conflict, your respect for the other person is critically important, as is the other person's respect for you. If there is mutual respect between you, then there is hope for resolving your differences. Mutual respect between disputing parties allows both individuals to *compromise* (the approach of the Fox) and to *confront* (the approach of the Owl) in order to overcome differences between them. In other words, mutual respect empowers both parties to resolve their conflict.

However, the respect you have for yourself is also an essential ingredient in conflict resolution. It is your self-respect that empowers you to prevent abuse from others or to end abuse from others. It is your self-respect that enables you to stand up for yourself and your rights when others ignore them or try to take them away. Unfortunately, those individuals who lack sufficient self-esteem and self-respect to defend themselves become the victims of others.

These two forms of respect — respect for others and self-respect — are the keys to effective conflict resolution between disputing parties. They enable both parties to compromise, to confront, and to collaborate in the resolution of their disagreements. Both respect for others and self-respect are at the heart of **assertive communication**, the kind of communication that is required to solve interpersonal disputes.

At one extreme, **passive persons** lack self-respect and do not stand up for their own rights in a conflict. They will not, for example, speak up for themselves to defend their interests. **Aggressive persons**, at the opposite extreme, take their own rights seriously but ignore the rights of others. They speak up for themselves but frequently don't listen to or care about others. In contrast to both passive and aggressive persons, **assertive persons** respect their own rights as well as those of others. They speak up, but they also listen respectfully. Some people communicate passively, others communicate aggressively, and still others communicate assertively. Like the Owl, you should communicate assertively with others.

assertive communication
communication between and among disputing group members in which self-respect, together with respect for others, aids in conflict resolution

passive person
one who lacks sufficient self-respect to defend his or her rights in a dispute and who withdraws from conflict

aggressive person
one whose concern for personal rights outweighs concern for the rights of others

assertive person
one whose self-interest is balanced by concern for others, who speaks up yet also listens

RULES FOR MANAGING CONFLICT EFFECTIVELY

The respectful, assertive communication that we described in the previous section is the communication style of the confronting Owl, who represents the ideal approach to conflict resolution. The rules below are consistent with the Owl's approach. If you follow these rules, you will bring the wisdom of the Owl to bear on the conflicts that you help to resolve.

Rule #1: Be Assertive

Most conflict involves some degree of aggression. Hostile words, for example, are a form of aggression in which inner anger is outwardly expressed. It's quite natural for people in disputes to react emotionally with anger. Unfortunately, words spoken in anger tend to intensify the conflict rather than resolve it. Frequently, the parties in a conflict behave like Sharks. The key to resolving conflicts lies in more rational behaviour, the assertive behaviour of the Owl.

In any conflict, you should *know* your rights and the rights of the other party. In addition, you should *respect* your rights and those of the other person. If you communicate assertively and choose an appropriate time and place for confronting the other person, there is a good chance that the dispute can be resolved. Healthy conflict resolution is characterized by assertive communication. In conflict, then, you should be assertive, not aggressive and not passive.

Rule #2: Use the Best Sending Skills

Conflict resolution is possible only when assertive communication is effective. In chapter 5 we noted six rules for sending messages effectively. These rules of effective communication need to be followed in the process of managing conflicts. In conflict, as in all situations, you should

- Use first-person pronouns in your messages.
- Convey your frame of reference.
- Present your ideas clearly and concisely.
- Describe your feelings, not express them.
- Describe behaviours, not judge persons.
- Request and pay attention to feedback.

Rule #3: Use the Best Receiving Skills

Active listening is critical to the resolution of conflicts. Chapter 5 presented three rules for receiving messages effectively. These rules should be followed to resolve interpersonal conflicts respectfully. Speaking assertively, you should

- Communicate your intention to listen.
- Listen with your whole person.
- Paraphrase the ideas and feelings of the sender.

Active listening is essential to conflict resolution. In a heightened emotional state, it is easy to talk but not listen. Often, we don't want to hear what the other person has to say. The third rule for managing conflict effectively reminds you to use your best listening skills when communicating in a conflict situation.

Rule #4: Jointly Define the Conflict

Conflicts will never get resolved if the disputing parties don't agree on the nature of the problem. Conflict resolution is a special kind of problem solving, and the first step in solving any problem is to define it clearly, concisely, and accurately. "What, exactly, is our problem?" is the important question. The answer to that question must be clear and acceptable to both parties in a dispute. In other words, they must jointly define the problem. Together, those in conflict define the exact nature of the dispute. In addition to jointly defining their problem, they should define the problem as one which can be solved in a win–win way. Win–lose approaches should be avoided. In conflict, then, you should define the problem together with the person with whom you are in conflict.

Rule #5: Encourage Negotiation in Good Faith

The win–win approach can be strengthened if both parties indicate, sincerely and clearly, that they want to resolve the dispute. Expressed differently, they need to encourage negotiation in good faith. Negotiations will succeed only if there is mutual trust between the parties in dispute. It is essential, therefore, to build and maintain trust between them. This can be done in part by expressing the intention to find a mutually acceptable solution.

In addition, good-faith bargaining will be encouraged if both parties understand the *benefits* to each party of finding a solution, and the *costs* to each party of not finding one. Notice, here, that the compromising Fox stands ready to accept certain costs in resolving the dispute. The Fox will lose a bit to win a bit. In contrast, the confronting Owl strives to have only benefits and no costs *for both parties*. This expectation — both will be winners and neither will be a loser — is why the Owl represents the ideal in conflict resolution. In your conflicts, encourage negotiation in good faith by expressing your intention to bargain in good faith and by identifying the costs and benefits of not resolving the dispute.

Rule #6: Confront in Order To Reach an Agreement

Being assertive, speaking and listening effectively, jointly defining the problem, and negotiating in good faith are all typical of both the Fox and the Owl. We noted earlier that while the Fox's position can be described as a lose–lose approach, it can also be viewed more positively as a win–win approach. The Fox compromises to resolve a dispute, winning some but also losing some.

The approach of the confronting Owl, however, places the emphasis more clearly on win–win solutions. Confrontation — communicating openly, honestly, and assertively — is the ideal, and it takes a great deal of maturity to engage in constructive confrontation. When you and the others in your group confront your interpersonal problems with the win–win hope of the Owl, your team will be in a position to handle virtually any problem that comes along. When conflict is seen as a problem to be solved, parties who respect one another can usually agree to a mutually beneficial solution. You should confront, then, to reach an agreement that benefits everyone concerned, both the disputants and the other members of your team.

CHAPTER SUMMARY

In this chapter we have examined conflicts of interest and their resolution. We defined conflict as an interpersonal dispute and noted four common forms of conflict that are problematic and need resolution — resource conflict, power conflict, status conflict, and personality conflict. We then described a fifth type of conflict, conceptual conflict, that is desirable and to be encouraged within groups. Conceptual conflict is a healthy critiquing of ideas that avoids criticizing people. It is essential for bringing out the best ideas in a group. Next, we identified five conflict styles that people typically employ in their disputes with others. The Turtle, the Shark, the Teddy Bear, the Fox, and the Owl each place different emphasis, in a conflict, on the importance of achieving personal goals versus the maintaining of good relationships. We then proceeded to emphasize the importance of respect and assertive communication in the resolution of disputes. We concluded by examining six rules for managing conflicts effectively. Together, these rules emphasized the importance of assertive and clear communication, mutually defining the problem, encouraging trust in negotiations, and constructively confronting in order to reach agreement on a resolution of the dispute.

KEY TERMS

aggressive person   conflict

assertive communication   conflict style

assertive person   passive person

MASTERING THE MATERIAL

Now that you have read this chapter, use the following guides to ensure that you
have mastered the material.

1. Identify the social role from chapter 1 that is most relevant to the subject
    of this chapter.

2. Define *conflict*.

3. Identify and describe the four types of conflict that are potentially
    harmful to groups.

    a.

    b.

    c.

    d.

4. Explain what conceptual conflict is and why it's important.

5. Conceptual conflict is also called _____ conflict and
    constructive _____.

6. The five conflict styles are distinguished by the different values that they
    place on two aspects of group experience. Identify these two aspects.

    a.

    b.

7. From memory, name the five styles of conflict and the distinguishing behaviour associated with each style. Use the various animals to name each style.

   a.

   b.

   c.

   d.

   e.

8. The two forms of respect that underlie assertive communication are _____ and _____.

9. Describe the characteristics of a passive person.

10. Describe the characteristics of an aggressive person.

11. Describe the characteristics of an assertive person.

12. From memory, list the six rules for managing conflict effectively.

   a.

   b.

   c.

   d.

   e.

   f.

APPLYING THE IDEAS IN POLICING

Exercise 6.1

Imagine that you are a constable working in a large regional police service. Give three examples of *resource conflict* that might occur between members of the service.

1.

2.

3.

Exercise 6.2

Imagine that you are a constable working in a large regional police service. Give three examples of *power conflict* that might occur between members of the service.

1.

2.

3.

Exercise 6.3

Imagine that you are a constable working in a large regional police service. Give three examples of *status conflict* that might occur between members of the service. (Provide examples other than ones given in exercise 6.2.)

1.

2.

3.

Exercise 6.4

Imagine that you are a constable working in a large regional police service. Give three examples of *personality conflict* that might occur between members of the service. Provide examples in which this kind of conflict could be very detrimental to members of the service.

1.

2.

3.

Exercise 6.5

Conceptual conflict is very different from the other types of conflict described in the chapter. Imagine that you are a constable in a large regional police service. Give three examples in which *conceptual conflict* would be desirable and should, therefore, be encouraged.

1.

2.

3.

Exercise 6.6

Are there any situations in which an on-duty police officer should adopt the *withdrawing* approach of the Turtle? If you think so, give an example and briefly explain your reasoning. If you think not, explain your reasoning.

Exercise 6.7

Are there any situations in which an on-duty police officer should adopt the *forcing* approach of the Shark? If you think so, give an example and briefly explain your reasoning. If you think not, explain your reasoning.

Exercise 6.8

Are there any situations in which an on-duty police officer should adopt the *smoothing* approach of the Teddy Bear? If you think so, give an example and briefly explain your reasoning. If you think not, explain your reasoning.

Exercise 6.9

Are there any situations in which an on-duty police officer should adopt the *compromising* approach of the Fox? If you think so, give an example and briefly explain your reasoning. If you think not, explain your reasoning.

Exercise 6.10

Give three examples of situations in which an on-duty police officer should take the *confronting* approach of the Owl.

     1.

     2.

     3.

Exercise 6.11

Imagine that you are a probationary constable in a large metropolitan police service. Two of the third-class constables routinely belittle you in various ways. They seem to enjoy harassing you because you're a rookie. Write out three things that you might say to them to "get them off your back." Be assertive in your statements, not aggressive.

1.

2.

3.

Exercise 6.12

Imagine that you have had an ongoing conflict with a peer in your police service. Both of you recognize that something is wrong and that it needs to be fixed. You are both willing to make the effort to resolve the dispute. Using each of the *six rules for managing conflict effectively*, give a statement that you might make as you attempt to resolve the dispute between you and your colleague. Make sure that the statement observes the respective rule in each case. Do not give the rule.

Statement #1 (follows rule #1):

Statement #2 (follows rule #2):

Statement #3 (follows rule #3):

Statement #4 (follows rule #4):

Statement #5 (follows rule #5):

Statement #6 (follows rule #6):

PRACTISING YOUR GROUP SKILLS

Purpose of This Section

The purpose of "Practising Your Group Skills" and the ultimate purpose of this book is to help you become a more effective participant in the groups to which you belong. This section is designed to provide opportunities for you and your fellow students to practise your group skills in a structured environment.

Team Responsibilities

A description of the team responsibilities for each of five different teams — the Executive Team, the Teaching Team, the Lesson Review Team, the Energizer Team, and the Evaluation Team — can be found in appendix A, pages 207–210. Your professor may have chosen to use from one to five of these teams to conduct the teaching and learning activities of the class. Units 2 and 3 of the Teacher's Guide provide your professor with additional information on the responsibilities of these teams.

Individual Role Responsibilities

A description of four individual role responsibilities — those of Leader, Recorder, Reporter, and Participant-Analyst — can be found in appendix A, pages 210–212. Your professor may have chosen to use from one to four of these roles within teams to give individuals experience leading, recording, reporting, and analyzing. Units 2 and 3 of the Teacher's Guide provide your professor with additional information on these individual role responsibilities.

Specific Team Assignments

Specific team assignments for this chapter appear immediately below. Specific team assignments for each of the subsequent chapters can be found in "Practising Your Group Skills" in each chapter.

CHAPTER 6 TEAM ASSIGNMENTS

The Executive Team

- *Executive Goal:* to provide leadership to your classmates for your class session on chapter 6.

- *Executive Objectives:* to facilitate the class session by (1) ensuring a good classroom setup, (2) welcoming the class, (3) introducing the lesson topic, (4) coordinating activities, and (5) bringing the session to a close.

- *Instructions:* Ensure that the classroom is set up to accommodate the class activities. Post an agenda for the session. Welcome people to class and announce the topic, "Conflict: Resolving Disputes in Your Group," in a creative and interesting way. Remind the class that conflict in groups is normal but must be handled effectively if groups are to become strong teams. Introduce and thank all speakers when appropriate. Coordinate the day's activities and bring closure at the end of the class. If necessary, return the classroom to its original configuration.

The Teaching Team

- *Teaching Goal:* to understand and demonstrate effective conflict resolution skills in a small group setting.

- *Teaching Objectives:* to describe, explain, and demonstrate (1) five different conflict styles and (2) six effective practices (rules) for managing conflict in small groups.

- *Instructions:* As the Teaching Team, you have the freedom to choose how you will teach your lesson. You can be as creative as you wish, but you must achieve the teaching objectives. Your lesson consists of two parts. The first part is the experiential exercise, and the second part is your explanation of the chapter information.

  - ❑ Your experiential exercise is called "Conflict Styles" and you'll find it described fully in appendix B, pages 224–225. Make sure that you refer to "Conflict Styles" when you teach and explain the five conflict styles and the six rules for managing conflict.

  - ❑ If time allows, you can also use exercises from "Mastering the Material" and "Applying the Ideas in Policing" in your lesson.

The Lesson Review Team

- *Review Goal:* to review chapter 5, "Messages: Communicating Effectively in Your Group."

- *Review Objectives:* to provide a review of (1) the experiential exercise, (2) six rules for sending messages effectively, (3) three rules for active listening, and (4) four rules for giving constructive feedback.

- *Instructions:* As the Lesson Review Team, you have the freedom to choose how you will do the review. You can be as creative as you wish, but you must achieve the review objectives. Remember that your time is very limited, so don't try to re-teach last chapter's lesson.

The Energizer Team

- *Energizer Goal:* to motivate your classmates by conducting an energizer activity.

- *Energizer Objectives:* to facilitate the energizing of your classmates by (1) planning an energizer activity and (2) implementing the plan at an appropriate time in the class session.

- *Instructions:* Your team doesn't have a specific, assigned activity to conduct. Rather, the team should remember its energizing purpose and conduct an activity that will provide a break in the class learning routine. Popular games like Simon Says, Heads Up Seven Up, and Murder Wink usually work well. So do various mixers and ice breakers. (Your professor's Teacher's Guide identifies a number of sources of energizer exercises.) Whatever you decide on, you must be prepared to give clear instructions and conduct the exercise effectively. When you lead the energizer, you are leading and directing the entire class. Plan well and execute professionally, even if the exercise is a "kid's game." Encourage everyone to get involved.

The Evaluation Team

As a member of the Evaluation Team, you need to review the information in chapter 10, pages 191–194, before you do anything else. There you will find helpful information on how to conduct your evaluation session. The most important thing to remember is that you are not to judge other people. Your role is to help the class make its own assessment of which practices worked well today and which didn't.

Note that the evaluation goal below is keyed to the content of this chapter. *If desirable or necessary, you can evaluate any other aspect of group experience.* Be sure, though, that you set the goal, develop appropriate objectives, and plan the evaluation session to achieve the goal and the objectives.

- *Evaluation Goal:* to assess group (or class) members' conflict resolution skills.

- *Evaluation Objectives:* to (1) assess the different conflict styles and conflict resolution skills within the group (or class) and (2) identify practices in need of improvement.

- *Instructions:* Create an evaluation instrument based on the selected focus behaviours identified in the objectives. See chapter 10, pages 192–193, for information on creating evaluation instruments. Figure 10.1 provides an example. Solicit feedback from the class using the evaluation instrument. Use the feedback to discuss the class session with the purpose of identifying improvements that can be made to individual, group, and class performance in future class sessions. Conclude by noting the specific actions that need to be repeated or avoided to make improvements.

REFERENCES AND RECOMMENDED READINGS

Blake, R.R., & Mouton, J.S. (1985). *The managerial grid III.* Houston: Gulf.

Deutsch, M. (1973). *The resolution of conflict.* New Haven, CT: Yale University Press.

Ellis, D.G., & Fisher, A.B. (1994). *Small group decision making* (4th ed.). New York: McGraw-Hill.

Filley, A.C. (1988). *Interpersonal conflict resolution* (2nd ed.). Glenview, IL: Scott, Foresman.

Guetzkow, H., & Gyr, J. (1954). An analysis of conflict in decision-making groups. *Human Relations, 7,* 367–381.

Johnson, D.W., & Johnson, R. (1987). *Creative conflict.* Edina, MN: Interaction Book Company.

Johnson, D.W., & Johnson, R. (1997). *Joining together: Group therapy and group skills* (6th ed.). Needham Heights, MA: Allyn & Bacon.

Rubin, J., Pruitt, D., & Kim, S. (1994). *Social conflict.* New York: McGraw-Hill.

Thomas, K.W., & Kilmann, R.H. (1974). *Thomas–Kilmann Conflict MODE Instrument.* Tuxedo, NY: Xicom

Cohesion: Building Your Group into a Team

Chapter Objectives

After completing this chapter, you should be able to:

- Define the terms *cohesion*, *identity*, and *cooperation*.

- Identify and describe five stages of group development.

- Explain the nature of trust.

- Explain the nature of trustworthiness.

- State and explain six rules for creating a climate of trust in a group.

- Describe how groups can meet an individual's need for affiliation, influence, and respect.

INTRODUCTION

Policing is teamwork. Even in the smallest of police services, officers must combine their knowledge and skills in a cooperative effort to ensure that the community is properly served and protected. Throughout police services, officers work together on a daily basis to get the job done. In addition, police officers often work closely with members of the community to ensure the safety and security of citizens. In these situations, teamwork is also essential in serving the public.

In this chapter, we examine the stages involved in building a group into a team. Future police officers need to understand this process to maximize their potential for building strong and effective teams. The same knowledge and skills can also be applied in an officer's private life — for example, in community service or in family life. Let's begin with a closer look at teambuilding.

TEAMBUILDING

As we saw in chapter 1, **cohesion** is a group's sense of oneness or togetherness. Sometimes groups form and get the job done, but group members don't feel a sense

cohesion
a group's sense of oneness or togetherness

of oneness or togetherness with other members of the group. Perhaps members of the group are only minimally committed and complete their tasks with a minimum of cooperation. The job gets done, we might say, but the group really doesn't function like a team. To become a team, members must move beyond minimal commitment and cooperation. Members of a team stick together and they want to stick together. They share a common spirit, team spirit.

identity
a shared sense of belonging when group members feel they are part of a team, and the team is part of them

The cohesion of an effective team comes from its sense of **identity**, of belonging together. When individuals begin to identify with their group and the group becomes a part of the identity of each individual, the group's cohesion is enhanced; it becomes a team. All successful professional teams attempt to develop this sense of cohesion. For example, management will invest time, money, and energy into events designed to bring individuals together to mould them into a team. They want individuals to bond and have a sense of oneness that will result in maximum commitment to team goals and maximum cooperation to achieve those goals. The military and the police also invest in the development of cohesion and a common identity for their members.

For individuals entering the police service, several factors immediately contribute to a sense of identity with other officers. Perhaps most obvious is the uniform, which clearly identifies the person wearing it as a police officer. While this is important to the public, it is also a visible sign, to the officers themselves, of unity and identity. More subtle factors are also at work. One is the commitment to service through police work. Despite occasional "bad press," the great majority of police officers are people of integrity, and most officers identify with others who have made a similar commitment to police service. They are proud to wear the badge. Within their many collegial groups, however, police officers need more than a uniform and a badge to help build the group into a team.

cooperation
working with other team members to accomplish a task and also to achieve a mutual feeling of accomplishment

Teambuilding, the development of a sense of cohesion, is accomplished through the cooperative efforts of the individuals in a group. **Cooperation**, as you well know, means working together with others to achieve common goals. Each individual combines her energy with that of others to get the job done. This collaborative effort contributes to a sense of mutual accomplishment and naturally generates good feelings among the collaborators. In addition to accomplishing its tasks, the group develops a sense of oneness. On the very best teams, members not only respect one another, they also like one another.

However, cohesion can be achieved even when team members don't become good friends. It can develop out of a sense of mutual respect as opposed to a sense of personal attraction. In an ideal world, all members of a team would like one another. In reality, though, many successful and cohesive teams are built on mutual respect among members. When some teams are able to add friendship to respect, they enjoy a great bonus.

We should also note that sometimes cooperation can stem from fear. Group members who cooperate solely out of a fear of being fired, for example, do cooperate with their fellow workers to get jobs done. Cooperation will be far more enjoyable and cohesion will be far stronger, however, if they are motivated by positive factors like respect, personal attraction, and the pursuit of excellence.

How does a group become a team? In order to develop clear strategies for teambuilding, let's look next at the stages that groups typically go through as they develop.

STAGES OF GROUP DEVELOPMENT

Social scientists have studied the stages that groups go through from the time they form to the time that they disband. Different researchers have described the process in different ways. One of the simplest, yet most useful, summaries identifies five typical stages in the development of a group. Since groups are as diverse as their members, we shouldn't assume that this pattern will always be the same. When you are a member of a newly formed group, chances are that you will experience the following stages as your group develops.[1]

1. Forming

Stage 1 is the *Forming Stage*, and it is marked by great uncertainty within the group. Since the group has just formed, people don't know one another yet and they are often reluctant to say very much. This is a time for sizing up the other members of the group. Many members will be tentative and some will be downright anxious. More assertive members may take advantage of this situation and try to give direction to the group, but, for the most part, no one is very sure how things will develop.

2. Storming

After a period of time, the group is likely to enter the *Storming Stage*. During this stage, members begin to express themselves more readily and differences of opinion surface. Consequently, members get angry and upset with one another. It quickly becomes evident that different members have different expectations for the group. Emotions begin to storm. Feelings run high and disputes occur frequently. Often there is a jockeying for positions of leadership and influence as different members try to get others to do things their way. Usually an absence of clear norms — rules, roles, expectations — contributes to the upset that members feel. This is often a challenging and upsetting time for group members. It is a time of emotional storms that result from both greater openness in the group and an absence of rules.

3. Norming

Before long, members realize that storming isn't getting the job done, and that it is creating an unhealthy climate within the group. Eventually, cooler heads prevail, and members begin to state their expectations for the group. Rules of conduct are established formally or informally, and the group begins to stabilize as members conduct themselves according to newly established norms. As rules are established and common goals are set, the group is in a position to begin to work together to get team tasks accomplished. The *Norming Stage* is characterized by the establishment of rules and the clarification of expectations. These actions prepare the group for the next stage, the stage of productivity.

4. Performing

Stage 4, the *Performing Stage*, is characterized by productivity. The group gets down to work as cooperation replaces conflict, and members work together to

---

1   Stage theories in group studies are numerous. This section reflects the work of Tuckman (1965, pp. 384–389).

achieve common goals. With the successful achievement of goals, the group often experiences a greater sense of cohesion and identity. Both task goals and social goals are accomplished as group members perform effectively as a team.

5. Adjourning

Some groups have a long life span, while others do not. At some time, most groups disband. Stage 5 is the *Adjourning Stage*. The experience of team members at the end of a group's life depends very much on how the group performed. The members of ineffective groups that have struggled throughout with ongoing difficulties may greet adjournment with relief. Members of highly productive and cohesive teams may reach adjournment and experience sadness as well as accomplishment.

Bearing in mind that not all groups will necessarily go through these stages in the order presented, let's now proceed to examine the essential elements of teambuilding.

TRUST

All positive human relationships begin with trust, and without mutual trust no positive relationship with another person is possible. "Trust" is a common word in our vocabulary, but the details of its meaning are not always clear. We'll begin this section with a simple but important question, and we'll try to provide a clear answer to that question. Our question is: What is trust?

trust
the act of placing confidence in another person without full assurance that the confidence is well placed; entails mutual disclosure, sharing, and reliance

Trust is an act in which we place confidence in another person without knowing whether our confidence is well placed or not. In other words, trust is an act of faith. We can call it an act of faith, because trusting another comes with no guarantees. When you trust someone, you may be disappointed. You place your confidence in them, but they may let you down. If you are let down, you are likely to feel disappointed and betrayed and may be unwilling to trust your betrayer again. However, if you place your trust in someone who doesn't let you down, then your relationship with that person is strengthened, and you are more likely to trust again. Trust creates trust when both parties keep their part of the bargain. In policing, as in many other areas of life, you have to place a great deal of trust in others on a regular basis.

Trust always involves taking a risk. It means making yourself vulnerable to others who may let you down, humiliate you, manipulate you, exploit you, or judge you. Because of these potentially nasty outcomes, many people are reluctant to place their faith in others, particularly if they have been hurt in the past. When individuals join new groups, they are often inhibited from fully contributing because they don't know whether others in the group can be trusted or not. This is quite natural. Some, however, have the additional burden of having been let down repeatedly in the past and they have learned to mistrust others. The Cynic from chapter 1 may be just such a person.

So far we've described trust as an act of faith and a risk-taking activity. We need to get more specific now by noting three particular actions that are associated with trust: *disclosure*, *sharing*, and *reliance*. Let's look at each of these actions in turn.

First, trust involves *disclosure*. To disclose something is to reveal it or make it known to others, and disclosure is the act of revealing or making something known. If you share a secret with someone, for example, you disclose some aspect of your personal life with him. If you trust another person, you are likely to reveal your thoughts and feelings to that person. When you trust a good friend, for instance, you may disclose your innermost thoughts and feelings. In our group life, we are not likely to reveal our deepest secrets, but we will regularly disclose our thoughts and feelings about many different things. Each time we disclose ourselves, we take a risk. We hope that others won't ridicule our views, but there's no guarantee that they won't. The police officer who reveals his fear to fellow officers in a dangerous situation takes the risk that others will ridicule or scorn him. He trusts.

Second, trust involves *sharing*. Sharing, of course, means lending or giving our possessions or resources to others. You will, for example, lend your car to a dear friend but not to a stranger. You trust the friend. You don't trust the stranger. Sharing the things we have with others is a sign that we trust them. In work groups, we often share resources with other members and usually there isn't a problem. It's the thing you do when you trust others.

Third, trust involves *reliance*. To rely on someone is to have confidence in them or depend upon them. For example, if you do a major school project with a classmate who promises to type, proof read, and submit the final draft by a certain date and time, you rely on her to do it. Another word for reliance is confidence, and in our example you place confidence in your classmate. Notice once again, relying on your colleague comes with no guarantees. She may or may not be worthy of your trust. If she keeps her promise, she has proved worthy of your trust. If she doesn't keep her promise, then she has proved unworthy of the confidence that you placed in her.

TRUSTWORTHINESS

Experience shows us that many, if not most, people can be relied upon. They keep their promises, return borrowed items, and do what they say they will. We use the word **trustworthy** to describe those people in whom we can confidently place our trust. Trustworthy people are reliable people, people who will not let us down. You can count on them and they won't disappoint you. Police officers, for example, who possess honesty and integrity are officers who are trusted implicitly by their colleagues. They are trustworthy. They are the kinds of people that you want to have around you in all circumstances.

trustworthiness
a quality that inspires the confident placement of trust; reliability

When all members of a group are trustworthy, everyone can take risks with little fear of being let down. All members can participate confidently in the group and the whole team benefits. Disclosure, sharing, and reliance become a way of life for the team, and it can do its work with confidence. All successful teams are built by trusting and trustworthy members. This is true of a police SWAT team as well as a police baseball team. Although the dangers are much higher for the SWAT team than for the baseball team, the group dynamics are essentially the same in both cases.

CREATING A CLIMATE OF TRUST

Effective teams foster a positive, supportive climate in which members can thrive, as the group accomplishes its various tasks and develops a sense of cohesion. In this section, you will find six rules for developing a positive group climate, a climate of trust.[2] If you and the other members of your group follow these rules, your team will create and enjoy a supportive climate in which trust and trustworthiness result in both increased productivity and an enhanced sense of cohesion.

Rule #1: Be Empathetic, Not Neutral

The emotional basis of all moral or ethical behaviour is *empathy*. In chapter 5, we defined empathy as feeling what another person feels. Empathy involves identifying emotionally with another person. The person who goes to the aid of someone in trouble, for example, identifies with the person in distress. The psychopath, in contrast, has no empathy. He is emotionally neutral and, consequently, does terrible things to others without feeling any remorse. Thankfully, most people have some degree of empathy and therefore do not deliberately hurt people or treat them as though they were objects. Most people are not emotionally neutral. They are empathetic and are able to identify with others.

This first rule for building a climate of trust encourages you and the others in your group to empathize with one another. It urges you to see things from the other person's point of view. It encourages you to get into the "emotional shoes" of your teammates so that you understand them better. The absence of empathy will contribute to a negative climate that will prove detrimental to your group. If you want to help build your group into a supportive team by creating a climate of trust, then be empathetic, not neutral.

Rule #2: Relate to Others as Equals, Not Inferiors

Respect is the cognitive and behavioural analogue to the emotion of empathy. In other words, while empathy is a matter of feelings, respect is a matter of attitude and behaviour. If you have the attitude that you are superior to others in your group, for example, then you are very likely to treat them as inferiors. Such an attitude and behaviour will, no doubt, provoke resentment and anger from others. People generally know when they are being treated as inferiors and they don't like it. All of this will, obviously, contribute to a negative climate within your group.

In contrast, if you feel that others are equals, you are likely to treat them as such. Rule #2 reminds us to treat others in our group with respect. It reminds us to relate to them as equals and not as inferiors. When we give respect, we usually get respect in return. Mutual respect among members of a group contributes enormously to the creation of a climate of trust.

At this point, it is important to note carefully what is *not* being said in this rule. In a very real sense, people are not all equals. When it comes to public speaking, for example, one person on your team may be superior to everyone else. So, too, with many other skills, we find a very real inequality among people. Rule #2 does not mean to say that there shouldn't be or that there are no differences among people with respect to knowledge and skill. And it doesn't say that we shouldn't honour those who have superior skills and knowledge. What it is saying is that any superior knowledge and skill that we possess does not make us *morally* superior persons. Our talents do not give us licence to treat others as inferiors. Despite any superior talents that you may have, you should relate to others as equals and not as inferiors.

---

2   The six rules presented in this section are based on the influential work of Gibb (1961, pp. 142–148), who examined behaviours that contribute to defensive and supportive climates within a group.

As mentioned previously, mutual respect, grounded in equality, contributes to the development of a climate of trust. The principle of equality, you will recall, was discussed in chapter 3 along with the other basic ethical principles of goodness, justice, truth, and freedom.

Rule #3: Be Cooperative, Not Competitive

In chapter 4, we discussed the importance of setting clear goals for your group. Among the things that we emphasized at that time was the importance of establishing cooperative goal structures and avoiding, for the most part, competitive and individualistic structures. Rule #3 requires that you cooperate with others in your group rather than competing with them. It encourages you to be an Owl, not a Shark.

As we saw in our examination of conflict, if you and your teammates approach challenges as problems to be solved in a win–win fashion, then you will contribute to the creation of a supportive climate within your group. You will foster a climate of trust, not suspicion. In contrast, when people approach their problems in a win–lose manner, then individuals become suspicious of one another and mistrust develops.

Effective groups emphasize cooperation among members rather than competition. By identifying problems together, mutually developing a range of solutions, reaching consensus on a course of action, and cooperatively implementing the chosen solution, your team will be able to tackle virtually any challenge successfully. You will enjoy the benefits of working in a supportive climate of trust.

Rule #4: Be Genuine, Not Manipulative

Sometimes individuals come to their groups with hidden agendas. An agenda is, of course, a schedule of items to be discussed by a group. Hidden agendas refer to things that members want to accomplish but in a secretive, dishonest, and manipulative manner. John, for example, says that he wants Mary to serve as leader, but he secretly wants Susan to become chair. His speech and behaviour are designed to get the group to think one way, when, in fact, John wants things to go a very different way. He is trying to manipulate the group to achieve the objectives of his hidden agenda.

Those members who have hidden agendas are dishonest. They lack integrity in that they are practising deception, and they illustrate how some people will attempt to manipulate groups to achieve their personal ends. It is not uncommon for others to catch on to what's happening. Needless to say, they can get very angry with those who are trying to use them or dupe them. Members who engage in manipulative behaviour undermine the trust that others have placed in them. Rule #4 is based on the principle that honesty and integrity build trust, while manipulative dishonesty destroys it. The rule urges you to be genuine and to refrain from dishonesty and manipulation. Truth telling and honesty are essential to building trust in your group, just as they are essential to building trust in any relationship.

Rule #5: Be Open, Not Closed, to New Ideas

Groups can very easily become closed to new ideas, especially if the group has been in existence for some time. "We've always done it this way" is a statement that is all too commonly heard in groups. It's a statement designed to shut down further discussion and new ideas. Whether motivated by laziness, the desire to control others, or the fear of new ideas, some group members are very closed to new ways of thinking and new ways of doing things.

As a group member, you may hold strong views about some issue that your group has to deal with. In your meetings, however, it is important for you to hear all points of view. It is important to remain open to the ideas of others. Perhaps others have also given thought to the issue, and they may have some useful ideas to share. If you are closed to their ideas, they may well close their minds to your ideas. Obviously, this creates a closed environment that can only work against the best interests of the group. The members of effective groups remain open to new and better ideas, regardless of their origin. This is the approach of all great thinkers and problem solvers. A positive climate within a group allows for honest and open sharing of all ideas with a view to finding the best solution to the group's problems. If you want your group to develop a climate of trust, then be open, not closed, to new ideas.

Rule #6: Be Supportive, Not Judgmental

One of the most difficult things to do in a group is to criticize ideas that you feel are weak. Much of the difficulty seems to lie in the fact that many people take the criticism of their ideas very personally. They seem unable to separate themselves from their ideas. You find it difficult to criticize their ideas, then, because you fear that it's going to cause a blow up. You fear that they'll take it personally.

For example, if I present an idea and someone points out its weaknesses, I may take it personally and see the criticism as an attack on me. I will likely react defensively, thus contributing to a negative climate. When you criticize the ideas of others, you should make it clear that you support the person but are critical of the idea. You might say, for example, "Tom, I'm not criticizing you personally, but I think that your suggestion won't work. Here's why." In words like these, you are expressing support for Tom and avoiding personal judgments.

In cases where we feel that someone's behaviour is inappropriate, we should describe their *actions* without imputing a motive. We've made this same point before, both in our study of communication in chapter 5 and our study of conflict resolution in chapter 6. We'll make the same point again in chapter 8 where we look at critical discussion. A non-judgmental approach within your group will do much to create a supportive climate. People will feel free to offer their views without fear of personal attack. If you want to contribute to the creation of a climate of trust in your group, then be supportive, not judgmental.

If you are empathetic, cooperative, honest, open, and non-judgmental, and respect others as equals, then you and the members of your group will be a powerful force for creating a climate of trust in which your group can become a team. When this occurs, your team is likely to achieve both its task goals and its social goals. It will be both productive and cohesive.

AFFILIATION, INFLUENCE, AND RESPECT

When teams create a climate of trust among their members, they allow individual members to satisfy three very important social needs. These needs are *affiliation*, *influence*, and *respect*.[3]

---

3 Schutz (1958) discussed group members' needs for inclusion, control, and affection. In this section, the focus is on the very similar concepts of affiliation, influence, and respect.

1. Affiliation

Most people have a need to belong to a group or groups. We are born into a group, the family, and we continue to live and work in groups throughout our lives. The need to associate with others is called **affiliation**. Membership in a group — be it a sports team, a social club, or a street gang — is often a source of pride and, in many instances, contributes to our sense of identity. The group becomes, in effect, a real part of who we are.

affiliation
a sense of association, connection, or identity with others

If you and the members of your group create the kind of supportive climate that we have discussed in this chapter, you will establish a social environment in which individuals can satisfy, at least in part, their need for affiliation. Individuals will enjoy being a part of the team and they will take pride in the team and its accomplishments.

2. Influence

Influence is the ability to affect circumstances and people. It is a form of power. Most of us feel good when we are successful at favourably affecting events around us. In groups, we respond positively when we see that we have influence on group outcomes, that our input makes a difference. However, if one or two others make all the decisions and ignore our views, then we feel impotent and may get discouraged or even resentful. Why belong to a group if you don't make a difference, if you don't really count?

influence
the ability to affect circumstances and people

If your team encourages everyone to contribute, takes everyone's views seriously, and allows all members to influence the actions of the team, then your members can satisfy their need to have influence. A supportive climate of trust empowers all members. Everyone will have the sense that they count, that they do have influence within the group. Members who have these kinds of feelings are members who will redouble their efforts on future tasks.

3. Respect

To **respect** someone means to hold that person in honour or esteem. One of the highest forms of respect that we can experience in life is to be honoured by our peers. When we are accepted as an equal within a group, we feel welcome. If, in contrast, we sense that others view us as inferiors and are disrespectful of us, then we will not want to associate with them. To respect others within your group is one of the best ways of involving them and gaining their commitment to the team.

respect
honour and esteem, particularly among peers

And, for you to enjoy the respect of others is, naturally, a tremendous feeling. When others show you that they respect you and the contributions that you make to the team, then you are likely to increase your involvement and commitment. The police officer who works to ensure that all members of the team feel that they belong (affiliation), that they have a contribution to make (influence), and that they are equals on the team (respect) will be an officer who, in turn, gains the respect of others.

CHAPTER SUMMARY

In this chapter, we first described the close connection between cohesion — the sense of togetherness on a team — and the concepts of identity and cooperation.

We then described five stages of development that groups typically go through. Members experience uncertainty in the forming stage, they vent feelings in the storming stage, they adopt rules for themselves in the norming stage, they become productive in the performing stage, and they eventually disperse in the adjourning stage. Next, we examined trust and trustworthiness, the bases for all healthy relationships and the fundamental ingredients in building a team. Then, we provided six rules for developing and maintaining a climate of trust within a group. These rules emphasized the importance of empathy, equality, cooperation, integrity, openness, and support. Finally, we noted how effective groups contribute to the satisfaction of the social needs of individual members by creating opportunities for experiencing affiliation, influence, and respect.

KEY TERMS

affiliation   influence

cohesion   respect

cooperation   trust

identity   trustworthiness

MASTERING THE MATERIAL

Now that you have read this chapter, use the following guides to ensure that you have mastered the material.

1. Define *cohesion.*

2. Define *identity.*

3. Define *cooperation.*

4. Cohesion occurs when group members have a sense of _____ and work together in a spirit of _____.

5. Briefly describe the five stages of group development.

    Stage 1: Forming

    Stage 2: Storming

    Stage 3: Norming

    Stage 4: Performing

    Stage 5: Adjourning

6. What is trust?

7. Identify the three actions that are associated with trust.

    a.

    b.

    c.

8. What is trustworthiness?

9. List, from memory, the six rules for creating a supportive climate in a group.

   Rule #1:

   Rule #2:

   Rule #3:

   Rule #4:

   Rule #5:

   Rule #6:

10. Identify and explain the three basic social needs that effective groups satisfy.

   a.

   b.

   c.

11. What is the word for the togetherness that occurs when police officers on a work team have a strong sense of identity with the team and also participate cooperatively in achieving the team's goals and objectives?

APPLYING THE IDEAS IN POLICING

Exercise 7.1

List three material (physical) things that police officers have in common in their work lives that contribute to their *sense of identity* as members of the policing team. (Give examples that were not mentioned in the text.)

   1.

   2.

   3.

Exercise 7.2

Identify three non-material (psychological) things that police officers have in common in their work lives that contribute to their *sense of identity* as members of the policing team. (Give examples not mentioned in the text.)

   1.

2.

3.

Exercise 7.3

Give three examples of important situations in policing where officers have to cooperate to get the job done.

1.

2.

3.

Exercise 7.4

Imagine that you have been assigned to a new team that is responsible for investigating a series of crimes that appear to be biker- and Mafia-related. This new team will work under the direction of a sergeant, but the nature of the work is such that there will be much interaction among teammates and much individual contribution as the group proceeds with its task. Show your understanding of the stages of group development by giving examples of statements or actions that might be expected in each of the five stages. Do not describe the stage.

Stage 1: Forming

Stage 2: Storming

Stage 3: Norming

Stage 4: Performing

Stage 5: Adjourning

Exercise 7.5

"Trust is an act of faith that has no guarantees." List six examples from a police officer's work life when an officer must trust fellow officers to get the job done. Give three examples of dangerous situations, and three examples in which there would be no immediate danger to the officer.

    1.

    2.

    3.

    4.

5.

6.

Exercise 7.6

Imagine that you are a police constable. List six things that you could do while on duty to ensure that others would respect you as a trustworthy person and colleague.

1.

2.

3.

4.

5.

6.

Exercise 7.7

Imagine that you are a member of a newly formed group of officers that has been given a special assignment over the next several months. For each of the six rules for creating a supportive climate within a group, write a statement or question that you could say or ask within the group during its initial stages of development to begin to build a supportive climate within the group. In each case, show that you understand the rule, but do not write the rule.

Rule #1:

Rule #2:

Rule #3:

Rule #4:

Rule #5:

Rule #6:

Exercise 7.8

Imagine that you are a first-class constable in a large police service. Several probationary constables will be working with you in various groups over the next few months. List three things that you could do or say to help these rookies meet their need for *affiliation*.

1.

2.

3.

Exercise 7.9

Imagine that you are a police service representative on a citizens' committee attempting to improve relations between the police and community members. The members of this ethnic community generally see police officers as authority figures whom they must obey. List three things that you could say or do to help others on the committee meet their need for *influence*. In other words, how could you help to empower them?

1.

2.

3.

Exercise 7.10

Imagine that you are a probationary constable in a police service. List three things that you would want your more senior colleagues to do or say that would indicate to you that they genuinely respect you. How, in other words, would you want others to help meet your need for *respect* within your group?

1.

2.

3.

PRACTISING YOUR GROUP SKILLS

Purpose of This Section

The purpose of "Practising Your Group Skills" and the ultimate purpose of this book is to help you become a more effective participant in the groups to which you belong. This section is designed to provide opportunities for you and your fellow students to practise your group skills in a structured environment.

Team Responsibilities

A description of the team responsibilities for each of five different teams — the Executive Team, the Teaching Team, the Lesson Review Team, the Energizer Team, and the Evaluation Team — can be found in appendix A, pages 207–210. Your professor may have chosen to use from one to five of these teams to conduct the teaching and learning activities of your class. Units 2 and 3 of the Teacher's Guide provide your professor with additional information on the responsibilities of these teams.

Individual Role Responsibilities

A description of four individual role responsibilities — those of Leader, Recorder, Reporter, and Participant-Analyst — can be found in appendix A, pages 210–212. Your professor may have chosen to use from one to four of these roles within teams to give individuals experience leading, recording, reporting, and analyzing. Units 2 and 3 of the Teacher's Guide provide your professor with additional information on these individual role responsibilities.

Specific Team Assignments

Specific team assignments for this chapter appear immediately below. Specific team assignments for each of the subsequent chapters can be found in "Practising Your Group Skills" in each chapter.

CHAPTER 7 TEAM ASSIGNMENTS

The Executive Team

- *Executive Goal:* to provide leadership to your classmates for your class session on chapter 7.

- *Executive Objectives:* to facilitate the class session by (1) ensuring a good classroom setup, (2) welcoming the class, (3) introducing the lesson topic, (4) coordinating activities, and (5) bringing the session to a close.

- *Instructions:* Ensure that the classroom is set up to accommodate the class activities. Post an agenda for the session. Welcome people to class and announce the topic, "Cohesion: Building Your Group into a Team," in a creative and interesting way. Remind the class that cohesion is a group's sense of togetherness or oneness, and that the topic includes instructions on how to create a climate of trust within groups. Introduce and thank all speakers when appropriate. Coordinate the day's activities and bring closure at the end of the class. If necessary, return the classroom to its original configuration.

The Teaching Team

- *Teaching Goal:* to understand and demonstrate effective team building skills in a small group setting.

- *Teaching Objectives:* to describe, explain, and demonstrate (1) cohesion, trust, and trustworthiness, (2) six effective practices (rules) for creating a climate of trust, and (3) the importance of affiliation, influence, and respect.

- *Instructions:* As the Teaching Team, you have the freedom to choose how you will teach your lesson. You can be as creative as you wish, but you must achieve the teaching objectives. Your lesson consists of two parts. The first part is the experiential exercise, and the second part is your explanation of the chapter information.

  - ❑ Your experiential exercise is called "Cohesion and Cooperation" and you'll find it described fully in appendix B, pages 225–226. Make sure that you refer to "Cohesion and Cooperation" when you teach and explain cohesion, trust, trustworthiness, the rules for creating a climate of trust, and the importance of affiliation, influence, and respect.

  - ❑ If time allows, you can also use exercises from "Mastering the Material" and "Applying the Ideas in Policing" in your lesson.

The Lesson Review Team

- *Review Goal:* to review chapter 6, "Conflict: Resolving Disputes in Your Group."

- *Review Objectives:* to provide a review of (1) the experiential exercise, (2) the five different conflict styles, and (3) the six effective practices (rules) that help to resolve conflicts in small groups.

- *Instructions:* As the Lesson Review Team, you have the freedom to choose how you will do the review. You can be as creative as you wish, but you must achieve the review objectives. Remember that your time is very limited, so don't try to re-teach last chapter's lesson.

The Energizer Team

- *Energizer Goal:* to motivate your classmates by conducting an energizer activity.

- *Energizer Objectives:* to facilitate the energizing of your classmates by (1) planning an energizer activity and (2) implementing the plan at an appropriate time in the class session.

- *Instructions:* Your team doesn't have a specific, assigned activity to conduct. Rather, the team should remember its energizing purpose and conduct an activity that will provide a break in the class learning routine. Popular games like Simon Says, Heads Up Seven Up, and Murder Wink usually work well. So do various mixers and ice breakers. (Your professor's Teacher's Guide identifies a number of sources of energizer exercises.) Whatever you decide on, you must be prepared to give clear instructions and conduct the exercise effectively. When you lead the energizer, you are leading and directing the entire class. Plan well and execute professionally, even if the exercise is a "kid's game." Encourage everyone to get involved.

The Evaluation Team

As a member of the Evaluation Team, you need to review the information in chapter 10, pages 191–194, before you do anything else. There you will find helpful information on how to conduct your evaluation session. The most important thing to remember is that you are not to judge other people. Your role is to help the class make its own assessment of which practices worked well today and which didn't.

Note that the evaluation goal below is keyed to the content of this chapter. *If desirable or necessary, you can evaluate any other aspect of group experience.* Be sure, though, that you set the goal, develop appropriate objectives, and plan the evaluation session to achieve the goal and the objectives.

- *Evaluation Goal:* to assess group (or class) members' team building skills.

- *Evaluation Objectives:* to (1) assess the levels of disclosure, sharing, and reliance within the group (or class) and (2) identify practices in need of improvement.

- *Instructions:* Create an evaluation instrument based on the selected focus behaviours identified in the objectives. See chapter 10, pages 192–193, for information on creating evaluation instruments. Figure 10.1 provides an example. Solicit feedback from the class using the evaluation instrument. Use the feedback to discuss the class session with the purpose of identifying improvements that can be made to individual, group, and class performance in future class sessions. Conclude by noting the specific actions that need to be repeated or avoided to make improvements.

REFERENCES AND RECOMMENDED READINGS

Deutsch, M. (1958). Trust and suspicion. *Journal of Conflict Resolution, 2.*

Deutsch, M. (1962). Cooperation and trust: Some theoretical notes. In M.R. Jones (Ed.), *Nebraska symposium on motivation.* Lincoln, NB: University of Nebraska Press.

Eadie, W.F. (1982). Defensive communication revisited: A critical examination of Gibb's theory. *Southern Speech Communication Journal, 47,* 163–177.

Fisher, R., & Ury, W. (1981). *Getting to yes: Negotiating agreement without giving in.* Boston: Houghton Mifflin.

Gibb, J.R. (1961). Defensive communication. *Journal of Communication, 11,* 142–148.

Robbins, S.P. (1994). *Supervision today.* Englewood Cliffs, NJ: Prentice Hall.

Schutz, W.C. (1958). *FIRO: A three-dimensional theory of interpersonal behavior.* New York: Holt, Rinehart & Winston.

Tuckman, B. (1965). Developmental sequence in small groups. *Psychological Bulletin, 63,* 384–399.

Walton, R. (1987). *Managing conflict.* Reading, MA: Addison-Wesley.

Wilmot, W.W., & Hocker, J.L. (1998). *Interpersonal conflict.* Boston: McGraw-Hill.

CHAPTER 8

Critical Discussion: Generating Ideas in Your Group

Chapter Objectives

After completing this chapter, you should be able to:

- Describe and explain critical discussion.

- Define *conceptual conflict*.

- Explain the difference between conceptual conflict and interpersonal conflict.

- Explain the concept of groupthink.

- Describe four factors that contribute to groupthink.

- Identify and explain three illusions associated with groupthink.

- Identify and explain the six steps of the process of critical discussion.

- Identify two benefits of critical discussion.

- State and explain eight rules for critical discussion.

INTRODUCTION

Policing has often been described as a paramilitary field, functioning in many ways like an army. There is a well-defined hierarchy of ranks, with each level of the system responding to directions from the level immediately above. Constables take their direction from sergeants who, in turn, take their direction from staff sergeants, and so on up the line to the highest authority, the chief. In many ways, policing is carried out autocratically. In chapter 2 we looked briefly at the autocratic approach to leadership. We noted that there are many situations in which autocratic leadership is appropriate. Many aspects of policing have to be managed autocratically, and that is why there is a clear chain of command. Someone has to give orders, and others have to follow them.

Even within autocratic organizations, however, there is plenty of room for democratic processes. In fact, it can be argued that any police service operating within a democratic society today will fail if it tries to function in an *entirely* autocratic way. Canadian society is based on democracy; people are used to having their say on important issues, in the public arena and in the workplace. Many organizations actively encourage the sharing of ideas among employees, recognizing that there are many benefits to be had from this open, democratic approach.

The subject of this chapter, critical discussion, applies to the many aspects of policing that require a democratic approach to groups and teams. For example, when sergeants meet with their peers to conduct business, they will engage in a democratic give-and-take. This is both natural and necessary; a sergeant who feels superior to his or her peers and tries to boss them around in an autocratic manner is highly likely to fail in the attempt. At all levels of the organization where there is more than one person of the same rank, democratic processes, including discussion, will be the norm.

Sometimes before making a decision, a senior officer requests feedback on a proposed course of action from those lower down the ranks. The senior officer will make the decision, but only after consultation. When senior officers invite feedback, they are opening up a genuine, albeit limited, democratic process. In such situations, within a generally autocratic organization, democratic approaches are both necessary and healthy.

In the broader community, police officers may be called upon to work with citizens' groups in settings where democratic discussion is expected. Citizens usually will not want their police representatives to act autocratically. If we add the many other situations in their personal lives when officers work with other citizens, we can appreciate the necessity for exploring the best ways to generate critical discussion.

Because police officers often function with their peers and the public on a democratic basis, they need to know as much as possible about making good decisions, and solving problems, within a group. Critical discussion is an important means to help a group do this. Decision making and problem solving (the subjects of chapter 9) require that group members share and implement their best ideas, and critical discussion is vital to this process.

CRITICAL DISCUSSION

critical discussion
a six-step process designed to encourage group members to engage in conceptual conflict

Critical discussion is a six-step process designed to encourage group members to engage in conceptual conflict on any particular issue that the group has to deal with. We will present the six-step process later in this chapter, but first we need to review and clarify what we mean by conceptual conflict.

In chapter 6, we discussed several forms of conflict. In particular, we described resource conflicts, power conflicts, status conflicts, and personality conflicts. Each of these forms of conflict, we emphasized, requires resolution. They need to be eliminated. We then went on to describe conceptual conflict, a form of conflict that should be encouraged within your group. **Conceptual conflict** refers to a disagreement or controversy about ideas, opinions, or points of view. This form of conflict is also called ideational conflict because of its focus on ideas, not people. When groups don't understand the nature of conceptual conflict and its importance, it can quickly degenerate into an undesirable personality conflict.

conceptual conflict
a disagreement or controversy about ideas or points of view

Conceptual conflict, as noted above, is desirable, and the reason for this is simple. When there is disagreement over ideas, your group is more likely to arrive at a good solution to a problem because it has considered a variety of ideas. Critical discussion is the process whereby your group can ensure that any decisions that it makes will be well thought out, using the best ideas that the group has to offer.

Unfortunately, some group members find it difficult to distinguish between a criticism of their ideas and a personal attack on them. This often causes conceptual conflict to degenerate into interpersonal conflict. It is strange that people associate their ideas so closely with their persons, since very few human beings have truly original ideas. Ideas are, for the most part, the common property of humanity. Those who have difficulty distinguishing between criticism and personal attack may have large egos or they may be insecure. Either way, conceptual conflict will suffer as a result.

In this chapter, we will examine the process of critical discussion with its emphasis on conceptual conflict. Our hope is that a clear understanding of this process will help you to engage in debates without taking criticism of your ideas as a personal affront. We will also discuss ways that you can be critical of other people's ideas while still supporting them as teammates and as persons. In order to see how important critical discussion is for you and your group, let's start by examining its opposite, groupthink. After we have done that, we will detail the six steps of the critical discussion process.

GROUPTHINK

Groupthink is a word coined to describe uncritical thinking within a group.[1] Groupthink can and does occur in groups of all kinds, and most often it is associated with poor decisions. For example, groupthink is often cited in the ill-fated, attempted invasion of Cuba at the Bay of Pigs in 1961. President John Kennedy of the United States, his brother Robert, and several close advisers agreed to support anti-Castro exiles in their attack against Cuba in the hope of removing the communist dictator Fidel Castro. Their discussion of the planned invasion apparently lacked critical analysis. It was assumed that the assault would be quick and effective; the results, however, were disastrous. The invading force was destroyed by Cuban forces in short order. How could such high-powered leaders fail so miserably? The likely answer is to be found in groupthink. Research into this case and others indicates that there are a number of factors that contribute to groupthink.

One factor is the presence of a *strong leader* whose views are firmly held and well known to group members. John Kennedy was just such a leader. His views were well known and, apparently in this situation, they were subject to little or no criticism. The essence of groupthink is an absence of critical discussion and conceptual conflict about the issue in question. Had someone challenged the president's assumption that the invasion would easily succeed, a different decision might have been reached. If your group has a strong leader with firmly held views that are known to your group, be on watch for groupthink.

groupthink
uncritical thinking within a group

---

1   Janis (1972, 1982) pioneered the study of uncritical thinking and decision making in small groups. Some of Janis's important ideas are included in this section.

A second factor is the presence of a *high level of cohesion* within the group. If a group is very cohesive, groupthink is much more likely to occur than if the group lacks cohesion. John Kennedy and his team members were a very cohesive group. When a group has this strong sense of identity and togetherness and also has a strong leader promoting a particular course of action, the group's cohesion tends to inhibit criticism. The group fails to engage in critical discussion and conceptual conflict, and poor decisions result. In chapter 7, we emphasized the importance of developing cohesion in your group. Here, we see the importance of ensuring that the cohesion within your group does not eliminate conceptual conflict.

A third factor is the *absence of procedural norms* within the group. Procedural norms are rules that require a group to proceed in certain ways. They are a group's rules of operation. If a group has rules that require it to give criticism of proposed ideas and courses of action, then critical analysis is a norm of group life. In contrast, a group that has no such procedural norm is less likely to engage in critical discussion. Perhaps John Kennedy's team had no rules requiring members to think about and discuss matters critically. Effective groups avoid groupthink partly by establishing rules that require critical discussion and conceptual conflict. To avoid groupthink, make sure that your group establishes norms that require critical thinking and critical discussion.

A fourth factor is *group isolation* from critics outside the group. Effective groups often invite outsiders to critique proposed courses of action, especially if the decision to be made is very important. Because the outsiders don't share the group's perspective on the issue, they can offer criticism from a different point of view. This different perspective can often identify drawbacks of the proposed course of action. In the case of John Kennedy and his group, their isolation from outside critics may well have contributed to their disastrous decision. If your group has to make a really important decision, invite outsiders to critique your proposed action. Don't isolate yourselves from outside critics.

In summary, four factors contribute to the uncritical thinking that we call groupthink: the presence of a strong leader, a high level of cohesion, an absence of rules requiring critical discussion, and the isolation of a group from outside criticism. You will do well to ensure that your group is familiar with these factors and avoids the pitfalls of groupthink.

Experiencing Groupthink

Researchers have studied groupthink with the hope of finding out what members experience as the group proceeds uncritically into disastrous circumstances. They have discovered that a number of misconceptions are prevalent when groups experience groupthink. The researchers call these misconceptions illusions. An illusion, of course, is a false perception or interpretation of an event. Successful illusionists on stage make us think that one thing is happening when, in fact, something quite different is taking place. What misconceptions are typical of people experiencing groupthink? We'll mention three such misconceptions or, as they're called, illusions of groupthink.

The first misconception is the **illusion of oneness**. In this illusion, individuals who have doubts or criticisms keep the doubts and criticisms to themselves. They keep silent because they believe, mistakenly, that nobody else has any doubts. In other words, they mistakenly believe that everyone else is in agreement with the

illusion of oneness
the mistaken belief that everyone is in agreement on an issue

proposed plan. They perceive a oneness or unity where, in fact, there isn't any. Because they are under the illusion of oneness, they proceed to censor their own criticisms. They keep quiet, thereby adding to the illusion of oneness. Self-censorship is a very important factor in this particular illusion.

The second misconception is the **illusion of invulnerability**. To feel invulnerable is to feel unbeatable and groups experiencing groupthink feel that they cannot fail, that they are unbeatable. In our example, the president of the most powerful nation in the world and his advisers apparently felt that they were unbeatable, that they just couldn't lose. Unfortunately for them and their troops, they were labouring under a misconception. They felt that Fidel Castro's military posed no threat to the US invasion force. Their belief in their own invulnerability was undoubtedly mistaken.

The third misconception is the **illusion of moral superiority**. This misconception is closely related to the illusion of invulnerability that we just described. In this third illusion, the group believes that it is morally superior to their opponents or competitors. They suffer from the illusion of moral superiority believing that they are better persons than their opponents. They believe that they are the good guys and that their enemies are the bad guys. In the case of the Bay of Pigs invasion, the presidential team may have believed that they, as god-fearing Americans, were morally superior to the godless, communist Fidel Castro. They probably thought they had right on their side because they planned the removal of a godless, communist dictator. In this case, their "rightness" was as illusory as their might was.

When uncritical thinking takes over in a group, then its members are likely to feel they are all of one mind, that they simply cannot fail, and that they are better people than their adversaries. To avoid groupthink on your team, do your best to ensure that critical discussion always takes place whenever your group deals with an issue of any importance.

illusion of invulnerability
the mistaken belief that one's team cannot fail

illusion of moral superiority
the belief that one's team is on the side of right

Groupthink and Policing

Is it possible for a group of police officers to engage in groupthink and experience its illusions? Imagine, for a moment, a special team assigned to carry out a raid on the headquarters of a biker gang. If the team has charted a course of action or has been ordered to proceed in a particular way, some or all of the officers may fall prey to self-censorship. They may refrain from questioning a potential flaw in the plan because they think that everyone agrees with the plan. In other words, because they are under the *illusion of oneness*, they stifle their own doubts and remain silent. Consequently, a potential flaw in the plan might go unchallenged.

Moreover, if the officers are equipped with the latest anti-gang weaponry and are convinced of their superior fire power, they may believe that the raid can't fail. Such a belief is consistent with the *illusion of invulnerability*. Critical thinking is set aside and criticism is stifled because everyone believes that there is no way that the operation can fail.

Now add to this scenario the fact that the officers are on the side of the law. They are on the side of right and the others are the bad guys. In these circumstances, it is not hard to see how they might experience the *illusion of moral superiority*. All three illusions could combine to create disastrous results just as they did at the Bay of Pigs.

In the example above, we are not in any way advocating insubordination or a challenge to the authority of a person giving lawful orders. However, *all* officers are required to think critically at all times, and to engage in critical discussion *whenever possible* in order to solve problems effectively. This applies both to the officer who gives the order and to those who carry it out. Everyone must work to avoid uncritical groupthink.

Another important point needs to be made. It might be argued that the officers in our example aren't under an illusion of moral superiority. In fact, they *are* morally superior to the lawbreaking bikers, and they *are* on the side of right. Whether the officers are *in fact* morally superior to the bikers is not the point, however. The point in this case is that their moral superiority doesn't automatically or necessarily give them an advantage in the upcoming raid; rather, it may contribute to the illusion of invulnerability. The fact that the police are the good guys does, in an odd way, make the situation more dangerous.

Clearly, not many readers of this book will be, as President Kennedy was, involved in planning the invasion of a foreign country. Also, you may never participate in a raid on biker headquarters. Virtually all readers will, however, be members of groups in which poor decisions are made because the group fails to evaluate its proposed course of action in a critical manner. In policing we can picture many dangerous situations, like the biker gang example above, in which officers need to make important decisions. Groupthink is both common and dangerous. It needs to be avoided.

In less dramatic situations, groups may make hasty and poor decisions because time is short. Members rush uncritically to a decision because they are under pressure of time. Or, they may act on the suggestion of the most vocal (talkative) member of the group, even when that person's ideas are weak. Sometimes groups defer to the most charming member, failing to evaluate that person's ideas in a critical manner. Groupthink can occur in many circumstances and at all levels in society. The antidote to groupthink is critical discussion.

THE PROCESS OF CRITICAL DISCUSSION

When your group is faced with important decisions, a simple six-step process can keep you from falling into groupthink. This process should be a natural part of every group member's thinking, and it should be included in your group's procedural rules. In addition to following these six steps, your group should solicit the views of outsiders whenever it faces a major decision. The six steps of the process of critical discussion are listed below.[2]

Step #1: Research

When faced with important decisions, your group should get individuals or subgroups to research different possibilities. If, for example, your group has to purchase a new computer, then you should have different members do research on different computers. Someone can investigate the IBM while someone else looks into the Hewlett-Packard (HP). For ease of illustration, we'll talk about only two computers; in reality, the group might research more. Regardless of how many computers are

---

2   Johnson and Johnson (1997, pp. 307–311) present a six-step process of constructive controversy based on the earlier work of Johnson and Johnson (1987). This section and the next, "The Benefits of Critical Discussion," rely extensively on their work.

being researched, each individual or subgroup takes the view, for the time being, that its computer is the best. The researchers dedicate themselves to learning as much as possible about their particular computer. Depending on the importance of the particular decision to be made, research may be more or less formal. Either way, it needs to be thorough.

Step #2: Presentation

After their research is complete, the individuals or subgroups in our example should present the merits of their computer to the whole group. Someone will make the case for purchasing the IBM and someone else will make the case for getting the HP. The details supporting each purchase are very important. Presenting the different points of view exposes your group members to all the relevant benefits of the two competing computers. Of course, you will begin to see the drawbacks of each as well.

Step #3: Discussion

Next, the IBM researchers should challenge the point of view of the HP researchers. The HP researchers should, in turn, challenge the point of view of the IBM proponents. Other members of your group who have not served as researchers should also enter into the discussion and debate. In all cases, criticism is directed not at the *persons* presenting their views, but toward the respective *merits* of the two computers. The debate is about ideas, not personalities. This conceptual conflict is, as we noted elsewhere, the heart of the critical discussion process.

Step #4: Reflection

When the merits of the two computers have been presented and challenged, it is important to allow time for members to reflect on the pros and cons of both computers. Persons who first favoured one computer may now experience second thoughts. They may see advantages in the other computer that they weren't aware of before. This time of "second thoughts" may be a time of conceptual conflict within one's own mind as each member weighs the pros and cons of the competing computers.

Step #5: Reconsideration

The conceptual conflict that develops in steps 3 and 4 can now continue in a reconsideration of your group's options. All members of the group have received the research results, they have had the opportunity to reflect on the information received, and they have together reconsidered their options. Consequently, everyone is in a position to make an informed choice. Critical thinking and critical discussion have been central to the process throughout. Now it's time for a decision.

Step #6: Decision

Having heard the merits of both computers, debated the pros and cons of each, explored some competing ideas, and taken time to rethink the matter, the group can now formulate a final point of view and arrive at a good decision. In chapter 9, we'll examine several ways that your group can arrive at its decisions. For the moment, however, we'll conclude our look at the process of critical discussion with an unanswerable question. If President Kennedy and his colleagues had followed this six-step process when considering the invasion of Cuba, would the disaster at the Bay of Pigs have been avoided?

THE BENEFITS OF CRITICAL DISCUSSION

Research shows that groups that use critical discussion enjoy two benefits:

- Despite the fact that critical discussion is time consuming, it ultimately leads to better decisions and greater productivity. As groups become more experienced at discussing issues critically, they become more efficient at making high-quality decisions. This results in greater productivity as teams get better at doing their various jobs. In summary, one benefit of critical discussion is greater effectiveness in achieving *task goals*.

- In addition, groups tend to experience an increased sense of cohesion, mutual respect and attraction, and increased individual self-esteem. These are all benefits associated with the social and emotional dimensions of group life. Healthy relationships are developed and maintained as groups become teams. The second benefit, then, is greater success in accomplishing *social goals*.

THE RULES OF CRITICAL DISCUSSION

Earlier in this chapter, we presented six steps of the critical discussion process. Here we present eight rules that should be observed throughout all six stages of the critical discussion process. The six steps of the critical discussion process are like your road map and the eight norms that follow are like the rules of the road.

Rule #1: Criticize Ideas, Not Persons

Conceptual conflict is about ideas, not personalities. The first rule of critical discussion reminds you of this important point, a point that has been made a number of times previously. If you critique ideas while supporting people, then you can identify the best ideas your group has while assuring members that they count, even when their views are rejected. Brainstorming, the very popular technique for soliciting ideas from a group, works on the principle that ideas are to be presented without criticism. Brainstorming seeks to get as many ideas out of the group as possible, and it is consistent with the spirit of this first rule of critical discussion. Note, however, that the process of critical discussion involves much more than brainstorming. Remember, criticize ideas, not people.

Rule #2: Focus on the Best Decision, Not on Winning

Effective teams emphasize cooperation and avoid competition among members. They encourage a win–win attitude among members who will "sink or swim together." This rule directs you to avoid win–lose approaches. After healthy conceptual conflict, everyone on your team will be a winner because you have together made the best decision possible. Always focus on making the best decisions. Never focus on beating fellow members in an idea game.

Rule #3: Encourage Everyone To Contribute

This rule applies to group life at any time, but it is particularly important when decisions are to be made. Sometimes a quieter member of the group has a great idea but is reluctant to share it. Perhaps the individual is shy or believes that her ideas aren't very good. If you encourage the reluctant member to contribute her ideas, then the group can benefit from them. If there is no encouragement, the ideas will be lost to the group. This rule urges you to be an Idea Seeker, an important role that we noted in chapter 1. It also urges you to be a Participation Encourager and a Participant Supporter, two more roles that we studied in the first chapter.

Rule #4: Listen to Everyone's Contribution

Encouraging contributions is vitally important. Equally important is listening to those contributions. This rule encourages you to listen actively to all who contribute to the discussion. Active listening, you will recall, involves conveying your intention to listen, listening with your whole person, and paraphrasing the speaker to ensure understanding. Often in groups, members give only half-hearted attention to the comments of others. Unfortunately, at times members don't listen at all. Listen actively to everyone's contribution.

Rule #5: Use Effective Communication Skills

Listening is a key communication skill. In addition, the sending skills and the feedback skills described in chapter 5 are essential to critical discussion. When it comes to speaking in your group, use first-person pronouns, convey your frame of reference, present ideas briefly and clearly, describe your feelings, don't judge others, and ask for feedback on your ideas. When you give feedback, don't force it on others, focus on their behaviour (not on their personalities), be specific, and avoid giving advice. When involved in critical discussion, always use your best communication skills.

Rule #6: Consider All the Facts

All too often, people are ready to go with the first idea or the quickest solution that is presented to the group. Effective groups take the time to gather all the information necessary to make good decisions. Each member of your group should think critically about all the facts that are brought forward in discussion. Careful assessment of these facts will ensure that your group develops an informed point of view. This rule reminds you to get the facts before making a decision or taking action, and it highlights the very close connection between critical thinking and critical discussion.

Rule #7: Understand All Points of View

Informed and high-quality decisions result from a thorough understanding by group members of the different points of view that can be taken on any issue before the group. An individual who has understood a particular point of view and determined its weaknesses can give informed support to an alternative view that is based on the facts. When the members of your group have a good understanding of alternative points of view, then you are in a position to make an informed decision. This rule emphasizes the importance of understanding all relevant points of view.

Rule #8: Change Your Mind If the Facts Dictate

The process of critical discussion allows time for individual members to reflect on the facts before them. Members need to be flexible in their thinking and they need to change their minds if the facts dictate. Too often, individuals remain stuck in their original point of view, even when an objective analysis suggests that they should change their minds. To be most effective, the members of your group should be open-minded and flexible, ready to change their positions if the facts support a change.

If your group follows these rules of critical discussion, it will experience the two benefits noted earlier — namely, greater cohesion and increased productivity. In chapter 9, we'll examine several ways in which your group can make its decisions as it attempts to solve the problems that come its way.

CHAPTER SUMMARY

In this chapter, we began our study of critical discussion by defining it as a six-step process that encourages group members to engage in conceptual conflict, a conflict about ideas. We continued by examining a form of uncritical thinking called groupthink. When groups engage in groupthink, they fail to do the critical thinking and discussing that is necessary to make informed and wise choices. Instead of critically thinking things through, members assume that they all agree, believe that they are invincible, and feel that they can do no wrong. Next we proceeded to describe the six steps of the critical discussion process. The steps are research, presentation, discussion, reflection, reconsideration, and decision. Then we pointed out two benefits that accrue to groups that regularly use critical discussion. These benefits are increased productivity and greater cohesion. Finally we presented eight rules of critical discussion. These rules require group members to criticize ideas constructively, to adopt a win–win attitude, to involve all members in discussion, to listen actively, to speak clearly and concisely, to consider the facts, to understand all points of view, and to change their minds if they have good reason to do so.

KEY TERMS

conceptual conflict   illusion of invulnerability

critical discussion   illusion of moral superiority

groupthink   illusion of oneness

MASTERING THE MATERIAL

Now that you have read this chapter, use the following guides to ensure that you
have mastered the material.

1. What is critical discussion?

2. What is conceptual conflict?

3. Why does conceptual conflict sometimes degenerate into interpersonal
    conflict?

4. What is groupthink?

5. Identify and explain the four factors that contribute to groupthink.

    a.

    b.

    c.

    d.

6. Name and explain the three illusions associated with groupthink.

    a.

    b.

    c.

7. List, from memory, the six steps of the critical discussion process.

    Step #1:

    Step #2:

    Step #3:

    Step #4:

    Step #5:

    Step #6:

8. What are the two benefits of critical discussion?

    a.

    b.

9. List, from memory, the eight rules of critical discussion.

Rule #1:

Rule #2:

Rule #3:

Rule #4:

Rule #5:

Rule #6:

Rule #7:

Rule #8:

APPLYING THE IDEAS IN POLICING

Scenario

Imagine that you are a member of a special police team planning a raid on the headquarters of a biker gang. The raid is not going to take place for a couple of days. A plan has been put forward by a very experienced sergeant who is highly respected by the group members. You begin to feel that the group may be under the *illusion of oneness*, as you yourself have unexpressed and serious reservations about the plan. There has also been a lot of talk about your team's ability to "outgun" the bikers, if it comes to that. You begin to wonder if the group isn't a bit too cocky, perhaps suffering from the *illusion of invulnerability*. Also, it is quite apparent to you that your group feels morally superior to these outlaws. In your mind, the *illusion of moral superiority* is clearly at work.

Exercise 8.1

Given the scenario above, write three statements or questions that you might make or ask that would contribute to critical discussion of the plan and, more specifically, help to determine whether the group is under the *illusion of oneness*.

1.

2.

3.

Exercise 8.2

Given the scenario above, write three statements or questions that you might make or ask that would contribute to critical discussion of the plan and, more specifically, help to determine whether the group is under the *illusion of invulnerability.*

1.

2.

3.

Exercise 8.3

Given the scenario above, write three statements or questions that you might make or ask that would contribute to critical discussion of the plan and, more specifically, help to determine whether the group is under the *illusion of moral superiority.*

1.

2.

3.

Exercise 8.4

Imagine that you have been assigned to a small committee of officers who are to recommend the purchase of a new type of pistol to be used by officers in your police service. For each of the six steps of the process of critical discussion, write a question or statement that you might ask or make at your committee meetings. Each statement or question should demonstrate that you understand the steps of the critical discussion process. Do not write the step.

Step #1:

Step #2:

Step #3:

Step #4:

Step #5:

Step #6:

Exercise 8.5

Imagine that you have been assigned to serve on a citizens' committee concerned about child abuse in the community. You will meet with them on a regular basis for a period of several months. It is in the best interests of the committee and the community to have free and open discussion on all pertinent matters. For each of the eight rules of critical discussion, write a question or statement that you might ask or make at your committee meetings. Each question or statement should demonstrate that you understand the rules of critical discussion. Do not write the rule.

Rule #1:

Rule #2:

Rule #3:

Rule #4:

Rule #5:

Rule #6:

Rule #7:

Rule #8:

PRACTISING YOUR GROUP SKILLS

Purpose of This Section

The purpose of "Practising Your Group Skills" and the ultimate purpose of this book is to help you become a more effective participant in the groups to which you belong. This section is designed to provide opportunities for you and your fellow students to practise your group skills in a structured environment.

Team Responsibilities

A description of the team responsibilities for each of five different teams — the Executive Team, the Teaching Team, the Lesson Review Team, the Energizer Team, and the Evaluation Team — can be found in appendix A, pages 207–210. Your professor may have chosen to use from one to five of these teams to conduct the teaching and learning activities of your class. Units 2 and 3 of the Teacher's Guide provide your professor with additional information on the responsibilities of these teams.

Individual Role Responsibilities

A description of four individual role responsibilities — those of Leader, Recorder, Reporter, and Participant-Analyst — can be found in appendix A, pages 210–212. Your professor may have chosen to use from one to four of these roles within teams to give individuals experience leading, recording, reporting, and analyzing. Units 2 and 3 of the Teacher's Guide provide your professor with additional information on these individual role responsibilities.

Specific Team Assignments

Specific team assignments for this chapter appear immediately below. Specific team assignments for each of the subsequent chapters can be found in "Practising Your Group Skills" in each chapter.

CHAPTER 8 TEAM ASSIGNMENTS

The Executive Team

- *Executive Goal:* to provide leadership to your classmates for your class session on chapter 8.

- *Executive Objectives:* to facilitate the class session by (1) ensuring a good classroom setup, (2) welcoming the class, (3) introducing the lesson topic, (4) coordinating activities, and (5) bringing the session to a close.

- *Instructions:* Ensure that the classroom is set up to accommodate the class activities. Post an agenda for the session. Welcome people to class and announce the topic, "Critical Discussion: Generating Ideas in Your Group," in a creative and interesting way. Remind the class that the topic includes both the dangers of groupthink and the importance of critical discussion for group success. Introduce and thank all speakers when appropriate. Coordinate the day's activities and bring closure at the end of the class. If necessary, return the classroom to its original configuration.

The Teaching Team

- *Teaching Goal:* to understand and demonstrate effective critical discussion skills in a small group setting.

- *Teaching Objectives:* to describe, explain, and demonstrate (1) groupthink, (2) the six steps of the critical discussion process, and (3) eight effective practices (rules) for critical discussion.

- *Instructions:* As the Teaching Team, you have the freedom to choose how you will teach your lesson. You can be as creative as you wish, but you must achieve the teaching objectives. Your lesson consists of two parts. The first part is the experiential exercise, and the second part is your explanation of the chapter information.

  - ❑ Your experiential exercise is called "Critical Discussion" and you'll find it described fully in appendix B, pages 226–227. Make sure that you refer to "Critical Discussion" when you teach and explain groupthink, the six steps of critical discussion, and the eight rules of critical discussion.

  - ❑ If time allows, you can also use exercises from "Mastering the Material" and "Applying the Ideas in Policing" to teach your lesson.

The Lesson Review Team

- *Review Goal:* to review chapter 7, "Cohesion: Building Your Group into a Team."

- *Objectives:* to provide a review of (1) the experiential exercise, (2) the three forms of trust, and (3) the six rules for creating a climate of trust in a group.

- *Instructions:* As the Lesson Review Team, you have the freedom to choose how you will do the review. You can be as creative as you wish, but you must achieve the review objectives. Remember that your time is very limited, so don't try to re-teach last chapter's lesson.

The Energizer Team

- *Energizer Goal:* to motivate your classmates by conducting an energizer activity.

- *Energizer Objectives:* to facilitate the energizing of your classmates by (1) planning an energizer activity and (2) implementing the plan at an appropriate time in the class session.

- *Instructions:* Your team doesn't have a specific, assigned activity to conduct. Rather, the team should remember its energizing purpose and conduct an activity that will provide a break in the class learning routine. Popular games like Simon Says, Heads Up Seven Up, and Murder Wink usually work well. So do various mixers and ice breakers. (Your professor's Teacher's Guide identifies a number of sources of energizer exercises.) Whatever you decide on, you must be prepared to give clear instructions and conduct the exercise effectively. When you lead the energizer, you are leading and directing the entire class. Plan well and execute professionally, even if the exercise is a "kid's game." Encourage everyone to get involved.

The Evaluation Team

As a member of the Evaluation Team, you need to review the information in chapter 10, pages 191–194, before you do anything else. There you will find helpful information on how to conduct your evaluation session. The most important thing to remember is that you are not to judge other people. Your role is to help the class make its own assessment of which practices worked well today and which didn't.

Note that the evaluation goal below is keyed to the content of this chapter. *If desirable or necessary, you can evaluate any other aspect of group experience.* Be sure, though, that you set the goal, develop appropriate objectives, and plan the evaluation session to achieve the goal and the objectives.

- *Evaluation Goal:* to assess group (or class) members' critical discussion skills.

- *Evaluation Objectives:* to (1) assess the group's (class's) understanding of the critical discussion process and the level of their critical discussion skills and (2) identify practices in need of improvement.

- *Instructions:* Create an evaluation instrument based on the selected focus behaviours identified in the objectives. See chapter 10, pages 192–193, for information on creating evaluation instruments. Figure 10.1 provides an example. Solicit feedback from the class using the evaluation instrument. Use the feedback to discuss the class session with the purpose of identifying improvements that can be made to individual, group, and class performance in future class sessions. Conclude by noting the specific actions that need to be repeated or avoided to make improvements.

REFERENCES AND RECOMMENDED READINGS

Janis, I.L. (1972). *Victims of groupthink.* Boston: Houghton Mifflin.

Janis, I.L. (1982). *Groupthink.* Boston: Houghton Mifflin.

Janis, I.L., & Mann, L. (1977). *Decision making.* New York: Free Press.

Johnson, D.W., & Johnson, R. (1987). *Creative conflict.* Edina, NY: Interaction Book Company.

Johnson, D.W., & Johnson, R. (1997). *Joining together: Group therapy and group skills* (6th ed.). Needham Heights, MA: Allyn & Bacon.

Decisions: Solving Problems in Your Group

Chapter Objectives

After completing this chapter, you should be able to:

- Define the terms *problem* and *decision*.

- Explain the connection between decision making and problem solving.

- Identify and explain the six steps of the problem-solving process.

- Name and describe eight methods for making decisions in a group.

- Describe six factors that improve group decision making.

INTRODUCTION

In many ways, policing is a matter of ongoing problem solving. A traffic tie-up, an accident scene, an empty cash register, a crowd turning ugly, or a shallow grave in the woods are all problems to be solved. In addition to these more dramatic scenarios, there are literally hundreds of smaller problems that on-duty officers deal with on a daily basis. Add to these work-related problems the many personal ones that all of us deal with in a given day, and you can see that a police officer's life is one of constant problem solving.

Because many of the problems faced in the course of duty are typical, it has been possible to establish clear strategies for dealing with them. For example, forensic teams proceed according to a careful plan, and traffic control is conducted according to well-developed principles and procedures. Specific strategies and procedures are in place because police have faced these problems many times before. This experience benefits today's officers and the communities they serve. Officers need to know these well-defined procedures for dealing with typical problems, and indeed much of police training consists of learning these procedures.

However, in policing — as in most of life — many problems arise for which there are no ready-made, predetermined strategies. This chapter reviews the basic steps that groups and individuals should follow when there are problems to be solved and there are no obvious precedents. Moreover, the problem-solving method described below is important to know even when specific strategies exist for dealing with a given problem. What first appears as a problem with a standard solution may be more complex than anticipated. The standard approach may not be appropriate. Swiftly changing circumstances may also render standard approaches ineffective. On duty and off, police officers do well to know and use the steps of the problem-solving method, the process that underlies all standard police procedures. In this chapter, we will concentrate on group problem solving and decision making with a view to highlighting the most effective ways that groups can make good decisions and solve problems effectively.

PROBLEMS AND DECISIONS

problem
any situation that requires consideration and a solution

In its most general sense, a **problem** is any situation that requires consideration and a solution. A problem can be big or small, routine or extraordinary. In order for us to solve problems of any kind, we have to consider certain information, formulate possible solutions, make choices among those possible solutions, and take actions to ensure that the chosen solution really is a solution. Fortunately, human experience at solving problems has produced a standard approach that we can use as we try to solve the problems that we face. Both individuals and groups can use this problem-solving method to deal with the many problems that occur in our lives. We'll study the problem-solving method in detail in the next section. Before we do, however, we need to review the role of decisions in the problem-solving process.

decision
a choice made between competing options

Decisions are choices made between competing options. In our efforts to solve problems, we always have to make decisions; we have to make choices among alternatives. If your sound system breaks down, for example, immediately you will be faced with a number of decisions, a number of choices. The first thing that you have to decide, of course, is whether to fix the system or not. Will you repair it or buy a new system? If you decide to buy new, what will you purchase?

Let's assume that you choose to buy a new system. Since you're not likely to be satisfied with a system of lower quality than you're accustomed to, you will likely consider comparable or better ones. You may look at the merits of particular Sony, Panasonic, or Toshiba systems. You will also have to decide exactly what features you want on the new equipment and what price you are willing to pay. If, after careful consideration and many choices, you purchase the Panasonic system and it is satisfactory, then you have solved your problem. You have made a series of decisions that has eventuated in a solution.

When you try to solve problems as an individual, you will have to make many decisions as you attempt to find a solution to them. The process may be quite complex. It will not, however, be as complex as the process is when groups attempt to solve problems. The complexity of group problem solving does not arise because of the problem-solving process itself, but because of the many decision-making methods that are available to groups compared with those available to individuals. Shortly, we will look at several decision-making methods that are available to groups. Before doing so, we'll examine the six steps of the problem-solving process.

THE PROBLEM-SOLVING PROCESS

The steps of the problem-solving process are well established. They are the same basic steps that scientists follow when they seek to understand something or try to find a practical solution to a particular problem. Different labels are used for these steps, but they share a common process. The well-established, effective procedures that policing has established over time were developed using these same problem-solving steps.

Step #1: Definition

Many experts have said that defining the problem is the most important step in the process. A problem clearly defined is a problem on the way to a solution. In contrast, a problem poorly defined is likely to result in wasted energy and time, not to mention frustration. The clearer the definition or description of the problem, the more likely it is that a solution will be found. Clear definition is critical regardless of whether the problem is being worked on by an individual or a group. A group's definition of a problem, however, requires the agreement of several minds. Although getting such agreement is sometimes difficult, it is always essential. Hopefully, as your group deals with its problems, you and your teammates can agree upon definitions that are both clear and accurate. That is the first step to solving your team's problems.

Step #2: Research

Having defined the problem, it is essential to gather relevant information. This research may be conducted formally or informally. Often, with smaller problems, the data gathering can be done informally with good results. If, however, the group is faced with an important issue, formal investigation may be required. Imagine a community task force composed of citizens, ambulance personnel, firefighters, and police officers, all trying, after a natural disaster, to establish an emergency response plan to deal with future disasters in their community.

In a case like this, formal research into all relevant aspects of the situation would be essential. In all likelihood, the group charged with the responsibility of developing the plan would do a great deal of formal research before recommending one. In our example, research into the existing plans of several communities of similar size would, no doubt, be a critical part of such information gathering. Whether your problems are serious or not, getting information relevant to a solution is essential.

Step #3: Alternatives

Once the relevant information has been collected, discussed, and analyzed, it is necessary to consider all feasible solutions to the problem. The more alternatives one has, the harder it may be to choose from among them, but any such difficulty is outweighed by the greater likelihood of arriving at an effective solution. When many alternatives are formulated, the chances are greater that those alternatives will include an effective solution. The best way to have good ideas, it has been said, is to have many ideas.

In our example of the task force and the emergency response plan, we can imagine research leading to a number of possible approaches. The variety of alternatives would emerge from the differing perspectives of the citizen representatives, paramedics, firefighters, and police. This variety is desirable. One approach, however, must ultimately be chosen. Using critical discussion, your group needs to identify a variety of alternatives before deciding on a course of action.

Step #4: Decision

Each of the alternatives from the previous step must be scrutinized, and a careful review of the pros and cons of each one must be undertaken. At this stage, your group should continue to engage in critical discussion to sift through the information associated with the alternative solutions. Conceptual conflict will ensure that the best ideas prevail. At some point, of course, you must make a decision. We've already noted that group decision making can be somewhat complex, and we'll examine the variety of options available to your group in the next section.

Hopefully, if the best ideas have surfaced and the drawbacks of the various proposals have been identified, the best decision will be made. However, this solution is only a *proposed* solution, and remains so until it is implemented and evaluated. As we will see in the final step of the problem-solving process, all solutions are tentative and subject to review. Only time will tell if your decision was truly the right one.

Step #5: Implementation

A proposed solution to a given problem requires a plan for implementing the solution. If the problem under consideration is a major one, as in our earlier example, a very detailed implementation plan will be required. Often, with minor issues, the plan is quite simple. Whether simple or complex, your plan should be clear, and it should include four essential elements. First, it should identify the scheduled start and finish times. Second, it should describe the details of the plan. Third, it should identify those responsible for implementation. And, fourth, it should indicate how success or failure will be determined. In other words, your team must be able to answer the following questions: *When* will we start and finish the project? *What* exactly is our game plan? *Who* is responsible for the plan? *How* will we know that we've succeeded? These are the minimal questions you must be able to answer. You will recall, no doubt, that these are exactly the same questions that we noted in our examination of goal setting in chapter 4.

Step #6: Evaluation

After the plan has been implemented, the situation has to be monitored to determine if, in fact, the proposed solution is effective. Often it is immediately clear that a good solution has been found. Sometimes, however, this is not immediately evident. Ongoing monitoring and evaluation of the plan are essential. If the evaluation is favourable and the "how" question of step 5 (*How* will we know that we've succeeded?) can be answered clearly, then a solution is in place. If the evaluation is unfavourable or the "how" question cannot be answered, then the problem is not yet solved. The plan may have to be modified, or perhaps even scrapped. In the latter instance, it's "back to the drawing board."

When faced with a problem, then, your team needs to define it very clearly, gather information relevant to a solution, formulate alternatives, decide on a course of action, develop a plan and implement it, and, finally, evaluate your results. As noted above, the six steps of the problem-solving method apply whether a problem is being solved by an individual or a group. Now we'll shift our focus to some of the special details of *group* decision making. When it comes to decision-making methods, groups have many more options than individuals do.

DECISION-MAKING METHODS

As an individual, when you make a decision on your own, you are limited to two general approaches. First, you can do your own research and then, on the basis of your personal standards, decide what you want to do. Second, you can flip a coin or otherwise let the fates decide for you. In contrast to these limited decision-making options, groups have many more ways of making decisions. We'll examine eight methods[1] in this section. Each method has its strengths and weaknesses, and we'll point them out as we survey the different approaches. We'll begin with the ideal method, consensus.

1. Decision by Consensus

We saw earlier that consensus means unanimous agreement. When consensus is achieved, then all members of your group agree with a decision. Whenever possible, your group should decide by consensus. Sometimes groups arrive at consensus easily, but at other times it takes a great deal of time to achieve. The fact that reaching consensus can be very time consuming is one of the criticisms that can be brought against it. Your group may not, for example, have the time to critically discuss an issue because members have other obligations that they have to meet. At other times, faced with an emergency, your group may have to act quickly and consensus-seeking may be impossible. However, when you do have time, and especially when critical decisions have to be made, then you should decide by consensus. The strength of consensus lies in the fact that it requires everyone to participate and allows everyone to contribute. In the end, there is no disagreement. Commitment to implementing the decision will be very strong. Both maximum participation and commitment make consensus the ideal method for group decision making.

2. Decision by Majority Vote

The second method, majority vote, is probably the most popular method for making group decisions in our society. This very popular method is sometimes confused with consensus, so note immediately that they are not the same. Indeed, as the example below will illustrate, they are very different.

In a democratic society like Canada, we learn early in life to respect the vote of the majority. Even when we disagree with the result, we are expected to abide by the decision. Federal, provincial, and local elections are conducted on this basis. So, too, are the decisions of countless groups in society. Majority vote often results in a good decision for a group. This happens when all points of view are expressed, the voting process itself has been conducted fairly, and voters are committed to the voting result. If the vote is a close one, however, this process has an inherent weakness. Let's look at an example to highlight the potential problem.

---

1   This review of decision-making methods elaborates on the summary provided by Wilson (1999, pp. 89–91).

Imagine a group trying to decide how to spend a $30 000 surplus. Some members want to renovate the group's recreation area. Others want to purchase a new van for a community outreach project. If a vote is taken on the renovation proposal and 51 percent are in favour, then the renovation proposal passes. That could mean, though, that 49 percent are opposed to the renovation project. If feelings have run high in the debate, then the 49 percent who have lost may not be committed to working on the winning project.

If your group uses majority vote, you may end up with close to half your members opposed to your team's decision. The majority vote may split your group into winners and losers, and the losers may not be committed to implementing the decision. Despite this danger, majority vote can work well. If you make sure that all points of view are expressed and considered prior to a vote, that the voting process itself is fair, and that everyone is encouraged to abide by and support the decision of the majority, then majority vote can work for your team.

3. Decision by a Minority

It often happens in groups that decisions are made by a minority of group members. The executive members of a group, for example, may make decisions on behalf of the whole team. In a group of ten, the executive members — the leader, reporter, and the recorder, for example — may make decisions for everyone. Three people decide for ten. If a group authorizes its executive to act on its behalf, there can be real advantages for the group. The executive can make decisions on routine matters, sparing the whole group the need to meet and deal with every last detail of business. Authorized minority decisions can be very practical and a real benefit to the team.

If an authorized minority oversteps its bounds, however, problems are likely to arise. If, for example, a minority on your team tries to take over the team or tries to use it to further personal agendas, then the rest of the group may very well be upset. Such "end runs," as they are sometimes called, are unfair and fly in the face of the democratic process.

Needless to say, if an unauthorized minority tries to decide matters on its own, your group is not very likely to appreciate its efforts. Unfortunately, this inappropriate minority action can and does occur. All your team needs, for example, is to have a couple of Rescuers (chapter 1) assume that they have to save your team from disaster and you will experience an unauthorized minority at work. If this happens, you'll have to confront the self-appointed saviours and find out why they think there's a disaster looming and why they feel that they are the ones to rescue the group.

Authorized minorities can work well for your group, provided that the minority stays within its authorized limits. Unauthorized minorities almost always lead to trouble.

4. Decision by a Leader Without Discussion

Sometimes a leader will make a decision for her group without discussing the matter with them. If the decision is a relatively minor one and the leader has the confidence of the group, this method can be effective. It can be a very practical way to get things done. But, if the leader makes an independent decision on a matter of importance without authorization from the group, problems are likely to arise.

Also, if some members of the group do not support the leader, an independent decision on even a minor matter may cause conflict. Needless to say, decision by authority without discussion is effective in only a very limited number of instances in groups that value democracy. Autocratic leaders (chapter 2) are the ones most likely to take action on their own. If you have a tendency to lead in an autocratic manner, you should pay close attention to the risks inherent in this particular method.

As suggested in an earlier chapter, policing frequently operates on autocratic rather than democratic principles. This is both natural, and appropriate, given the hierarchical chain of command in a police service. In many group situations within policing, however, the autocratic approach is not an effective approach, and decision by consensus or majority vote is a leader's most prudent course of action.

5. Decision by a Leader After Discussion

This method, for obvious reasons, is much less likely to result in conflict. In this case, a leader discusses a course of action with the group before he makes a decision on an issue. If the decision reflects the views of all or a majority of group members, difficulties are not likely to arise. If, however, a minority of members of your group disagrees with the decision and they do not support the leader, then problems may occur. When all or a majority agree with the leader, then the discussion that precedes the decision is often seen as the group's authorization of the leader's subsequent action. Leaders are wise, if they need to use this method, to ask the group to support whatever decision they finally make. If the leader has such support, then the decision that he makes after discussing the issue with his group has been authorized, in advance, by the group.

6. Decision by a Leader Based on the Most Frequently Expressed Opinion

This method is a special one that looks, at first glance, like majority vote. It's not the same, however, and the following example shows why. Imagine that a group leader has to reply to someone outside the group, a salesperson for example, and the leader doesn't have time to bring the group together to have members make a decision. The outsider has submitted three prices on three different models of copier and needs a quick answer if the group is to benefit from a time-limited special.

If the team leader calls all the group members individually by telephone and asks whether they support model A, model B, or model C, she might get the following responses: of the 10 group members, four support model A, three support model B, and three support model C. Obviously, the group is split almost equally. If the leader decides to reply to the salesperson on the basis of *the most frequently expressed opinion*, she will purchase model A. Four people supported model A, while models B and C each got support from only three members. The leader in this case has decided on the basis of the most frequently expressed opinion, not majority vote.

A potential problem is obvious. A majority of members support models B and C, so the leader is acting on the opinions of a minority. If the issue is minor, there may be no ensuing difficulty in the group. If, however, the issue is more important, problems are likely to develop. In groups strapped for time, this is a tempting method for leaders to use. It should be applied cautiously, however, for the reason noted.

7. Decision by an Expert Member

Sometimes a decision is best left to an expert within the group. Imagine a group in which there is only one person who is very knowledgeable about computers. If the group is going to purchase a computer for group use, it makes sense to ask the most knowledgeable individual to decide which computer to purchase. If the group wants this and the expert is willing to do the job, this method is likely to work. If, however, the expert is self-appointed, or if some members do not support the expert, problems may develop. In either case, it's possible that a good computer will be purchased, but interpersonal problems may occur. If you are the expert in a given situation, you will want to ensure that everyone supports you as the decision maker. You may also want to point out that while you are an expert, you are not necessarily infallible.

In policing, a given service may have many experts — for example, in forensics, crowd control, or negotiation — and these experts will be *assigned by a commanding officer* to do certain tasks at certain times. This is a different situation from the one described above. Our fourth decision-making method, therefore, applies only to the many instances within policing where groups are operating democratically.

8. Decision by an Arbitrator

arbitrator
an unbiased third party
that makes a decision for
a group that cannot reach
a decision on its own

When a group is divided and group members cannot come to an agreement on an issue, the group may ask an **arbitrator**, an unbiased third party, to make a decision for the group. The ideal arbitrator is someone respected by all parties and considered to be a fair dealer. The arbitrator hears the reasoning of all parties, gives careful consideration to the differences, and makes an independent determination in the matter. Sometimes, as in union–management negotiations, the arbitration is legally binding on the parties involved. In many groups adherence to the arbitrator's decision will be voluntary and not legally binding. This fact underscores the importance of having an arbitrator who is accepted by both parties as being a fair dealer.

Our review of these eight methods of decision making has included an appraisal of the strengths and weaknesses of each method. As suggested earlier in this chapter, these decision-making methods are designed to assist you when making decisions in democratically oriented police groups. Hopefully, it will also benefit you in the many situations in your personal life in which you will contribute to group decisions.

FACTORS THAT IMPROVE GROUP DECISION MAKING

Having examined several different methods of making group decisions, consider the following six factors that will increase your team's chances of making high-quality decisions. As with many things in life, there are no guarantees. Groups that include the following in their deliberations, however, will improve their chances of making the best decisions possible.

1. Participation

As always in your group life, encourage everyone to participate in the decision-making process. When member participation is high, your group is more likely to make good decisions. This is particularly true when members function as Idea

Seekers, Idea Sharers, Direction Suggesters, Progress Summarizers, Comprehension Checkers, and Group Motivators. These are, of course, the basic task functions that we first studied in chapter 1.

2. Cooperation

Groups that establish goals and norms that promote cooperation will create win–win attitudes in the minds and hearts of their members. This cooperative spirit is extremely valuable when solving problems and making decisions. As we saw in chapter 7, competitive, win–lose approaches weaken group cohesion and are ultimately counterproductive. Groups that establish cooperation as the norm are far more likely to make good decisions than those that don't. As your group makes its decisions, try to ensure that it adopts a cooperative win–win approach.

3. Heterogeneous Makeup

Groups that have a heterogeneous makeup are more likely to make better decisions than homogeneous groups. *Heterogeneous* means *having variety*, and *homogeneous* means *lacking variety*. When groups are homogeneous, members may be too much alike and, consequently, may not engage in critical discussion. They may be inclined to fall into groupthink. In contrast, heterogeneous groups — for example, those composed of both men and women, and persons of different ethnic backgrounds — are much more likely to have a variety of points of view on any given issue. Your group should, whenever possible, encourage a healthy mix of members who offer a variety of points of view as the group makes its decisions.

Notice again the point that we made about guarantees at the beginning of this section. We said that there are none. If a team, for example, has a difficult mathematical problem to solve and the team has a heterogeneous makeup with gender, racial, and ethnic diversity, but none of the members has any math skills, then heterogeneity is of no value. It would be better to have a homogeneous group — all women, all men, or all blacks, for example — of people with math skills than to have a heterogeneous group without math skills. In summary, if people have the requisite skills to do a job, then heterogeneous makeup is more desirable than homogeneous makeup.

4. Critical Discussion

The use of critical discussion and conceptual conflict, as we noted in chapter 8, will help to prevent a group from falling into groupthink. This is especially important for homogeneous groups. While it might be desirable to have a mix of people on a team, this is not always possible. Because relatively homogeneous groups are frequently the reality, it is essential that they engage in critical discussion in their decision-making sessions. Criticizing ideas while supporting the persons who offer them is the best way to ensure that the group will generate many ideas that, hopefully, lead to the best decisions.

5. Use of the Problem-Solving Process

Conscious use of the problem-solving process will assist your group in staying on track as it deliberates. Proven by its success in the sciences, the six-step method is a tool that effective groups use regularly. The strength of the process lies in the fact that it provides a structure for dealing with issues. That structure ensures that your group will cover all the necessary steps in a systematic manner.

If your group uses the process, it will have a structured way in which to deal with the problems and tasks that it has to face. As described above in this chapter, your group will define the problem, research relevant information, formulate alternative solutions, decide on a course of action, implement the proposed solution, and evaluate the results. As you can see, the problem-solving process includes a time for decision making in its fourth step.

6. Use of the Eight Decision-Making Methods

An understanding of the various decision-making methods and their strengths and weaknesses will help your group as it makes its decisions. A thorough grasp of these methods will equip you with a number of options when it comes to making decisions. Requiring consensus on very important matters, for example, is more likely to result in a better decision than moving quickly to a vote. Your group should understand the pros and cons of each method discussed in this chapter and use the most appropriate method for the circumstances that you face at any particular time.

Effective groups take all six of these factors into consideration as they attempt to make good decisions to solve the various problems that they face.

CHAPTER SUMMARY

We began this chapter by defining the terms *problem* and *decision*, and showing the connection between problem solving and decision making. Next, we reviewed the six steps of the standard problem-solving process developed by scientists in their pursuit of knowledge and practical solutions to human problems. The steps, in order, are definition, research, alternatives, decision, implementation, and evaluation. Then we described eight methods by which groups can make decisions, noting some of the benefits and limitations associated with each. We held up consensus as the ideal method by which to make group decisions. The other methods included decision by a majority, by a minority, by a leader without discussion, by a leader after discussion, by a leader using the most frequently expressed opinion, by an expert, and by an arbitrator. Finally, we presented six factors that can improve decision making and problem solving within groups. The factors include maximizing participation, promoting cooperation, ensuring heterogeneity, using critical discussion, and using the problem-solving process and the various decision-making methods.

KEY TERMS

arbitrator

decision

problem

MASTERING THE MATERIAL

Now that you have read this chapter, use the following guides to ensure that you have mastered the material.

    1. Define *problem.*

    2. Define *decision.*

    3. List, from memory, the six steps of the problem-solving process.

        Step #1:

        Step #2:

        Step #3:

        Step #4:

Step #5:

Step #6:

4. In step #4 of the problem-solving process, group members are encouraged to challenge one another's ideas while remaining supportive of one another. Members are encouraged to engage in _____ discussion that generates _____ conflict.

5. What four questions are essential in the implementation plan of step #5?

   a.

   b.

   c.

   d.

6. Name and describe the eight methods of making decisions in groups.

   a.

   b.

   c.

   d.

   e.

   f.

   g.

   h.

7. Majority vote is one of the most common methods of group decision making. What is the main weakness of this popular method?

8. The ideal method for making decisions in a group is _____.

9. Define *consensus*.

10. What is an arbitrator?

11. An arbitrator should have the _____ of both parties, and he or she should be _____-minded.

12. Identify the six factors that improve group decision making.

   a.

   b.

   c.

   d.

   e.

   f.

13. Define *heterogeneous*.

14. Define *homogeneous*.

15. Critical _____ and _____ conflict can keep a group from falling into groupthink.

APPLYING THE IDEAS IN POLICING

Exercise 9.1

Imagine that you have been assigned to a special investigative task force in a large metropolitan area. You are charged with the responsibility of investigating a series of sexual assaults in the community. For each of the steps of the problem-solving method, write a statement that you might make to members of the task force that demonstrates your understanding of the relevant step. Do not write the steps.

Step #1:

Step #2:

Step #3:

Step #4:

Step #5:

Step #6:

Exercise 9.2

In police service, the distinction between legitimate *autocratic* decisions and legitimate *democratic* decisions is an important one. Show that you understand this distinction by giving three examples of situations in policing where the autocratic approach is necessary, and three examples of situations where the democratic approach is necessary.

Autocratic #1:

Autocratic #2:

Autocratic #3:

Democratic #1:

Democratic #2:

Democratic #3:

Exercise 9.3

For each of the eight decision-making methods described in the text, give one example from policing and one from civilian life where, in your view, the method would be both appropriate and effective.

1. Decision by a leader without discussion

   Policing:

   Civilian life:

2. Decision by a leader after discussion

   Policing:

   Civilian life:

3. Decision by a leader based on the most frequently expressed opinion

   Policing:

   Civilian life:

4. Decision by an expert

    Policing:

    Civilian life:

5. Decision by a minority of group members

    Policing:

    Civilian life:

6. Decision by majority vote

    Policing:

    Civilian life:

7. Decision by consensus

   Policing:

   Civilian life:

8. Decision by an arbitrator

   Policing:

   Civilian life:

Exercise 9.4

Imagine that you have been assigned to assist a committee of citizens who are interested in preventing child abuse in their community. They have elected you as chairperson of their committee. For each of the factors that improve group decision making, write a statement or a question that you might make or ask at your first few meetings that demonstrates your understanding of that factor.

Factor #1 (Participation):

Factor #2 (Cooperation):

Factor #3 (Heterogeneity):

Factor #4 (Critical discussion):

Factor #5 (Problem-solving process):

Factor #6 (Decision-making methods):

PRACTISING YOUR GROUP SKILLS

Purpose of This Section

The purpose of "Practising Your Group Skills" and the ultimate purpose of this book is to help you become a more effective participant in the groups to which you belong. This section is designed to provide opportunities for you and your fellow students to practise your group skills in a structured environment.

Team Responsibilities

A description of the team responsibilities for each of five different teams — the Executive Team, the Teaching Team, the Lesson Review Team, the Energizer Team, and the Evaluation Team — can be found in appendix A, pages 207–210. Your professor may have chosen to use from one to five of these teams to conduct the teaching and learning activities of the class. Units 2 and 3 of the Teacher's Guide provide your professor with additional information on the responsibilities of these teams.

Individual Role Responsibilities

A description of four individual role responsibilities — those of Leader, Recorder, Reporter, and Participant-Analyst — can be found in appendix A, pages 210–212. Your professor may have chosen to use from one to four of these roles within teams to give individuals experience leading, recording, reporting, and analyzing. Units 2 and 3 of the Teacher's Guide provide your professor with additional information on these individual role responsibilities.

Specific Team Assignments

Specific team assignments for this chapter appear immediately below. Specific team assignments for each of the subsequent chapters can be found in "Practising Your Group Skills" in each chapter.

CHAPTER 9 TEAM ASSIGNMENTS

The Executive Team

- *Executive Goal:* to provide leadership to your classmates for your class session on chapter 9.

- *Executive Objectives:* to facilitate the class session by (1) ensuring a good classroom setup, (2) welcoming the class, (3) introducing the lesson topic, (4) coordinating activities, and (5) bringing the session to a close.

- *Instructions:* Ensure that the classroom is set up to accommodate the class activities. Post an agenda for the session. Welcome people to class and announce the topic, "Decisions: Solving Problems in Your Group," in a creative and interesting way. Remind the class that the topic includes instruction on the problem-solving process and a variety of decision-making methods. Introduce and thank all speakers when appropriate. Coordinate the day's activities and bring closure at the end of the class. If necessary, return the classroom to its original configuration.

The Teaching Team

- *Teaching Goal:* to understand and demonstrate effective problem-solving and decision-making skills in a small group setting.

- *Teaching Objectives:* to describe, explain, and demonstrate (1) the six steps of the problem-solving process and (2) the eight decision-making methods that groups can use when solving problems.

- *Instructions:* As the Teaching Team, you have the freedom to choose how you will teach your lesson. You can be as creative as you wish, but you must achieve the teaching objectives. Your lesson consists of two parts. The first part is the experiential exercise, and the second part is your explanation of the chapter information.

  - Your experiential exercise is called "Comparing Decision-Making Methods" and you'll find it described fully in appendix B, pages 227–228. Make sure that you refer to "Comparing Decision-Making Methods" when you teach and explain the six steps of problem solving and the eight methods for making decisions.

  - If time allows, you can also use exercises from "Mastering the Material" and "Applying the Ideas in Policing" in your lesson.

The Lesson Review Team

- *Review Goal:* to review chapter 8, "Critical Discussion: Generating Ideas in Your Group."

- *Objectives:* to provide a review of (1) the experiential exercise, (2) groupthink, (3) the six steps of the critical discussion process, and (4) eight effective practices (rules) for critical discussion.

- *Instructions:* As the Lesson Review Team, you have the freedom to choose how you will do the review. You can be as creative as you wish, but you must achieve the review objectives. Remember that your time is very limited, so don't try to re-teach last chapter's lesson.

The Energizer Team

- *Energizer Goal:* to motivate your classmates by conducting an energizer activity.

- *Energizer Objectives:* to facilitate the energizing of your classmates by (1) planning an energizer activity and (2) implementing the plan at an appropriate time in the class session.

- *Instructions:* Your team doesn't have a specific, assigned activity to conduct. Rather, the team should remember its energizing purpose and conduct an activity that will provide a break in the class learning routine. Popular games like Simon Says, Heads Up Seven Up, and Murder Wink usually work well. So do various mixers and ice breakers. (Your professor's Teacher's Guide identifies a number of sources of energizer exercises.) Whatever you decide on, you must be prepared to give clear instructions and conduct the exercise effectively. When you lead the energizer, you are leading and directing the entire class. Plan well and execute professionally, even if the exercise is a "kid's game." Encourage everyone to get involved.

The Evaluation Team

As a member of the Evaluation Team, you need to review the information in chapter 10, pages 191–194, before you do anything else. There you will find helpful information on how to conduct your evaluation session. The most important thing to remember is that you are not to judge other people. Your role is to help the class make its own assessment of which practices worked well today and which didn't.

Note that the evaluation goal below is keyed to the content of this chapter. *If desirable or necessary, you can evaluate any other aspect of group experience.* Be sure, though, that you set the goal, develop appropriate objectives, and plan the evaluation session to achieve the goal and the objectives.

- *Evaluation Goal:* to assess group (or class) members' problem-solving and decision-making skills.

- *Evaluation Objectives:* to (1) assess the group's (class's) use of decision by consensus, decision by majority vote, and decision by a minority and (2) identify practices in need of improvement.

- *Instructions:* Create an evaluation instrument based on the selected focus behaviours identified in the objectives. See chapter 10, pages 192–193, for information on creating evaluation instruments. Figure 10.1 provides an example. Solicit feedback from the class using the evaluation instrument. Use the feedback to discuss the class session with the purpose of identifying improvements that can be made to individual, group, and class performance in future class sessions. Conclude by noting the specific actions that need to be repeated or avoided to make improvements.

REFERENCES AND RECOMMENDED READINGS

Frey, L.R., & Barge, J.K. (Eds.). (1997). *Managing group life: Communicating in decision-making groups.* Boston: Houghton Mifflin.

Gordon, W.W.J. (1961). *Synectics.* New York: Harper & Row.

Hirokawa, R.Y., & Poole, M.S. (Eds.). (1986). *Communication and group decision-making.* Beverly Hills, CA: Sage.

Janis, I.L. (1989). *Crucial decisions: Leadership in policymaking and crisis management.* New York: Free Press.

Watson, G. (1931). Do groups think more effectively than individuals? In G. Murphy & L. Murphy (Eds.), *Experimental social psychology.* New York: Harper.

Wilson, G.L. (1999). *Groups in context: Leadership and participation in small groups.* Boston: McGraw-Hill.

Evaluation: Improving Your Group's Performance

Chapter Objectives

After completing this chapter, you should be able to:

- Explain the difference between describing behaviours and judging people.

- Describe the difference between formal and informal evaluation.

- Design and create an evaluation instrument.

- State and explain five rules for conducting formal group evaluations.

- Describe ten aspects of group work that should be evaluated regularly.

INTRODUCTION

For many probationary constables, the thought of a sergeant assessing their performance on the job is an uncomfortable one, and worries of failure are often at the heart of that discomfort. Many veterans experience similar concerns. Whether we like them or not, performance reviews are a fact of life in many organizations, including policing organizations. This practice is designed to ensure that employees work to the standards of the organization and develop their full potential.

While performance reviews strike fear in the hearts of some workers, others see them as beneficial, provided that they are conducted in a fair manner and allow opportunity for improvement where necessary. Most often, any initial fears of the process give way in time to confidence as such reviews become routine.

A fair evaluation of a person's performance carried out in a supportive manner is a healthy organizational practice. For example, the sergeant who helps a junior constable to improve her performance is contributing to that constable's future, the improvement of the police service, and the welfare of the community served. Similarly, officers in small work groups who evaluate their group's performance cooperatively and supportively can improve the group's effectiveness and develop a real sense of team. This peer evaluation in small groups can benefit the team, the police service, and the community.

The most effective teams in policing, and every area of life, are those that make performance evaluation a regular part of their group life. In this chapter we will detail the elements of constructive evaluation that should exist in any small group, whether in the workplace or in the community, that wishes to enhance its productivity and the relationships among its members.

TASK GOALS AND SOCIAL GOALS

The twin goals of an effective group have been prominent throughout our discussions. Those twin goals are task accomplishment and team development. Every group has as one of its goals the goal of getting the job done, whatever that job might be. This is the group's *task goal*. Every effective group also has a second goal, that of building and maintaining good relationships among its members. This is the group's *social goal*.

When trying to improve your group's performance, you should look at the degree to which you are completing your tasks and the degree to which members feel good about being on the team. In this chapter, we will focus our attention on the various steps that your group can take to measure and improve its performance in both the task and the social dimensions of its life. While these two goals are very general, we will see that there are many specific aspects of a group's activities that require ongoing evaluation if performance is to be enhanced.

THE CHALLENGE OF EVALUATION

Before we turn to the specific areas of group life that require evaluation, let's review a critically important point that we first made in chapter 5 and have repeated a number of times since. The challenge of evaluation lies in describing behaviour without judging members themselves. Some people are very sensitive and they tend to take things personally. If we describe behaviour and refrain from making judgments about people or their character, we contribute to the development or maintenance of a supportive climate in which group performance can be assessed and improved. If Ned, for example, is late for three consecutive meetings, we can describe the fact of his lateness without making judgments about the reasons for his lateness. We can stick with the facts and avoid attributing his behaviour to laziness, lack of interest, or some other personality factor.

Throughout our study of group dynamics and interpersonal relationships, we have repeatedly made this most important point. In chapter 5, the fifth rule for sending messages effectively was: "*Describe the behaviour; don't judge the person,*" and the second rule for giving effective feedback was: "*Focus feedback on behaviour, not personality.*" In chapter 8, the first rule of critical discussion directed us to "*Criticize ideas, not persons.*" Also, in our review of group cohesion (chapter 7), we noted that trust is built and maintained when judgments are avoided. And, finally, the sixth rule for building a supportive climate (chapter 7) tells us to "*Be supportive, not judgmental.*"

Your group's evaluation of its performance will be most effective when your members *describe the actions* of group members that prevent the group from accomplishing its task goals, *without attributing motives* to those persons. The same is true when your group looks at how well it is doing in terms of building a team — that is, accomplishing its social goals. Supportive environments free of judgments are the best environments in which to measure and improve group performance. When assessing your team's performance, the members of your group should describe behaviour and avoid judging people.

FORMAL EVALUATION

Effective groups use both *formal* and *informal* evaluation on an ongoing basis. We'll describe the formal evaluation first. The performance evaluation sessions of professional sports teams illustrate the formal evaluation process well. A professional football team, for example, meets the day after a game to review videotapes of the game just played. The coaching staff have viewed the tapes, and they have some specific points to make. They have isolated key plays to highlight a particular problem, or they have noted specific plays that were especially successful. Two things make this kind of review a formal review. One is that it is a scheduled part of the team's overall operations, and the other is that it focuses on predetermined and specific aspects of the team's play.

To enhance your team's performance, your group should schedule regular times for evaluating its performance, just as professional sports teams do. Setting time aside for regular performance assessment is the first step toward improving performance. The second step is to identify specific aspects of performance to review and assess. The professional football team, we said, zeroes in on specific plays that were a failure or a success. You and the other members of your team should do the same. Later in this chapter we will identify the areas that need to be evaluated, but for the moment let's detail the basic steps of the formal evaluation process.

STEPS OF THE FORMAL EVALUATION PROCESS

In order to evaluate and improve its performance, your team should take the five important steps described below. Each step covers a key aspect of the formal evaluation process.

Step #1: Identify the Focus Behaviours

If you want to be able to improve your group's performance, then you need to be very specific about what needs to be reviewed. To say, for example, "We were awesome!" is very positive and will no doubt motivate team members to some degree. But, because the evaluative remark is very general, it doesn't isolate or highlight specific things that the group should repeat in order to be awesome again next time. Similar remarks are relevant to the negative evaluation, "We were lousy!" The first thing that needs to be done in evaluation, then, is to identify the specifics to be examined by the group. Decide, for example, that you will evaluate how well members *give feedback* (specific) rather than how well members *communicate* (general).

Imagine, for a moment, that your team wants to evaluate the participation of its members in a critical discussion. Since participation is a very general concept, you will want to be much more specific. The six task actions from chapter 1, for example, are quite specific, and they could become your focus for evaluation purposes. Do your members share their ideas? Do they seek the ideas of others? Do they suggest directions that the group might take? Do they summarize the group's progress? Do they check to see that "everyone is on the same page"? Do they motivate one another to complete the task at hand?

To continue with this example, your group might list these specific behaviours as the focus behaviours that you will evaluate at a future meeting:

- Sharing ideas
- Seeking ideas
- Suggesting direction
- Summarizing progress
- Checking comprehension
- Motivating others

When you create a list such as this one, you have identified precisely what you want to evaluate. These behaviours are called the **focus behaviours**, the behaviours of group members that you are going to concentrate on and evaluate.

focus behaviours
the specific behaviours to be evaluated by a group

Step #2: Create an Evaluation Instrument

instrument
a tool used to observe and rate group performance

This step involves the creation of an evaluation **instrument**, which is a tool, often a single sheet of paper, that provides questions or statements that members use to rate group performance. In the example from step 1, the six task actions were identified as the focus behaviours to be assessed. An evaluation instrument designed to help assess these actions would include the specific task actions, the names of group members, and a rating scale. Figure 10.1 provides an example of a simple evaluation instrument that takes this approach. The main purpose of the instrument is to focus attention on the specific behaviours that are to be assessed — the focus behaviours — so that the group can provide feedback on them, discuss possible improvements, and set goals for improvement. When doing formal evaluations, your group should create an evaluation instrument to help you with the assessment process.

Step #3: Use the Instrument To Observe and Rate Performance

Having included the focus behaviours on your evaluation instrument, it is now time to observe members in a discussion to see how often and how well they employ the task actions in a critical discussion. Remember that the task actions are only an example of what might be evaluated. In reality, a group could be assessing the social actions, aspects of communication, conflict resolution, or any number of other behaviours. If necessary, all members are reminded of the particular focus behaviours before the discussion begins. At the end of the discussion, the evaluation instrument is distributed and members are given time to rate everyone with respect to their contributions to the discussion.

FIGURE 10.1   Sample Evaluation Instrument

INSTRUCTIONS: Using the scale below, rate each member's performance in the critical discussion.

1 = minimal
2 = good
3 = very good
4 = excellent
5 = exceptional

TASK ACTIONS	Mary	Tom	Sue	Doug	Dana	Pat	Jim
Shares Ideas							
Seeks Ideas							
Suggests Direction							
Summarizes Progress							
Checks Comprehension							
Motivates Others							

Another approach involves the appointment of observers who have the special task of observing the discussion, making note of who contributes what to the discussion, and then rating everyone's performance using the evaluation instrument. Since the observers do not participate in the discussion, they can be much more attentive to the contributions of each participant. One of the main benefits of having observers is that participants do not have to concern themselves with observation. They can simply get involved in the discussion.

Another approach employs "secret" observers, identified long before a particular evaluation session. They secretly make their observations and report them at an appropriate time after the discussion has concluded. To ensure that this method isn't an unethical and unwanted intrusion into the lives of members, the entire team should agree to this kind of approach well in advance of implementation. In other words, if there is consensus on using this approach as one of a number of evaluation strategies, then it will not be ethically offensive when it is employed.

Regardless of the method you use to observe the focus behaviours, the point of the exercise is to get data on the contributions of your members so that those contributions can be discussed by your team to improve the team's performance. As we'll see in the next step, the purpose is not to judge individuals. The purpose is to collect information by observing the focus behaviours, the specific aspects of the group's dynamics to be evaluated.

Step #4: Discuss the Observations and Ratings

After identifying the focus behaviours, creating a tool for rating them, and observing the focus behaviours, your group is in a position to assess its performance. The rating scale on the evaluation instrument becomes particularly relevant at this point.

Using the rating scale, your team can arrive at some numbers that represent your evaluation results. The numbers, however, should be viewed only as a starting point for the discussion and goal setting that takes place in step 5.

In the sample instrument in Figure 10.1, the scale ranges from "minimal" contribution through "very good" to "exceptional" contribution with numbers ranging from 1 to 5, respectively. While evaluation instruments frequently use numbers in their rating scales, other approaches can be used. The ever popular "happy face," for example, can represent the highest rating on a scale where the equally popular "sad face" represents the weakest performance.

Regardless of whether the tool uses numbers or symbols, the ratings are only a starting point for group discussion. Your group should never, for example, average a bunch of numbers, announce the result, and end the assessment session. You should always use the ratings to focus discussion on ways that your team can improve its performance. The ratings are just one more step in the overall process that leads to the setting of goals for performance improvement.

Step #5: Set Goals for Improvement

The last step in the formal evaluation process is devoted to goal setting. The critical discussion that takes place at this stage is dedicated to setting specific targets for team improvement. Since performance evaluation identifies both strengths and weaknesses, your team can establish objectives that encourage the repetition of strong performance and the elimination of weak performance.

When your team sets goals for performance improvement, you should seek consensus among members. Critical discussion of your performance that leads to consensus will help to ensure commitment to improvement. Having had their say and having agreed upon improvement goals, all members of your team are likely to work toward the achievement of your objectives.

Throughout the formal evaluation process, but particularly in steps 3, 4, and 5, it is vitally important for your team to follow the primary rule of group evaluation: *"Describe behaviours; don't judge people."* In a supportive climate of trust, your group can take the steps necessary to become the very best. Like a professional sports team, you can work regularly on getting better at what you do.

INFORMAL EVALUATION

The steps described above outline the formal evaluation process. Often, however, evaluation takes place informally. In many cases, informal evaluation can be as effective or more effective than formal evaluation. For example, when the coach behind the bench gives immediate feedback to a player returning to the bench after a play, such informal feedback can be very helpful. The returning player will be clear on the specific action or aspect of performance that needs to be repeated or changed.

In group meetings, informal evaluation can occur at any time, and it should occur regularly. For example, words of praise and support that are given to another member for making a particular contribution are a type of informal evaluation. Furthermore, group members can take a time-out at virtually any point for informal evaluation of specific aspects of their performance. Effective teams encourage informal evaluation at any time, and schedule formal evaluations on a regular basis.

EVALUATING SPECIFIC AREAS OF GROUP WORK

In the previous section, we described *how* to evaluate performance. Now we will examine *what* to evaluate. Because group work is complex, there are many possible aspects to assess. It's possible, however, to narrow things by homing in on the basic areas of group experience that we have studied. Let's return to these topics to highlight the essential aspects of group work requiring regular evaluation, both formal and informal. Note that the areas are described in fairly general ways. In any area that your team chooses to evaluate, you will need to get very specific. Each of the following broad areas includes many specific focus behaviours that you can assess.

1. Member Roles

Your group should monitor its task roles and social roles to ensure that it is performing well in these two critical areas, which are the subject of chapter 1. In the area of task accomplishment, your group should evaluate idea seeking, idea sharing, summarizing, comprehension checking, direction suggesting, and energizing. In the area of relationship development, you should evaluate participation encouragement, the support and praise of member contributions, communication facilitation, stress relief, conflict mediation, and process observation. These 12 roles were identified as the essential member roles in an effective group and they should be evaluated regularly.

2. Leader Roles

In chapter 2, we pointed out that different situations may require different styles of leadership. Recognizing this fact, your group should regularly evaluate the appropriateness of its leadership actions. For example, is your leader becoming overly task-oriented and neglecting the social needs of the group? Or, in contrast, is she encouraging team development at the expense of team productivity? Is there a healthy balance between concern for tasks and concern for people? Is the ideal-leader approach being employed within the group? To a large degree, the evaluation of leadership roles within the group is an evaluation of the appropriate use of power. Regular evaluation of leadership is necessary to improve your group's effectiveness. In evaluating leadership, as with all areas of group performance, describe behaviours and avoid judging people.

3. Norms

In chapter 3, we defined norms as the rules of the group and noted that they may be established by outside authorities or determined by the group itself. Usually both conditions prevail, some norms being imposed and others being developed from within. All norms over which your group has any influence should be the subject of regular evaluative reviews. As conditions change within your group, norms may need to change as well. Just as societies sometimes retain outdated laws on their books, so do groups. The old objection "We've always done it this way" is an appeal to the rules that have governed the past. Adherence to such rules may well inhibit group progress. Consequently, your group needs to be aware of the norms that continue to serve it well and those that are in need of change. Regular evaluation of group norms is essential to healthy group development.

4. Goals

Goals and objectives identify the targets at which a group is aiming. Both are the subject of chapter 4. Goals are the broad targets that lie ahead; objectives are the specific, measurable targets whose achievement brings the group closer to its ultimate goals. Your team's goals and objectives need to be evaluated regularly. Are the established targets still appropriate? Are they in need of revision in the light of changing circumstances? Answers to such questions are most important. When the goals and objectives are appropriate, they serve as benchmarks for assessing your group's performance. Objectives that are stated clearly allow you to determine whether you have hit your targets or not. They are essential points of reference for evaluating your team's performance.

5. Messages

In chapter 5, several rules for sending and receiving messages effectively were presented. We also noted the rules for giving feedback. Communication is critical for any group's task accomplishment and social development. Ongoing evaluation of communication practices is another essential aspect of group work. If your group frequently uses written communication, the practices and systems associated with written messages will require regular monitoring. You also need to assess your oral communication practices. Are messages being sent, received, and responded to in the best ways possible, or is there room for improvement?

6. Conflict

Chapter 6 made the point that conflict within your group is inevitable. We noted that the important thing is how your team handles conflicts when they do occur. Are constructive solutions being found to disputes? Are relationships strengthened through effective conflict resolution by all members of your group? Conflict management is another important subject for group evaluation, and effective groups regularly examine their strategies for dealing with conflict. Some build "gripe sessions" into their agendas so that members will have an opportunity to air their concerns about the group. While the label "gripe session" is not particularly positive, the concept of regularly providing time to assess interpersonal relationships is a good one. If your group evaluates its conflict resolution abilities and regularly provides members with a chance to vent their feelings, you will establish a supportive climate in which conflict can be dealt with constructively.

7. Cohesion

Team spirit is another focus for periodic evaluation. In chapter 7, the importance of trust, affiliation, influence, respect, and the creation of a supportive climate were detailed. In addition, six rules for creating a supportive climate were reviewed. These rules can, for example, serve as a focal point for assessing the climate in your group. Are your members cold and neutral or warm and empathetic? Do you treat one another as equals? Are members cooperative? Are members genuine and honest, refraining from manipulation? Are members open to new ideas? Are they supportive and non-judgmental? Work to ensure that, among other things, your group keeps examining its climate and its sense of cohesion.

8. Critical Discussion

In order to generate the best ideas possible, your group needs to engage in critical discussion, the subject of chapter 8. A regular review of your use of critical discussion can prevent members from falling prey to groupthink. It can also help you to avoid making decisions prematurely at times when groupthink is not a factor. Regular appraisal of your group's handling of conceptual conflict is essential to improving its performance. Conceptual conflict is a fundamental ingredient in effective problem solving, because it encourages a group to make good decisions based on critical analysis of members' suggestions. In your strategies for assessing your performance, make sure that your group includes evaluations of its critical thinking.

9. Decisions

Effective decision making, as described in chapter 9, is essential for solving the many problems that your group faces. Consequently, your team needs to evaluate its decision-making practices and its successes and failures in problem solving. Does your group employ the problem-solving process as it deals with various issues? Does it take time to define the problem, research it, formulate alternative solutions, consciously decide on a solution, implement the solution plan, and evaluate the success of the plan? In addition, does your group use effective decision-making methods? Does it, for example, know when to use majority vote and when to use consensus? All the elements of decision making and problem solving are worthy of regular assessment by your team.

10. Evaluation

It may seem redundant to suggest evaluating the evaluation practices of a group. Isn't this overkill? Not really. If, for example, your group has poor evaluation strategies, then your assessments are not likely to produce much improvement. It's possible for a group to evaluate regularly yet do so ineffectively. This could happen if the group neglects to assess specific aspects of its work. If the group continually deals in generalities, progress is not likely. As suggested earlier in this chapter, general comments about group performance may motivate if they're positive or discourage if they're negative, but they won't do much to help members alter specific practices in ways that lead to improvement. Analysis of your group's evaluation practices is, therefore, absolutely necessary.

We have now reviewed the many subjects that require regular evaluation within small groups. Obviously, evaluating them all at one time or in one session would be impossible. All of your group's time would be expended in evaluation, none in performance. Effective groups will consider one aspect at one time and other aspects at other times. Sometimes circumstances will dictate the subject for evaluation. At other times, a well-planned agenda will do so. Effective groups assess their performance in all these areas both formally and informally as a regular part of their work.

When it comes to evaluation, your group will want to develop a checklist to ensure that all major areas of its experience are evaluated. Your checklist should include all of the following broad areas:

- Member roles
- Leadership

- Group rules
- Goals and objectives
- Communication skills
- Conflict strategies
- Teambuilding
- Critical discussion
- Decision making and problem solving
- Performance evaluation

CHAPTER SUMMARY

We began this chapter by reviewing the fundamental distinction between task goals and social goals. Our purpose was to note the two broad areas in which performance evaluation is essential. Having made that distinction, we underscored the cardinal rule of group evaluation: "Describe behaviours; don't judge people." Next, we described both formal and informal evaluation, pointing out the similarities and differences between them. Further, we emphasized the importance of both. We then presented five steps for effective formal evaluation. Groups should identify the focus behaviours, create an evaluation tool, use the tool to observe and rate performance, discuss the observations and ratings, and set goals for improvement. Finally, we described the 10 areas of group experience that require regular evaluation if a group wants to be an effective team, improving its performance throughout its life. Each of these areas, we pointed out, has been the subject of one chapter of this examination of interpersonal and group dynamics.

KEY TERMS

focus behaviours

instrument

MASTERING THE MATERIAL

Now that you have read this chapter, use the following guides to ensure that you have mastered the material.

1. The two basic goals of an effective group are _____ accomplishment and _____ development. These goals are called the _____ goal and the _____ goal.

2. The critical skill of describing the behaviour of others without judging them personally underlies five specific rules presented in various chapters throughout this text. Identify the five rules.

   a.

   b.

   c.

   d.

   e.

3. Name and describe the two forms of evaluation discussed in this chapter.

   a.

   b.

4. List, from memory, the five steps of the formal evaluation process for groups.

   Step #1:

   Step #2:

   Step #3:

   Step #4:

   Step #5:

5. Name and describe the ten areas of group work that require regular evaluation.

   a.

   b.

   c.

   d.

   e.

f.

g.

h.

i.

j.

APPLYING THE IDEAS IN POLICING

Exercise 10.1

Imagine that you are a member of a team considering ways to improve the relationship between your police service and the community. After several meetings, you feel that the group is not really getting down to work. A couple of members don't appear to be taking the job as seriously as you think they should. Remembering the challenge of evaluation, write three statements that you might say to your teammates that would *describe member behaviours without judging persons.*

1.

2.

3.

Exercise 10.2

Imagine that you have been assigned to work with a citizens' group concerned with improving security in their neighbourhood. You sit on their committee as a peer and, after a couple of meetings, you feel that the group is not getting anywhere. Most members are not speaking up, and there seems to be no sense of cohesion. You know the rules for formal evaluation of small group performance and decide to introduce the idea at the next meeting with the hope that it might get the group moving. Using the task actions and social actions from chapter 1, identify three specific task actions and three specific social actions that could be evaluated by your committee. Following step #1 for formal evaluations, identify the focus behaviours to be assessed. Write them in the spaces below. Do not write the step.

Focus task actions to be evaluated:

1.

2.

3.

Focus social actions to be evaluated:

1.

2.

3.

Exercise 10.3

Using your responses from exercise 10.2, create an evaluation instrument on a sheet of letter-sized paper that you could use at the next meeting of your committee. Assume that your committee includes you and Larry, Mary, Moe, Jo, Curly, and Shirley.

Exercise 10.4

Imagine yourself as a member of various small groups within your police service. For each of the 10 aspects of group work that require regular evaluation, identify one specific item that might be evaluated by the groups to which you belong. Write one question that you might ask your fellow members to help them evaluate the groups' performance with respect to the focus behaviours that you have identified.

1. Member roles

2. Leader roles

3. Norms

4. Goals

5. Communication

6. Conflict

7. Cohesion

8. Critical discussion

9. Decisions

10. Evaluation

PRACTISING YOUR GROUP SKILLS

Purpose of This Section

The purpose of "Practising Your Group Skills" and the ultimate purpose of this book is to help you become a more effective participant in the groups to which you belong. This section is designed to provide opportunities for you and your fellow students to practise your group skills in a structured environment.

Team Responsibilities

A description of the team responsibilities for each of five different teams — the Executive Team, the Teaching Team, the Lesson Review Team, the Energizer Team, and the Evaluation Team — can be found in appendix A, pages 207–210. Your professor may have chosen to use from one to five of these teams to conduct the teaching and learning activities of your class. Units 2 and 3 of the Teacher's Guide provide your professor with additional information on the responsibilities of these teams.

Individual Role Responsibilities

A description of four individual role responsibilities — those of Leader, Recorder, Reporter, and Participant-Analyst — can be found in appendix A, pages 210–212. Your professor may have chosen to use from one to four of these roles within teams to give individuals experience leading, recording, reporting, and analyzing. Units 2 and 3 of the Teacher's Guide provide your professor with additional information on these individual role responsibilities.

Specific Team Assignments

Specific team assignments for this chapter appear immediately below. Specific team assignments for each of the subsequent chapters can be found in "Practising Your Group Skills" in each chapter.

CHAPTER 10 TEAM ASSIGNMENTS

The Executive Team

- *Executive Goal:* to provide leadership to your classmates for your class session on chapter 10.

- *Executive Objectives:* to facilitate the class session by (1) ensuring a good classroom setup, (2) welcoming the class, (3) introducing the lesson topic, (4) coordinating activities, and (5) bringing the session to a close.

- *Instructions:* Ensure that the classroom is set up to accommodate the class activities. Post an agenda for the session. Welcome people to class and announce the topic, "Evaluation: Improving Your Group's Performance," in a creative and interesting way. Remind the class that the topic includes instruction on five steps of the formal evaluation process. Introduce and thank all speakers when appropriate. Coordinate the day's activities and bring closure at the end of the class. If necessary, return the classroom to its original configuration.

The Teaching Team

- *Teaching Goal:* to understand and demonstrate effective group evaluation skills in a small group setting.

- *Teaching Objectives:* to describe, explain, and demonstrate (1) the five steps of the formal evaluation process and (2) the ten areas of group experience that require evaluation.

- *Instructions:* As the Teaching Team, you have the freedom to choose how you will teach your lesson. You can be as creative as you wish, but you must achieve the teaching objectives. Your lesson consists of two parts. The first part is the experiential exercise, and the second part is your explanation of the chapter information.

  - ❑ Your experiential exercise is called "Creating Evaluation Instruments" and you'll find it described fully in appendix B, pages 228–230. Make sure that you refer to "Creating Evaluation Instruments" when you teach and explain the five steps of the formal evaluation process and the ten areas of group life that need evaluation.

❑ If time allows, you can also use exercises from "Mastering the Material" and "Applying the Ideas in Policing" in your lesson.

The Lesson Review Team

- *Review Goal:* to review chapter 9, "Decisions: Solving Problems in Your Group."

- *Objectives:* to provide a review of (1) the experiential exercise, (2) the six steps of the problem-solving process, and (3) the eight decision-making methods that groups can use when solving problems.

- *Instructions:* As the Lesson Review Team, you have the freedom to choose how you will do the review. You can be as creative as you wish, but you must achieve the review objectives. Remember that your time is very limited, so don't try to re-teach last chapter's lesson.

The Energizer Team

- *Energizer Goal:* to motivate your classmates by conducting an energizer activity.

- *Energizer Objectives:* to facilitate the energizing of your classmates by (1) planning an energizer activity and (2) implementing the plan at an appropriate time in the class session.

- *Instructions:* Your team doesn't have a specific, assigned activity to conduct. Rather, the team should remember its energizing purpose and conduct an activity that will provide a break in the class learning routine. Popular games like Simon Says, Heads Up Seven Up, and Murder Wink usually work well. So do various mixers and ice breakers. (Your professor's Teacher's Guide identifies a number of sources of energizer exercises.) Whatever you decide on, you must be prepared to give clear instructions and conduct the exercise effectively. When you lead the energizer, you are leading and directing the entire class. Plan well and execute professionally, even if the exercise is a "kid's game." Encourage everyone to get involved.

The Evaluation Team

As a member of the Evaluation Team, you need to review the information in chapter 10, pages 191–194, before you do anything else. There you will find helpful information on how to conduct your evaluation session. The most important thing to remember is that you are not to judge other people. Your role is to help the class make its own assessment of which practices worked well today and which didn't.

Note that the evaluation goal below is keyed to the content of this chapter. *If desirable or necessary, you can evaluate any other aspect of group experience.* Be sure, though, that you set the goal, develop appropriate objectives, and plan the evaluation session to achieve the goal and the objectives.

- *Evaluation Goal:* to assess group (or class) members' team evaluation skills.

- *Evaluation Objectives:* to (1) assess group (or class) knowledge of and use of the formal evaluation process and (2) identify practices in need of improvement.

- *Instructions:* Create an evaluation instrument based on the selected focus behaviours identified in the objectives. See chapter 10, pages 192–193, for information on creating evaluation instruments. Figure 10.1 provides an example. Solicit feedback from the class using the evaluation instrument. Use the feedback to discuss the class session with the purpose of identifying improvements that can be made to individual, group, and class performance in future class sessions. Conclude by noting the specific actions that need to be repeated or avoided to make improvements.

REFERENCES AND RECOMMENDED READINGS

Coffey, R.E., Curtis, W.C., & Hunsaker, P.L. (1994). *Management and organizational behaviour*. Burr Ridge, IL: Austin Press/Irwin.

Gibb, J.R. (1961). Defensive communication. *Journal of Communication, 11*, 142–148.

Harris, E.T., & Sherblom, J.C. (1999). *Small group and team communication*. Needham Heights, MA: Allyn & Bacon.

Robbins, S.P. (1994). *Essentials of organizational behavior* (4th ed.). Englewood Cliffs, NJ: Prentice Hall.

Wilson, G.L. (1999). *Groups in context: Leadership and participation in small groups*. Boston: McGraw-Hill.

The Experiential Model: Teaching and Learning Group Skills

Appendix Objectives

Upon completion of this appendix, you should be able to:

- Explain experiential learning.
- Describe the experiential model.
- Identify the responsibilities of the teams used in the model.
- Identify the individual role responsibilities used in the model.
- Describe a typical model-based class session.
- Locate specific team assignments.
- Locate more information on the model and how it works.

EXPERIENTIAL LEARNING

Practical Learning

Experiential learning is learning by doing. It is practical, hands-on learning that moves from practice to theory, not the other way around. It is the kind of learning that is best suited to acquiring skills. Learning to ride a bicycle, for example, can't be done by attending classroom lectures and being tested on the lecture material. It requires doing. The student must get on a bicycle and give it a try. Once the learner has mastered some basic skills, then it's a matter of practice, practice, practice. In this regard, learning interpersonal and group skills is much like learning to ride a bicycle.

As its name suggests, experiential learning refers to the acquisition of knowledge and skills through experience. It is experiential learning — learning by doing — that forms the foundation of the learning model that is described below. In each of the ten chapters of the text, the "Practising Your Group Skills" section is devoted to developing the various skills discussed in the chapter by having students work together in teams to practise those skills.

The material in this appendix explains how "Practising Your Group Skills" can create the experiences from which students will acquire the skills essential to working cooperatively with others in groups. Students practise group skills in a meaningful way as they carry out their various assignments in designated teams. By using student teams in a structured environment, we create a situation in which interpersonal skills can be explained, understood, and practised.

Effective Teachers

Consider, for a moment, the various tasks that an effective teacher does when teaching a typical lesson in the traditional teacher-centred fashion. First, the teacher welcomes the students to class and reminds them of the lesson topic of the day. He then reviews basic ideas from the last class. Next he presents the new lesson. Somewhere in the proceedings there is time for a break, a time for everyone to get refreshed for the next part of the class session. After break, the lesson continues until the session is close to an end. Before concluding the class, however, the teacher takes a few minutes to summarize the key ideas of the day's lesson. Finally, he reminds students of their homework assignment and wishes them a good day.

Student Teams

Imagine how the dynamics of the class would change if student teams were responsible for the tasks that the teacher normally directs or coordinates — an introduction to the class, a review of the previous lesson, the teaching of the new lesson, the coffee break, and a concluding summary. Imagine the learning experiences that students would have if they were responsible for planning and implementing the class activities that usually fall to the teacher. With the teacher serving as a coach and consultant, student teams can both teach and learn essential group skills as they host one another, review their own lessons, teach one another new lessons, energize one another, and work together to evaluate and improve their performance in the class.

THE EXPERIENTIAL MODEL

The experiential model provides a structure and directions whereby student teams complete the various classroom tasks that are normally done by teachers. In this model, the teacher becomes a consultant who assists the students with the planning and implementation of their assigned tasks. Throughout the rest of the description of the model, I will refer to the teacher as the consultant or the professor. Instead of directing the class in the traditional manner, the consultant coaches and guides the student teams who practise their group skills within the parameters of the model. Professors can choose to employ one or more teams to do the experiential learning prescribed by the model.

If a professor wishes to have classes that are built almost entirely on experiential learning, then she will want to use all five of the teams. In contrast, if a professor wishes to employ the model in a more modest way, then she will use fewer than five teams to help conduct the class and deliver the lessons. As professors become familiar with the teams and their responsibilities, they will see that it's also possible to have one team carry out two different sets of responsibilities. The model allows for a variety of different applications.

Professors who choose to have a group of students rotate through all five of the team functions in the course of a semester will provide that group with five distinctly different sets of responsibilities that require students to practise their interpersonal and group skills on an ongoing basis. In this approach, each group of students functions as the Executive Team at one time, the Lesson Review Team at another time, the Teaching Team at another time, the Energizer Team at another time, and the Evaluation Team at yet another time. In the next section, we'll provide the job descriptions for all five teams.

Note that the group members stay together as a group throughout the course. The membership of each team remains the same, but a team's responsibilities change from time to time according to a predetermined schedule. At any given time, for example, one team will be responsible for teaching while the other teams are responsible for hosting and coordinating, reviewing the last lesson, energizing their classmates, and evaluating class performance.

The model also includes individual role responsibilities for each of four different roles, those of leader, recorder, reporter, and participant-analyst. If individual students are required to serve as leaders, recorders, reporters, and analysts on their teams, then both teams and individuals will be involved in experiential learning at virtually all stages of the course. This skills-focused, practical approach to acquiring and developing interpersonal and group skills provides powerful motivation for and reinforcement of student learning.

Take note that the time frames included in the "Specific Responsibilities" sections below are based on the assumption that all five teams are working within a two-hour block of time. Consequently, each team has a time limit within which it has to meet its particular responsibilities for the class session.

THE TEAM RESPONSIBILITIES

The Executive Team

As hosts for the class session, the Executive Team begins the class with an appropriate welcome to members of the class. Team members introduce themselves so that the rest of the class knows who the executive members are. They may also wear name tags or dress distinctively to help others recognize them as the hosts for the class session. Then they introduce the lesson topic for the day in some interesting way and, if required, call for reports from each team, including their own team. The reports are very brief updates by each team, describing their progress on the various tasks for which they are responsible. Someone from the Executive Team introduces and thanks each of the reporters. At appropriate times throughout the class session, the Executive Team introduces and thanks all the other teams — the Lesson Review Team, the Teaching Team, the Energizer Team, and the Evaluation Team — as those teams carry out their responsibilities. Finally, the Executive Team brings closure to the class session.

SPECIFIC RESPONSIBILITIES

- Ensure that the classroom is properly set up.

- Provide an agenda for the class session.

- Introduce the chapter topic in a creative way.

- Introduce and thank all teams and speakers.

- Coordinate the class activities.

- Bring closure to the class session.

- Ensure that the classroom is returned to its standard form.

The Lesson Review Team

After the opening welcome by the Executive Team, the Lesson Review Team assists the class in reviewing the previous week's lesson. The team's specific lesson review assignment is found in "Practising Your Group Skills" in each chapter. Team members can choose to do the review in any way they wish, provided that they achieve the learning objectives of the review. Students can be very creative in their review, and their creativity should be encouraged as long as it serves the learning process. While the lesson review is in progress, the Lesson Review Team is in charge of the class. Their leaders give direction to the review process while members of all the other teams participate in the review. When the Lesson Review Team concludes its review, the Executive Team thanks the members and then introduces the next team.

SPECIFIC RESPONSIBILITIES

- Provide a review of the lesson taught at the previous class session.

- Explain the experiential exercise and its purpose.

- Summarize the key topics taught.

- Complete the review in 10 to 15 minutes.

The Teaching Team

The Teaching Team has the biggest responsibility of any team. During the lesson, the Teaching Team is in charge of the class, and team members teach the assigned lesson to the rest of the class. The specific teaching assignment is provided in each chapter of the text in "Practising Your Group Skills." The consultant works with the team to help plan its lesson. Note that the assigned experiential exercise is a very important part of that lesson in that it provides the class with a common group experience. In addition, the Teaching Team uses the experiential exercise to illustrate various topics from the assigned chapter. In other words, the Teaching Team employs experiential learning, the same kind of learning that forms the basis of the entire experiential learning model. When the Teaching Team has conducted the experiential exercise and presented the assigned chapter material, members call on the consultant to clarify or elaborate. The consultant has a chance, at this time, to highlight key points and clarify any misunderstandings. When the Teaching Team has finished the lesson, the Executive Team thanks the members and introduces the next team.

SPECIFIC RESPONSIBILITIES

- Introduce the goals and objectives of the assigned lesson.
- Conduct the assigned experiential exercise.
- Explain the assigned chapter material, linking it to the experiential exercise.
- Call on the consultant (the professor) for any necessary clarification.
- Conclude the lesson with a brief summary.
- Complete the lesson in 40 to 60 minutes.

The Energizer Team

The Energizer Team is responsible for conducting a brief, motivational exercise that follows the work of the Lesson Review Team and the Teaching Team. The Energizer Team's motivational exercise may be upbeat and active or quiet and meditative. Team members plan the kind of energizer activity that they feel will best help students with the learning activities of the class session. Often these are ice-breaker activities that get the class members to move around and intermingle. These fun experiences provide a necessary change of pace after the more serious activities associated with the lesson review and the lesson of the day. The Energizer Team is in charge of the class when team members are conducting their activity. Energizer activities must be safe, relatively quiet, and professional. When the energizer is over, the Executive Team thanks the Energizer Team and introduces the next team.

SPECIFIC RESPONSIBILITIES

- Conduct a brief energizer exercise that involves the whole class.
- Choose an energizer that is either active or meditative.
- Ensure that the exercise is safe, quiet, and professional.
- Ensure that the exercise is conducted respectfully.
- Complete the exercise in 10 to 15 minutes.

The Evaluation Team

The last major activity of the class session is an evaluation of the class's performance. Under the leadership of the Evaluation Team, the whole class assesses its performance in the class session and identifies goals for improving performance in future classes. The Evaluation Team facilitates the evaluation process, but it does not stand in judgment of the other teams or of any individuals. Team members are responsible for assisting the entire class in assessing its performance on some specific aspect of the class's experience that day.

The steps of the formal evaluation process are detailed in chapter 10 and members of the Evaluation Team need to read this material *before* facilitating an evaluation session. In addition, each chapter provides a specific evaluation assignment that is keyed to material in that chapter. The evaluation assignment is found in the chapter's "Practising Your Group Skills."

Evaluation teams can depart from the chapter assignment and assess other practices if there is a need to do so. If, for example, conflict arises while the class is studying goal setting in chapter 4, the need to deal with the conflict may override the assigned evaluation on goal setting. Such overriding will be an exception though, an exception occasioned only by a very important class need.

When the Evaluation Team concludes its task, the Executive Team brings closure to the day's activities in some appropriate way.

SPECIFIC RESPONSIBILITIES

- Create an instrument to evaluate the assigned focus behaviours.

- Collect class input using the evaluation instrument.

- Conduct a class discussion of the input collected.

- Assist the class in identifying the successes of the current session.

- Assist the class in identifying specific things that need improvement.

- Complete the session in 15 to 20 minutes.

THE INDIVIDUAL ROLE RESPONSIBILITIES

Team Leader

Every group needs a leader. In the experiential approach to learning group skills, each student serves as Team Leader at some point during the course. In this setting, Team Leaders are not dictators who boss others around. Rather, they are individuals who demonstrate leadership through the coordination of a group's activities, ensuring that the group's responsibilities are being met. When teams meet to do their planning, the Team Leader plays a key role as chair of the meeting, facilitating discussion and ensuring that the team gets its work done. The Team Leader may also be required to communicate with the consultant by way of a written memorandum, informing the consultant of the team's progress during its meeting. A standard memorandum form is available in the Teacher's Guide. The memorandum can be graded if the consultant desires.

SPECIFIC RESPONSIBILITIES

- Chair team meetings.

- Encourage individuals to complete their tasks.

- Ensure that the team meets its responsibilities.

- Communicate with other teams as necessary.

- Identify yourself to the consultant before each class.

- If required, send a memorandum to the consultant.

Team Recorder

A written record of team discussion and decisions is very important. From parliament to courtrooms throughout the country, individuals are responsible for keeping an accurate record of proceedings. Groups of all sizes, in virtually all circumstances, do well to maintain a written record of their meetings. In this experiential model, the Team Recorder performs this function for the team.

A record is kept for all group meetings. Recorders use full, clear, and concise sentences when creating the record. The emphasis is placed on accurately recording both the decisions made by the group and the names of those responsible for implementing the decisions. Not everything said in a meeting is necessary to record. Students who have never served as secretary for a group may need special coaching to be able to identify what should be a part of the record and what should not.

There is an advantage to having individuals record for two consecutive classes. The record from the first meeting can serve as a practice run for inexperienced Recorders. By giving the Recorder feedback on the first effort, the consultant puts the student in a position to write a more polished record on the second effort. A standard record form is available in the Teacher's Guide. One or both records can be graded if the consultant desires.

SPECIFIC RESPONSIBILITIES

- Keep a written record of team meetings.
- Include the following in your record
  - ❏ Team name
  - ❏ Your name (printed and signed)
  - ❏ Date, time, and length of meeting
  - ❏ Members present and absent
  - ❏ Team decisions and actions
  - ❏ Members responsible for implementing decisions.
- Check the accuracy of your record with team members.
- If required, submit your record to the consultant.

Team Reporter

Written and spoken reports are a fact of group life, and they are required for a variety of reasons. Sometimes it is simply a matter of keeping others informed regarding the work of the reporting group. At other times, the reporting group has been charged with the responsibility of making a recommendation to a larger group. The safety sub-committee of city council, for example, may recommend that city council install street lights in a particular part of town.

In the experiential model, the Team Reporter typically gives a status report to the other groups, highlighting the work that the Reporter's team did in its last meeting. A team that has solved a particular problem, for example, can advise other teams on how to avoid the problem should the other teams face it in the future. Most often, however, the Reporter will simply inform other groups as to the current status of the Reporter's group.

The Team Reporter prepares a written report on the proceedings of her group, and reports orally to the class when the Executive Team requests the report. Usually the report is made early in a class session. Once the report has been presented orally, the Reporter may be required to hand in the written report to the consultant. A standard report form is available in the Teacher's Guide. Both the oral and the written reports can be graded if the consultant desires.

SPECIFIC RESPONSIBILITIES

- Write a report summarizing your team meeting(s).

- Present your report orally to the class when requested.

- If required, submit the written report to the consultant.

Team Participant-Analyst

Actively involved group members carefully observe their groups in order to assess two important things. They analyze their group's progress regarding tasks to be accomplished, and they analyze their group's social-emotional status. These are the two broad goals of all successful groups: task completion and team development.

To help students learn to analyze their groups from these two perspectives, the experiential model requires each student to be a Participant-Analyst at various times throughout the course. Whenever a student is not the Team Leader, Team Reporter, or Team Recorder, she is by default a team Participant-Analyst.

The word "participant" in the label reminds students that they are to *participate* fully in the activities of the group. Being a Participant-Analyst doesn't mean that the student now has time off from group work responsibilities to observe others doing the work. Analysts participate fully, contributing to all aspects of the team's work.

The word "analyst" captures the additional responsibility of monitoring the group's progress with respect to its task and social goals. By requiring students to keep a record of team progress in the areas of task completion and relationship development, the experiential model encourages group members to monitor these critical aspects of group life. The Participant-Analyst shares her observations with the team and leads the team in an evaluation of its performance. If required, she submits her notes to the consultant. A standard form for a Participant-Analyst's notes is available in the Teacher's Guide. The notes can be graded if the consultant desires.

SPECIFIC RESPONSIBILITIES

- Participate fully in the work of your team.

- Observe and record your team's use of task actions.

- Observe and record your team's use of social actions.

- Lead your team in an evaluation of its performance.

- If required, submit your notes to the consultant.

A TYPICAL CLASS SESSION

- Opening, welcome, and introduction (Executive Team)

- Reports (Team Reporters)

- Review of the previous lesson (Lesson Review Team)

- Teaching of the new lesson (Teaching Team)

  - Part 1 — the experiential exercise

  - Part 2 — the explanation of chapter material

- Motivational activity (Energizer Team)

- Assessment of class performance (Evaluation Team)

- Closure (Executive Team)

- Team planning time (individual teams working independently)

SPECIFIC TEAM ASSIGNMENTS

Specific team assignments that are keyed to the material presented in each chapter of the text are found in the "Practising Your Group Skills" section of each chapter.

MORE INFORMATION ON THE MODEL

Units 2 and 3 of the Teacher's Guide provide the professor with more information on the experiential model and how it can be put to use in class. Unit 2 gives a general description of the model, and unit 3 presents a detailed account of the model.

The Experiential Exercises

Appendix Objectives

Upon completion of this appendix, you should be able to:

- Locate ten experiential exercises, one for each chapter of the text.

- Describe the specific experiential exercise that you will conduct.

- Identify the Teacher's Guide source for more information about your exercise.

- Identify the Teacher's Guide source for any handouts required for your exercise.

INTRODUCTION

Purpose and Connections

The purpose of appendix B is to provide members of the Teaching Team with detailed instructions on how to conduct their assigned experiential exercise. The assignments are given in "Practising Your Groups Skills" in each chapter. Unit 9 of the Teacher's Guide provides further information about each exercise. It also includes resources for duplication and use in the conduct of the exercises. Appendix A describes experiential learning in general and provides a detailed statement of responsibilities for the teaching team.

Exercise Format

Each exercise in this appendix is presented using a standard format. First, the chapter number and the name of the experiential exercise are identified. Next, the general goal of the exercise is presented, followed by specific objectives. Then, the necessary resources are listed. The detailed instructions for the exercise then follow in two sections on procedures. A brief statement on general procedure is followed by detailed, step-by-step procedures for conducting the exercise.

Variations

The detailed procedures include time frames for the various parts of each exercise. The entire exercise is, in each case, limited to 30 minutes. The experiential exercise is the first part of the Teaching Team's responsibility, and it has to be time-limited in order to allow for the rest of the Teaching Team's presentation. You may need to vary the time or the content of your experiential exercise to get everything done in the maximum 60 minutes allotted for the total teaching assignment. If your professor isn't using the full experiential model with five student teams, then you may have more time to devote to the assigned exercise and the subsequent presentation. Work with your professor to determine what is best for your circumstances.

Creativity and Fun

While the procedures for each exercise are spelled out in fairly fine detail, your exercise still allows for some creativity on your part. Conduct your assigned exercise as creatively as you can, but always ensure that your creativity helps to achieve the goal and the objectives of the exercise. Some exercises are more fun than others. You should strive to make your exercise an enjoyable learning experience.

Teaching Tip

Often the experiential exercise requires groups to report to the class at the end of the exercise. Here's a tip. If you tell each individual member of a group to be prepared to report when you request it, you are more likely to get everyone paying attention to the exercise. If participants know in advance that they may have to report, then they are much more likely to concentrate on the activity.

In contrast, if you allow groups to select their own reporters, you are more likely to have some people tuning out because they will not be responsible for reporting. Moreover, you are likely to get the most outgoing and talkative people speaking to the class. They will be happy to talk, and quieter members will be happy to let them do so. Try to involve everyone and be supportive of all who do contribute.

THE EXPERIENTIAL EXERCISES

Chapter 1   Member Roles: Participating Effectively in Your Group

EFFECTIVE PARTICIPATION

Goal: to demonstrate the effects of different contributions to a discussion within a small group.

Objectives: to demonstrate the positive effects on discussion in a small group of both (1) member task actions and (2) member social actions.

Time Limit: 30 minutes.

Resources:
- An adequate supply of Member Role Play sheets per group
- An adequate supply of Discussion and Ranking Worksheets per group
- 1 Scoring the "I Am Canadian" Rankings sheet

- 1 Original Survey Results overhead transparency
- 1 overhead slide with the original survey rankings
- 1 overhead projector
- The Teacher's Guide, which provides additional information and resources for this exercise

Procedure

This is a five-step exercise. First, you will randomly divide the class into groups of five or six players each, and locate the teams around the room with as much space between groups as possible. Second, you will instruct group members regarding the roles that they are to play during the discussion. Third, you will give specific instructions for the "I Am Canadian" discussion and then observe the groups as they discuss the topic. Fourth, you will provide the original (correct) rankings and then lead a discussion of the group dynamics within each team. Finally, you will lead the class in a debriefing session.

Step 1: Selecting and Locating the Groups (2 minutes)

Randomly divide the class into groups of five or six members each. Locate them around the room with as much space as possible between groups.

Step 2: Giving the Role Play Instructions (3 minutes)

When the groups are in place, remind them that chapter 1 describes the six task actions and the six social actions that effective group members use to contribute to the success of their groups.

Next, direct the groups as follows, regarding the role play instruction sheets that you distribute to them:

> You are each getting a role play instruction sheet that reviews the six task actions and the six social actions from chapter 1 and asks you to practise them in the "I Am Canadian" discussion exercise. In the exercise, try to demonstrate the very best group skills that you can. In order to get the most out of today's discussion, please follow your instructions carefully. You are to role play excellence in group member participation.

Distribute the instruction sheets and give each member a minute to silently read her instructions. There is to be no discussion among members at this point.

Step 3: Giving the "I Am Canadian" Discussion Instructions (12 minutes)

Give the following instructions for the "I Am Canadian" discussion:

> Each year Canadians are surveyed to see what's most important to them. In a moment, each team will receive a sheet that lists 15 items from the latest survey. Using your best group skills, discuss and rank the items in the order of the importance that your group thinks Canadians placed on each item in the survey. Do not give your personal ranking or your team's ranking. Rather, rank the items the way that you believe other Canadians ranked them in the original survey. Use the number 1 for most important and the number 15 for least important. Rank all 15 items. Try to decide by consensus (unanimous agreement). The objective is to see how accurately your team can identify the original rankings.

Distribute one ranking sheet to each team and direct them to start the discussion and the ranking. Tell them that they will have 12 minutes to finish the assignment. Observe the groups throughout the discussion session. Call time at the end of 12 minutes.

Step 4: Discussing the Group Dynamics (10 minutes)
Use the overhead slide to show the original survey results. Allow a minute or two to determine which group came closest. Congratulate the group that has done the best job of identifying the original survey results.

Point out, however, that the overall purpose of the experiential exercise is not to identify the original survey results, as interesting as that may be. The purpose is to examine the interpersonal and group dynamics that occurred during the "I Am Canadian" discussion exercise.

Ask the members in each group to comment on the group dynamics within their groups. For example, ask them who spoke most, who spoke least, who used the task actions, who used the social actions, etc. Teaching team observers should also comment on the group dynamics during the discussion.

Step 5: Debriefing (3 minutes)
Conclude the experiential exercise by emphasizing the importance of the task actions and the social actions for group success. Point out that the teaching team presentation that follows will look at both the 12 helpful actions and the 6 harmful actions.

Chapter 2   Leader Roles: Leading Effectively in Your Group
LEADERSHIP STYLES

NOTE: The following exercise was created by Professor Maureen Murphy-Fricker of Conestoga College Institute of Technology and Advanced Learning and is used by permission.

Goal: to demonstrate different leadership styles in the process of teaching a lesson.

Objectives: to demonstrate (1) autocratic leadership, (2) democratic leadership, and (3) laissez-faire leadership in the teaching of lessons to small groups.

Time Limit: 30 minutes.

Resources:

- 4 teaching stations
- Appropriate materials for each station
- 1 timing device
- 1 bell or other signaling device
- The Teacher's Guide, which provides additional information and resources for this exercise

Procedure

This is a five-step exercise. First, you will identify and prepare four different locations in the classroom as learning stations. Second, you will randomly divide the class into four different groups. Third, you will give instructions for the overall exercise.

Fourth, you will signal the start and finish of each round, and coordinate the rotation of groups. Finally, you will facilitate the debriefing session.

Step 1: Establishing the Teaching Stations (1 minute)
Identify four different locations in the room and set up a teaching station at each. Put all necessary teaching materials at each station in advance of the first round.

Step 2: Selecting and Locating the Groups (1 minute)
Randomly divide the class into four different groups. Indicate to each group the station at which they will start the exercise when you give the signal to start.

Step 3: Giving the Overall Instructions (3 minutes)
Tell the class how the exercise will work overall. Indicate that the lesson at each station will be taught by a teaching team member and timed by the teaching team. Inform the class that you will give everyone the signal to rotate to the next station at the appropriate time.

Step 4: Coordinating the Rotations (20 minutes)
Ensure that the learning groups move from station to station at the appropriate time. Do this four times, once for each station.

Step 5: Debriefing (5 minutes)
After thanking the four teachers and the four learning groups, ask participants to comment on the three different leadership styles used by the teachers at their stations. Remind the class that the three leadership styles are discussed in chapter 2 and that the teaching presentation that follows will discuss the styles further.

Chapter 3   Norms: Establishing Effective Rules in Your Group
MUTUAL EXPECTATIONS

NOTE: The following exercise was created by Professor Maureen Murphy-Fricker of Conestoga College Institute of Technology and Advanced Learning and is used by permission.

Goal: to demonstrate a process that a small group can use to develop a set of expectations (norms or rules) for its members.

Objectives: to demonstrate (1) the individual expectations step, (2) the critical discussion step, (3) the consensus step, and (4) the publishing step of a four-step process for establishing effective rules for the members of a small group.

Time Limit: 30 minutes.

Resources:

- 1 Individual Expectations sheet per group member
- 1 Team Expectations sheet per group
- 1 blank write-on, erasable overhead transparency per group
- 1 erasable transparency pen per group
- 1 or more overhead projectors

- The Teacher's Guide, which provides additional information and resources for this exercise

Procedure

This is a five-step exercise. First, you will randomly divide the class into groups of five or six players each, and locate the teams around the room with as much space between groups as possible. (Note: If the class has been or will be working in a number of established teams over an extended period of time, then you should use the established teams for this exercise, rather than randomly creating new teams.) Second, you will instruct group members regarding the completion of the Individual Expectations sheet. Third, you will give instructions for the critical discussion and consensus steps. Fourth, you will facilitate a session in which each group presents or publishes its results. Finally, you will lead the class in a debriefing session.

Step 1: Selecting and Locating the Groups (2 minutes)
Randomly divide the class into groups of five or six members each. Locate them around the room with as much space as possible between groups. As noted above, if the class has been or will be working in a number of established teams over a continuous period of time, then you should use the established teams for this exercise, rather than randomly creating new teams.

Step 2: Instructing the Use of the Individual Expectations Sheet (8 minutes)
Tell the groups that this step requires individuals to work independently. There is to be no discussion or consultation with others. Provide each individual with a blank Individual Expectations sheet, and give them five minutes to complete it.

Step 3: Discussing and Deciding on Team Expectations (15 minutes)
Give each group a Team Expectations sheet. Direct each group to share their individual expectations and to critically discuss what they have produced. Encourage them to reach consensus on the expectations that the team would include in a code of conduct for its members. Ask them to record their mutual expectations on the Team Expectations sheet.

Direct the groups to write a summary of their expectations on an overhead transparency for viewing and discussion by the class. Ask all individuals to stand ready to explain their team's work should you call on them to do so.

Step 4: Presenting the Results (4 minutes)
Take each team in turn, and ask one member of the team to present the team's expectations to the class, using the overhead transparency prepared earlier. Ask for comments from the class and look for the similarities among the statements of the different groups.

Step 5: Debriefing (1 minute)
Conclude the experiential exercise by emphasizing how important it is for group members to know what others in their group expect of them. Point out that the teaching team presentation that follows will further examine the role that norms play in the life of a small group.

Chapter 4   Goals: Setting Clear Targets for Your Group

WRITING CLEAR OBJECTIVES

Goal: to write clear and concise objectives that would support the achievement of a stipulated goal.

Objectives: to (1) carefully consider a stipulated goal, (2) write a number of objectives that would support the achievement of that goal, and (3) create an overhead transparency of the goal and its related objectives for viewing and discussion by the class.

Time Limit: 30 minutes.

Resources:

- 1 blank 8.5 × 11 inch (21.6 × 27.9 cm) sheet of paper per goal per group

- 1 blank write-on, erasable overhead transparency per goal per group

- 1 overhead, erasable transparency pen per group

- 1 or more overhead projectors

- The Teacher's Guide, which provides additional information and resources for this exercise

Procedure

This is a four-step exercise. First, you will randomly divide the class into groups of three to five members each and locate them around the room with as much space as possible between groups. Second, you will instruct the groups on the steps of the objective-writing assignment. Third, you will facilitate a class discussion of each team's work. Finally, you will lead the class in a debriefing session.

Step 1: Selecting and Locating Groups (2 minutes)
Randomly divide the class into groups of three to five members each. Locate them around the room with as much space between groups as possible.

Step 2: Giving the Objective-Writing Instructions (12 minutes)
Give each group a goal statement for their consideration. Remind the group that properly written objectives must answer the four specific questions discussed in chapter 4. Instruct each group to use a blank 8.5 × 11 inch (21.6 × 27.9 cm) sheet to draft three specific objectives that would support the achievement of their assigned goal.

Next, direct the groups to transfer their assigned goal and the objectives to an overhead transparency. Tell them that later you will randomly call on a member of the team to explain the team's overhead to the class. All members should stand ready to provide the explanation if called upon.

Step 3: Discussing the Results (12 minutes)
Ensure that you have everyone's attention. Proceed to view the team results, in each case asking a team member to describe the group's thinking and work. Invite class comments on and discussion of each presentation. When all groups have presented, thank them for their work in this part of the experiential exercise.

Step 4: Debriefing (4 minutes)

Use one of the best overhead transparencies to remind the class of the specifics that must be a part of a properly written objective. The specifics are, of course, captured by the four questions. Point out the relationship between this experiential exercise and the teaching team presentation that will follow.

Chapter 5   Messages: Communicating Effectively in Your Group

ONE-WAY AND TWO-WAY COMMUNICATION

Goal: to demonstrate the drawbacks of one-way communication and the benefits of two-way communication.

Objectives: to demonstrate (1) the drawbacks of spontaneous one-way communication, (2) the drawbacks of effective one-way communication, and (3) the benefits of two-way communication.

Time Limit: 30 minutes.

Resources:

- 3 legal-sized file folders, numbered #1 through #3

- 3 different figures, one for each file folder

- 3 overhead slides, one for each figure

- 1 tip sheet, for folder #2

- The Teacher's Guide, which provides additional information and resources for this exercise

Procedure

This is a five-step exercise. First, you will select volunteers and introduce the exercise. Second, you will direct the one-way, unassisted communication exercise. Third, you will direct the one-way, coached communication exercise. Fourth, you will direct the two-way, open communication exercise. Finally, you will lead the class in a debriefing session.

Step 1: Introducing the Exercise (3 minutes)

Tell the class that the experiential exercise is an exercise in oral communication, the subject of chapter 5. Identify three volunteer communicators who will come forward individually when you ask them. Instruct class members to take out three, blank 8.5 × 11 inch (21.6 × 27.9 cm) sheets of paper and a pen or pencil.

Step 2: Directing the One-Way Unassisted Communication (5 minutes)

Direct class members to get their first blank sheet ready, to await the instructions of the volunteer communicator, and to do so silently.

Direct the first volunteer to come forward to sit in a designated seat at the front of the class that you have positioned to face away from the class. With his back to the class, the volunteer is prevented from making eye contact with the class. Thus, he will not be able to receive non-verbal messages from class members.

Tell the volunteer that he will have to speak clearly and loudly so that everyone can hear him. Give him folder #1, open it with him, and make sure that class members cannot see the figure inside the folder. Tell the volunteer that he is to describe the figure so that the class members can draw (duplicate) the figure on their sheets. The volunteer must not show the figure to the class, or use any gestures or any aids, such as a white board. Do not give the volunteer any further help.

Remind the class that there is to be absolutely no feedback, either verbal or non-verbal. There are to be no comments, no questions, no moans, and no groans. Tell the volunteer to start. When you call time, ask the class members to set their first sheet aside until later.

Step 3: Directing the One-Way Coached Communication (5 minutes)

Direct class members to get their second blank sheet ready, to await the instructions of the volunteer communicator, and to do so silently.

Direct the second volunteer to come forward, to sit in the designated seat at the front of the class, facing away from the class. The procedure for this stage is exactly the same as the last stage except for one difference. The exception is as follows. Before the volunteer begins, give her one minute to read silently the tip sheet that is included in folder #2. When she has read the tips, encourage her to follow them when she describes her figure to the class.

Remind the class that there is to be no feedback, either verbal or non-verbal. There are to be no comments, no questions, no moans, and no groans. Tell the volunteer to start. When you call time, ask the class members to set their second sheet aside until later.

Step 4: Directing the Two-Way Open Communication (5 minutes)

Direct class members to get their third blank sheet ready and to await the instructions of the volunteer communicator.

Direct the third volunteer to come forward, and to sit in the designated seat that you have now turned to face the class. Tell the volunteer that he will have to speak clearly and loudly so that everyone can hear him. Give him folder #3, open it with him, and make sure that class members cannot see the figure inside the folder. Tell the volunteer to describe the figure so that the class members can draw the figure on their sheets. The volunteer must not reveal the figure, or use any gestures or any aids, such as a white board. He can, however, respond to class questions and comments as they arise.

Encourage the class to give helpful feedback to the volunteer, either verbally or non-verbally. They should ask questions and make comments as necessary. Tell the volunteer to start. When you call time, ask the class members to set their third sheet aside for a moment.

Step 5: Debriefing (10 minutes)

Project slide #1 onto a screen and invite class members to compare their drawings with the original on the screen. Congratulate the person who has achieved the greatest likeness. Do the same for slides #2 and #3. Thank the volunteer communicators and highlight the different types of communication that they were required to use. Remind the class that the teaching team's presentation that follows this exercise will describe the ideal way of communicating orally in a group; namely, through two-way, open communication.

Chapter 6   Conflict: Resolving Disputes in Your Group
CONFLICT STYLES

Goal: to demonstrate different conflict styles in a small group setting.

Objectives: to demonstrate (1) withdrawing, (2) forcing, (3) smoothing, (4) compromising, and (5) confronting reactions to conflict in a small group.

Time Limit: 30 minutes.

Resources:

- 1 Role Play Instruction sheet per group
- 1 large bag of potato chips
- 1 designated role-play area in the classroom
- An adequate supply of animal masks (optional)
- The Teacher's Guide, which provides additional information and resources for this exercise

Procedure

This is a five-step exercise. First, you will randomly divide the class into five groups, and locate them around the room. Second, you will instruct each group regarding its role-play assignment. Third, you will coordinate the presentation of five preliminary skits. Fourth, you will coordinate the grand finale skit. Finally, you will lead the class in a debriefing session.

Step1: Selecting and Locating the Groups (2 minutes)
Randomly divide the class into five different groups and locate them around the room with as much space as possible between them.

Step 2: Instructing the Role Play (10 minutes)
When the groups are in place, remind them that chapter 6 discusses five different styles of conflict. Provide each group with its role-play assignment sheet, and ensure that they understand their responsibilities. Tell them that they have five minutes to prepare their two-minute skit.

Step 3: Coordinating the Preliminary Skits (12 minutes)
Request that all skit preparation stop and get everyone's attention. Randomly select the first team and invite members to present their silent skit in the designated role-play area. When their skit is over, thank them and invite a second team to present its silent skit. Follow the same procedure with the remaining three groups, ensuring that the class is attentive to the efforts of all teams.

Step 4: Coordinating the Grand Finale Skit (4 minutes)
Ask for one volunteer from each of the existing groups to form a new group of five members. Take them aside and provide them with the role-play assignment for the grand finale skit. Give them two minutes to prepare their silent skit, and then invite them to present their silent skit to the class.

Step 5: Debriefing (2 minutes)
Conclude the exercise by thanking all the teams and individual actors. Remind the class that the five conflict styles demonstrated in the skits are commonly used by members of small groups when conflict arises in a group. Inform the class that the five conflict styles will be discussed further in the teaching team presentation that will follow.

Chapter 7   Cohesion: Building Your Group into a Team

COHESION AND COOPERATION

Goal: to demonstrate cohesion in a cooperative effort to reach a common goal.

Objectives: to demonstrate (1) mutual need, (2) mutual trust, and (3) mutual cooperation in the achievement of a common goal.

Time Limit: 40 minutes.

Resources:

- 1 clean, comfortable blindfold per triad

- 1 one-metre piece of wide masking tape per triad

- 2 one-metre pieces of string per triad

- 1 deck of 20 word cards per triad

- The Teacher's Guide, which provides additional information and resources for this exercise

Procedure

This is a four-step exercise. First, you will randomly divide the class into groups of three people (triads) and locate them around the room with as much space between triads as possible. Second, you will read the scenario and start the exercise. Third, you will compare and discuss the outcomes of the exercise. Finally, you will lead the class in a debriefing session.

Step 1: Selecting, Locating, and Preparing the Triads (5 minutes)
Randomly divide the class members into triads. Locate the triads around the classroom with as much space as possible between triads. Clear a space on the floor where two members of each triad can complete the exercise.

Identify one member of each triad as A, another as B, and the third as C. A and B are participants and C is an observer. Blindfold A and gently place a 10-centimetre piece of tape over her mouth. (If participants object to the tape, they must promise to remain silent throughout the exercise.) Loosely tie B's hands behind his back with one piece of string, and tie his legs together loosely with the other piece. Do not blindfold, tape, or tie C.

Step 2: Reading the Scenario and Starting the Exercise (15 minutes)
A special deck of cards is used in this exercise. It is extremely important to keep the deck of cards hidden until the signal to start has been given. Once A and B have been appropriately tied, taped, and blindfolded, read the scenario clearly and loudly

so that all triads hear the scenario and the instructions. If everyone understands the rules of the exercise, then shuffle the cards and spread them randomly on the floor in front of A.

Step 3: Comparing Results (8 minutes)

After 15 minutes, call time, remove all blindfolds, and untie all participants. Allow a minute or two to examine the quality and accuracy of the notes that have been created. Next, call on the observers (the Cs) to report on what they observed. Then, ask the players (the As and Bs) to share their experience of the game.

Step 4: Debriefing (2 minutes)

Finally, you will conclude the experiential exercise by pointing out how it provides a metaphor for real life. On every team, different individuals bring different talents to the group. Point out that this exercise relates to the teaching team's presentation on chapter 7 that will follow, particularly to the material on trust and cooperation.

Chapter 8   Critical Discussion: Generating Ideas in Your Group

CRITICAL DISCUSSION

Goal: to demonstrate mutual support among members of a small group in the discussion of controversial issues.

Objectives: to demonstrate (1) assertive communication, (2) active listening, (3) criticism of ideas, and (4) personal support in a small group discussion of a controversial issue.

Time Limit: 30 minutes.

Resources:

- An adequate supply of Controversial Issues sheets
- 1 Rules of Critical Discussion sheet per person
- The Teacher's Guide, which provides additional information and resources for this exercise

Procedure

This is a five-step exercise. First, you will randomly divide the class into groups of five or six members each and locate the groups around the room with as much space between groups as possible. Second, you will instruct group members regarding the rules that they are to observe in the discussion of their topic. Third, you will monitor the critical discussion. Fourth, you will facilitate a post-discussion session in which participants share their experience of the exercise. Finally, you will lead the class in a debriefing session.

Step 1: Selecting and Locating the Groups (2 minutes)

Randomly divide the class into groups of five or six members each, and locate the groups around the room with as much space between groups as possible.

Step 2: Instructing the Discussion Groups (5 minutes)

Tell the groups that they will engage in a two-stage discussion of a controversial social issue. In stage one, the discussion will be free-wheeling without any particular rules in force or any set goal to achieve. In stage two, the participants must (a) proceed according to specified rules and (b) try to achieve consensus. Inform the groups that you will interrupt the free discussion after five minutes, distribute and explain the rules for stage two, and begin the stage-two discussion that will be limited to ten minutes. Finally, assist the group in selecting a controversial topic and begin the free discussion.

Step 3: Monitoring the Critical Discussion (16 minutes)

Observe the free-wheeling discussion for five minutes, allowing participants to discuss the issue as they choose. After five minutes, interrupt the discussion and distribute and explain the rules for stage two. Remind the groups to follow the rules and seek consensus on the issue. Begin stage two and monitor the discussion, ensuring that participants follow the rules of critical discussion that you distributed.

Step 4: Facilitating the Sharing of Experiences (5 minutes)

Facilitate a class discussion of the exercise. Invite participants to comment on both the free-wheeling stage and the rule-governed stage. Offer comments on the teaching team's observations.

Step 5: Debriefing (2 minutes)

After thanking participants for their contributions, conclude the experiential exercise by highlighting the importance of critical discussion for group success. Remind the class that both critical discussion and uncritical groupthink will be discussed further in the teaching team presentation that follows.

Chapter 9   Decisions: Solving Problems in Your Group

COMPARING DECISION-MAKING METHODS

Goal: to demonstrate and compare several different decision-making methods that groups can use when solving problems.

Objectives: to demonstrate and compare (1) decision by consensus, (2) decision by majority vote, (3) decision by a minority, and (4) decision by an expert with respect to the solution of a common problem.

Time Limit: 30 minutes.

Resources:

- An adequate supply of pencils
- An adequate supply of blank 8.5 × 11 inch (21.6 × 27.9 cm) paper
- 1 Problem Sheet per group
- 1 Role Play Assignment sheet per group
- The Teacher's Guide, which provides additional information and resources for this exercise

Procedure

This is a four-step exercise. First, you will randomly divide the class into four groups of approximately equal size and locate the groups around the room with as much space between groups as possible. Second, you will instruct group members regarding the role play that forms the basis of the exercise and assign the problem to each group. Third, you will observe the groups as they carry out their assignments. Finally, you will lead the class in a debriefing session.

Step 1: Selecting and Locating the Groups (2 minutes)

Randomly divide the class into groups of five or six members each. Locate them around the room with as much space as possible between groups.

Step 2: Giving the Role-Play Instructions (6 minutes)

When the groups are in place, remind them that chapter 9 describes several methods by which groups can make decisions. Inform the class that each group will be assigned a particular method to use in solving the problem that you will give them.

Distribute the role-play instructions to each group, give them sufficient time to read them, and ensure that they understand how the method works. Remind them that they are to use the assigned method to decide their group's solution to the problem.

Step 3: Solving the Problem (10 minutes)

Give each team a copy of the problem sheet and instruct them to solve the problem as quickly as they can, using the assigned decision-making method.

Observe each team and ensure that it adheres to the assigned method. Keep time and call time at the end of 8 minutes, or sooner if all teams are finished. Collect each team's answer and determine whether it is correct or not.

Step 4: Debriefing (12 minutes)

Get the class's attention, give the correct answer to the assigned problem, and congratulate any successful teams. Having done that, remind the class that the overall purpose of the experiential exercise was to compare different methods of group decision making, not to solve the given problem. In other words, the exercise was about group dynamics, not word puzzles.

Randomly select a person from each group to describe that team's assigned method and to comment on how members felt about the process. Discuss the strengths and weaknesses of the method. Repeat this process with each team and each method.

Remind the class that these are only four of eight decision-making methods discussed in chapter 9. Be sure to link this experiential exercise with the presentation from the teaching team that will follow.

Chapter 10   Evaluation: Improving Your Group's Performance

CREATING EVALUATION INSTRUMENTS

Goal: to create an evaluation instrument for use in a small group evaluation session.

Objectives: to (1) design an evaluation instrument, (2) create an overhead transparency of the instrument, and (3) discuss the instrument's value as an assessment tool.

Time Limit: 30 minutes.

Resources:

- 1 blank 8.5 × 11 inch (21.6 × 27.9 cm) sheet of paper per group

- 1 blank write-on, erasable overhead transparency per group

- 1 overhead, erasable transparency pen per group

- 1 overhead projector

- The Teacher's Guide, which provides additional information and resources for this exercise

Procedure

This is a four-step exercise. First, you will randomly divide the class into groups of three to five members each and locate them around the room with as much space as possible between groups. Second, you will instruct each group to design and create an evaluation instrument on an overhead transparency. Third, you will facilitate a class discussion of the assessment tools that have been created. Finally, you will lead the class in a debriefing session.

Step 1: Selecting and Locating Groups (2 minutes)

Randomly divide the class into groups of three to five members each. Ten working groups is the ideal but not absolutely necessary. Locate them around the room with as much space between groups as possible.

Step 2: Designing and Creating the Instruments (10 minutes)

Each team should have one or more textbooks for use during this exercise. Randomly assign each group a different chapter from the text. The assigned chapter will provide the group with focus behaviours for its evaluation instrument. Each group will probably have to make a choice of focus behaviours from its assigned chapter in order to narrow the scope of their assessment tool. If there are not enough groups to cover all 10 chapters, then assign only as many chapters as there are groups.

Direct each group to use the blank 8.5 × 11 inch (21.6 × 27.9 cm) sheet to design its instrument carefully before transferring the design to an overhead transparency. Once the group is satisfied that its design is of high quality, instruct them to transfer the design to the overhead transparency for viewing by the class in the next step of the exercise. All members should stand ready to explain the team's evaluation instrument if called upon to do so.

Step 3: Discussing the Creations (15 minutes)

Ensure that all members of the class are focused for discussion. Remind them that evaluation has been an essential part of each class session from the beginning of the course. Underscore the importance of formal evaluation for the improvement of group performance.

Randomly select a person from one of the groups to come forward, to project her team's instrument on the screen, and to explain the features of the instrument. The person should do this in approximately one minute. Ask the class to provide constructive feedback on the instrument as an assessment tool. Repeat this process with each of the groups.

Step 4: Debriefing (3 minutes)

Congratulate all groups on the evaluation instruments that they have created, and remind the class that this experiential exercise is an introduction to the teaching team's presentation that will follow.

Glossary of Terms

A

active listening
the conscious use of cognitive, affective, and behavioural cues to encourage and clarify communication between and among people

affiliation
a sense of association, connection, or identity with others

aggressive person
one whose concern for personal rights outweighs concern for the rights of others

arbitrator
an unbiased third party that makes a decision for a group that cannot reach a decision on its own

assertive communication
communication between and among disputing group members in which self-respect, together with respect for others, aids in conflict resolution

assertive person
one whose self-interest is balanced by concern for others, who speaks up yet also listens

autocratic leader
a take-charge leader who tells others what to do and sees that they do it

C

charismatic power
power resulting from a leader's personal qualities

coercive power
power resulting from the use of punishment to influence conduct

cohesion
a group's sense of oneness or togetherness

commitment
a willingness to stick with things over the long term

communication
the successful exchange of information and feelings between people in a group

conceptual conflict
a disagreement or controversy about ideas or points of view

conflict
an interpersonal dispute between or among members of a group

conflict style
the manner in which a group member typically engages in disputes with others

consensus
unanimous agreement within a group

consistency
being in agreement with

cooperation
working with other team members to accomplish a task and also to achieve a mutual feeling of accomplishment

critical discussion
a six-step process designed to encourage group members to engage in conceptual conflict; the healthy exchange of differing views on an issue

culture
the way of life of people in a given society or group

D

decision
a choice made between competing options

decode
to interpret a spoken or written message accurately

democratic leader
a leader who involves all members of a group in discussion of issues and decisions

designated leader
a leader chosen by or for a group

developed norm
a rule established by a group to govern behaviour within the group

dysfunctional role
negative behaviours that cause an individual to become a harmful group member

E

emergent leader
a leader who assumes a temporary leadership role because of his or her special talents

empathy
feeling what another person feels; feeling with another person

encode
to express a message in spoken or written words

equality
the moral principle of treating each member of a group equally

expert power
power resulting from particular knowledge or skill

F

feedback message
a return message sent by a receiver to the original sender

focus behaviours
the specific behaviours to be evaluated by a group

folkways
the least important norms of a group

frame of reference
the context from which a person speaks or listens

freedom
the moral principle of mutual respect for group members' choices

functional role
behaviours associated with being a good or helpful group member

G

goal
a desired state of future affairs, a target; goals are expressed in general, rather than specific, terms

goodness
the moral principle of doing good to others and not doing harm

group maturity
a group's achievement orientation, level of responsibility, and expertise

groupthink
uncritical thinking within a group

I

ideal leader
a leader who has equal respect for both task completion and social relationships

identity
a shared sense of belonging when group members feel they are part of a team, and the team is part of them

illusion of invulnerability
the mistaken belief that one's team cannot fail

illusion of moral superiority
the mistaken belief that one's team is on the side of right

illusion of oneness
the mistaken belief that everyone is in agreement on an issue

imposed norm
a rule established by an authority outside the group

influence
the ability to affect circumstances and people

instrument
a tool used to observe and rate group performance

J

justice
the moral principle of fair dealing among group members

L

laissez-faire leader
a leader who consciously adopts the non-leader approach with a specific purpose in mind

legitimate power
power that flows from the designated positions within a group

long-term goal
a target that requires planning and strategies implemented over an extended period of time

M

message
the thoughts and feelings communicated by a sender, whether verbally or non-verbally

model
a simplified description of a process, often expressed as a diagram

mores
the most important norms of a group

N

noise
any physical, physiological, or psychological interference that impedes communication

non-leader
a leader who places little or no emphasis on either task goals or social goals

non-verbal communication
a message expressed without the use of words, by gestures, eye contact, or body posture

norm
a written or unwritten rule of a group

O

objective
a target that is specific and readily measurable

P

paraphrasing
the skill of accurately restating another's position in words different from the original

passive person
one who lacks sufficient self-respect to defend his or her rights in a dispute and who withdraws from conflict

people-oriented leader
a leader who sees teambuilding as the most important aspect of leadership

power
the ability to influence a situation in desired directions

problem
any situation that requires consideration and a solution

principles
the standards by which a group evaluates a course of action

R

receiver
the person in the communication process who interprets the sender's words

respect
honour and esteem, particularly among peers

reward power
power resulting from the use of rewards to influence conduct

role
a set of expectations associated with a particular responsibility

S

sanctions
powers to reward or punish members of a group

sender
the person who begins the communication process by expressing thoughts and feelings in words

short-term goal
a target that requires planning and strategies implemented over a brief period of time

social action
an action by a group member that helps to build and maintain a cohesive team

social goal
the goal of building relationships among group members

society
a large, identifiable community of individuals who fulfill a variety of differing and interdependent roles

subculture
a smaller culture within a larger culture

T

task action
an action by a group member that enables the group to get the task done

task goal
the goal of getting the job done

task-oriented leader
a leader who is most interested in productivity, or getting the job done

trust
the act of placing confidence in another person without full assurance that the confidence is well placed; entails mutual disclosure, sharing, and reliance

trustworthiness
a quality that inspires the confident placement of trust; reliability

truth
the moral principle of mutual integrity and trustworthiness

V

values
whatever is of importance or worth to an individual or a group

verbal communication
a message expressed in words (speech or writing)

Index